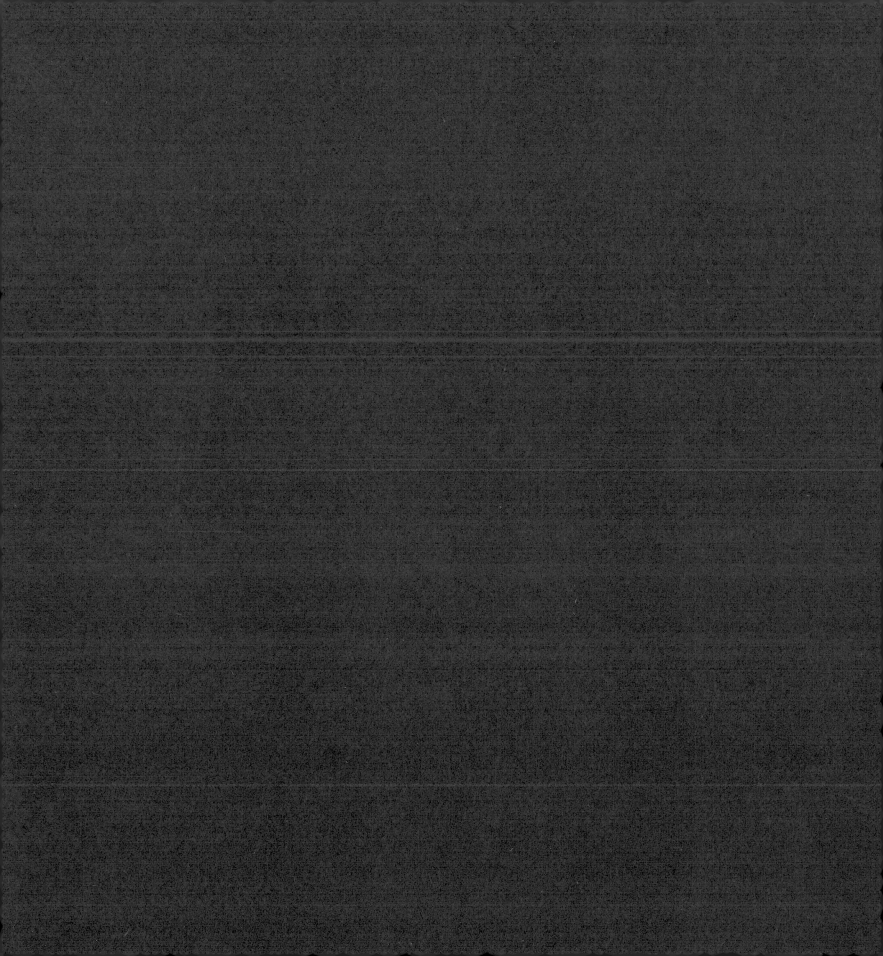

Voices of the Civil War

Voices of the Civil War · The Seven Days

By the Editors of Time-Life Books, Alexandria, Virginia

Contents

BATTLE AT RICHMOND'S DOORSTEP

This artist's rendering of the area east of Richmond shows the battlegrounds of the Seven Days. Robert E. Lee's operations to turn back the threat of McClellan's Federal army against the Confederate capital were conducted among the farmlands and swamps between the Chickahominy and James Rivers.

N
E
W
S
Pamunkey River
White House
Landing
Richmond &
York River Railroad
Chickahominy River
ite Oak
wamp
Glendale
Frayser's Farm
Malvern
Hill
James River
Westover
Harrison's
Landing
City
Point

Lee Takes Command

In early June 1862, a pall hung over the Confederate capital of Richmond, Virginia. General Joseph E. Johnston's recent counterattack against the left wing of Major General George B. McClellan's Army of the Potomac on June 1 had produced a great bloodletting but scant results. Whether called by its Southern name, Seven Pines, or its Northern name, Fair Oaks—after a nearby railroad station where the Yankees had fought to best effect—the battle had cost the Confederates more than 6,000 casualties, including 980 dead, and left them right where they had started, with their backs against Richmond. McClellan's huge army was still so close to the capital that some troops could set their watches by the chimes of its churches.

Worse for the Confederates, they had lost Johnston, who was severely wounded on the first day of fighting. And his replacement, Major General Gustavus W. Smith, had promptly shown himself unequal to the task, suffering virtually a nervous breakdown.

The Rebel side had fought bravely, but command breakdowns had ruined Johnston's well-laid plans. "Seven Pines should have been a magnificent victory for us," one Confederate officer lamented. "It was really far from that, and while encouraging the soldiers in fighting and the belief in their ability to beat the enemy, it was a waste of life and a great disappointment."

Inside the threatened capital, anxious crowds gathered around public bulletin boards to scour the casualty lists for the names of family and friends. Wagons filled with the dead rolled through the streets. The wounded, too numerous for the hospitals to handle, spilled over into public buildings and private homes. Looking back on that bleak time, a Confederate veteran would write: "No city in the world was sadder than Richmond in those days."

Over the next month, however, the mood of apprehension and pessimism would change to one of pride and hope—thanks to the debut of a bold new leader whose influence on the course of the war was to be greater, perhaps, than that of any other general on either side. At two o'clock on the afternoon of June 1, a few hours after the last shots were fired at Seven

Major General Edwin V. Sumner (fourth from right), commander of the II Corps, poses with members of his staff before historic St. Peter's Church near White House Landing during the Army of the Potomac's advance on Richmond.

Pines, President Jefferson Davis relieved Gustavus Smith and announced the name of the new commander. It was Robert E. Lee.

Although Lee's family name was celebrated in Virginia lore and American history, few cheers greeted the appointment. The Richmond newspapers were skeptical, one of them referring to Lee as "a general who had never fought a battle." Even a few of Lee's own new subordinates muttered that they were now to be led by a staff officer who had never demonstrated the forcefulness and talent required for high command in the field.

Much of the criticism arose from the fact that a great deal had been expected of Lee. At the outbreak of the war Lee had been offered command of the U.S. Army, sign of the high regard in which he was held at the top governmental and military levels. But in the year since he had resigned from that army and accepted command of Virginia's troops, as far as most Southerners could tell, he had had little influence on events. It was widely felt that he had failed to live up to his promise.

Charged with preserving western Virginia for the Confederacy, Lee had evolved a bold plan of military action. But it had miscarried, and in September 1861 Confederate troops withdrew after a defeat at Cheat Mountain. Lee's setback in western Virginia was followed by what he described as "another forlorn expedition" supervising the building of fortifications along the coasts of South Carolina and Georgia.

Next came the job of military adviser to President Davis. Lee performed masterfully in this position, launching Major General Thomas J. "Stonewall" Jackson's brilliant campaign in the Shenandoah Valley and arranging for Joseph Johnston's month-long defense of the Yorktown line on the Peninsula. Few outside the government, however, knew of these behind-the-scenes efforts. Robert E. Lee seemed to be just one more big name from the prewar Army who had not panned out.

But there were dissenters from this view. One man who appreciated Lee's talents was Colonel Joseph Ives, who had known the general in South Carolina. Ives was riding that June among Richmond's defenses when a fellow officer, Major E. Porter Alexander, asked him a crucial question: "Has General Lee the audacity that is going to be required for our inferior force to meet the enemy's superior force—to take the aggressive and to run risks and stand chances?"

Ives stopped and faced the other man. "Alexander," he said, "if there is one man in either army, Confederate or Federal, head and shoulders above every other in audacity, it is General Lee! His name might be 'Audacity.' He will take more desperate chances, and take them quicker, than any other general in this country, North or South; and you will live to see it, too."

Joseph Johnston, in an unusual display of self-effacement, also supported the choice. When a friend suggested to Johnston that his wounds spelled disaster for the Confederates, he replied: "No, sir! The shot that struck me down is the very best that has been fired for the Southern cause yet. For I possess in no degree the confidence of our government, and now they have in my place one who does possess it, and who can accomplish what I never could have done—the concentration of our armies for the defense of the capital of the Confederacy."

The task facing Lee was formidable. At the time of his appointment he had only about 65,000 troops. Although full of fight, they were inexperienced and poorly supplied. Facing them was McClellan's magnificently equipped force of 100,000. The Army of the Potomac's 2-to-1 manpower advantage seemed insuperable: Once it began its siege, Richmond would be doomed.

But days passed and to the wonderment of observers on both sides the Union juggernaut remained stuck in place. Always the careful-minded military engineer, McClellan had brought the Army of the Potomac a long distance, and he did not want things to go wrong now. Indeed, the amphibious movement he had organized to deliver his army to the Virginia Peninsula was unprecedented in American military annals—a British observer had called it "the stride of a giant." But once McClellan was ashore his pace had become, in the words of the same observer, "that of a dwarf." Three months had passed since his troops had landed at Fort Monroe, 100 miles from Richmond, and begun their fighting advance up the Peninsula toward Richmond.

McClellan had proclaimed the Battle of Seven Pines a great victory. "You are now face to face with the rebels, who are at bay in front of their Capital," he told his troops in a printed address. "Let us meet and crush him here in the very centre of the rebellion. The final and decisive battle is at hand."

But in fact the tough fight at Seven Pines had made the hesitant "Young Napoleon" even more timid. McClellan remained convinced that he faced vastly superior numbers. "I have to be very cautious now," he informed President Abraham Lincoln on June 4. "I mention these facts now merely to show you that the Army of the Potomac has had serious work & that no child's play is before it."

Still, McClellan was confident of at least one thing: He had plenty of time to prepare for what he predicted would be "one of the great historic battles of the world," an American Waterloo that would win the war with one blow. The Confederates, he was certain, would remain in their earthworks. Thus he spent the next two weeks after the Battle of Seven Pines constructing elaborate defenses, rebuilding his 11 jury-rigged or flooded-out bridges over the Chickahominy, and waiting for the muddy roads to harden so that he could move up his big guns.

All the while he kept up a demand to Washington that Major General Irvin McDowell's 30,000-man Army of the Rappahannock be sent south to reinforce him. For a time it appeared that the War Department would comply, and in expectation of McDowell's arrival McClellan extended his lines northward. But the threat posed by Stonewall Jackson's army in the Shenandoah Valley induced the administration to hold back all but one of McDowell's divisions.

Lee, meanwhile, used the respite to craft a Confederate strategy that would include Jackson's forces. Lee had inherited a loose-knit force—for which he formalized the name Army of Northern Virginia. It was composed of Johnston's Manassas veterans, the original Peninsula defense force under Major General John B. Magruder, and a hodgepodge of reinforcements now arriving from southern Virginia, North Carolina, South Carolina, and Georgia.

Lee was building his own grand army, which, when all the troops en route arrived, would total more than 92,000 men. He worked to integrate the new forces into the army and to improve its discipline and overall fighting quality. Lee obtained better rations and uniforms for his troops and strengthened his officer corps, promoting deserving men and sacking incompetents. The artillery, which had fought poorly at Seven Pines, was strengthened with nine new batteries. By the time the reorganization was complete, no fewer than 30 regiments from Johnston's old army had been placed in new brigades, and a number of new divisions created.

Lee also tackled a troubling attitude of defeatism. At his first meeting with his four dozen or so generals, Lee found that a surprising number of them favored pulling back even closer to the outskirts of Richmond. Brigadier General William H. C. Whiting, a division commander and an excellent engineer, sought to demonstrate mathematically the inevitability of McClellan's advance. As Whiting drew diagrams of the Union's powerful siege guns inching ever nearer, Lee's forbearance snapped. "Stop! Stop!" he exclaimed. "If we go to ciphering we shall be whipped beforehand."

Lee had no intention of withdrawing. Instead, he set the troops to work with pick and shovel, building miles of new earthworks in an arc between White Oak Swamp, east of Richmond, and the Mechanicsville bridges, north of the capital. Lee, who had commanded the young McClellan in the Mexican War, correctly divined that his former subordinate would try to tighten his grip on Richmond gradually, through siege work. Lee had a counterplan, and on June 5 he explained it in a message to President Davis.

The new defenses, he said, would allow him to take the offensive. "McClellan will make this a battle of posts," Lee wrote. "He will take position from position, under cover of his heavy guns. I am preparing a line that I can hold with part of our forces in front, while with the rest I will endeavor to make a diversion to bring McClellan out."

"Diversion" was a modest word for what Lee had in mind. He intended nothing less than a full-scale attack north of the Chickahominy River. He would cross the river near Mechanicsville and strike McClellan's extended right wing on the north bank. Such a maneuver would threaten the Federal supply line, which ran along the Richmond & York River Railroad from White House Landing on the Pamunkey River. The counterstroke would pry McClellan from his entrenchments south of the Chickahominy and force him to fight in the open. It would, Lee assured Davis, forestall McClellan's projected siege—and "change the character of the war."

But it would also be an enormous gamble. Lee was risking everything in order to gain the initiative on the battlefield. He would leave fewer than 25,000 men under Magruder to defend Richmond. If the Federals mounted a major attack from their line northeast of the city, the capital of the Confederacy would be lost.

Before planning the details of his attack, Lee had to know the dispositions of the Federal right wing. The tip of this wing consisted of Brigadier General Fitz-John Porter's V Corps, which had initially been deployed to link up with McDowell's long-awaited troops marching south from Fredericksburg. To map Porter's whereabouts, Lee ordered his cavalry chief, Brigadier General James E. B. "Jeb" Stuart, to conduct a reconnaissance in force. Thus was set in motion one of the war's most dramatic episodes.

Only 29, stockily built, with a thick, curled mustache and a wide-spreading reddish brown beard, Jeb Stuart was a storybook cavalryman with a swashbuckling air. His charge from Lee suited his style of mounted war-making.

Shortly after 2:00 a.m. on June 12 Stuart set out with 1,200 men and two pieces of horse artillery. The force included Colonel Fitzhugh Lee, a 26-year-old nephew of the commanding general, and Colonel William Henry Fitzhugh Lee, known to everyone as "Rooney," Lee's 25-year-old second son. The half-mile-long column headed northwest from Richmond to create the impression that it was merely a body of cavalry being sent to Jackson in the Shenandoah Valley.

The column crossed the headwaters of the Chickahominy, then turned sharply east and camped that night a few miles short of Hanover Court House. The next morning, Stuart flushed a handful of Federal cavalry pickets, then sliced southeastward on back roads. This route took him behind Porter's corps, on the flank of McClellan's right wing.

Early in the afternoon, Stuart's column surprised and overwhelmed a detachment of the 5th U.S. Cavalry. The Rebel troopers then rode on several miles to Old Church crossroads, destroyed a lightly defended Yankee cavalry camp, taking some prisoners, and then paused. Here at Old Church Stuart faced a decision. His semicircular route from Richmond had taken him perhaps 35 miles—around and behind Porter's V Corps, and now to a point a few miles to the rear of Brigadier General William Franklin's VI Corps. It seemed to be time to turn around and retrace his steps to Richmond. He had gathered all the information Lee wanted. But from the beginning of the mission, Stuart had harbored a wild and splendid notion: to ride all the way around McClellan's army.

Union forces would have been alerted to his presence by now, Stuart reasoned, and would likely be waiting in ambush if he returned by the same route. It would actually be safer, he figured, to ride on. That afternoon, the ride took on the trappings of a triumphal tour. Many of the troopers had homes in the area, and as they headed southeast, women poured from the houses to bring food and to embrace sons, brothers, husbands, and sweethearts they had not seen since the war began.

About nine miles southeast of Old Church the gray-clad horsemen swooped down on Tunstall's Station, a stop on the Richmond & York River Railroad. They seized two parties of guards and set about wrecking the place. Stuart then led the column four miles to Talleysville, where he left unmolested a Union field hospital caring for several hundred wounded; but he allowed his men to refresh themselves with sausages, figs, and other victuals from a sutler's store.

It was midnight before Stuart left Talleysville on the next leg of the journey, to the lower Chickahominy, seven miles to the south. The column was slowed by its burden of 165 Union prisoners —riding double on captured horses and mules — and by the troopers' own exhaustion. The moon was dangerously bright, and the slow-moving horsemen expected Union cavalry to pounce on them at any moment. In fact, the Federals were in hot pursuit, under the command of none other than Stuart's father-in-law, Brigadier General Philip St. George Cooke, a Virginian whose own nephew was on Stuart's staff. When Stuart left Talleysville, Cooke's column was just four miles back, at Tunstall's Station.

Shortly after dawn on the 14th, Stuart's men reached the Chickahominy but found the river too deep to ford. Stuart led the column along the bank, looking for a crossing. A mile downriver, the Confederates discovered an old skiff and anchored it in the middle of the 40-foot-wide channel to serve as a makeshift pontoon. They bridged the stream with timbers salvaged from a nearby warehouse and filed across. Then the rear guard, under Fitzhugh Lee, set fire to the bridge. As Lee was leaving the scene at about 2:00 p.m., he saw a squad of Union cavalrymen pulling up on the far bank.

Richmond was still 35 miles away. Stuart cut south, then swung northeastward on a path paralleling the James River. After a night's sleep, the column reached Richmond on Sunday, June 15. In three days, the troopers had ridden nearly 100 miles. Stuart had lost only a single man and one artillery limber.

Stuart's dashing exploit gave an enormous boost to Southern morale. But far more significant was the effect it had on McClellan. All along he had felt apprehensive about his supply line to White House Landing. Now Jeb Stuart had easily cut that line—if only temporarily—demonstrating its vulnerability. McClellan decided to move his supply base south of the Chickahominy, along with the two corps that remained on the north bank. On June 18, the first supplies left White House Landing for a new base on the James River. That same day, Franklin's VI Corps moved to the south bank; Porter's V Corps would remain north of the river to guard the transfer of matériel.

Stuart, meanwhile, had reported good news to Lee. The northern tip of Porter's line was vulnerable to a flanking movement. Lee could now proceed. The key was Stonewall Jackson's 18,500-man army in the Shenandoah Valley. Lee wanted Jackson to march from the Valley and outflank Porter. At the same time three divisions, about 47,000 men, commanded by Major Generals James Longstreet, Ambrose Powell Hill, and Daniel Harvey Hill, would attack from the west and sweep eastward along the north bank, threatening McClellan's supply line to White House Landing.

Lee already had sent Jackson reinforcements—William Whiting's infantry division, which included a brigade of Texans under Brigadier General John B. Hood and a brigade of Georgians under Brigadier General Alexander Lawton. He hoped that their departure from Richmond would confuse the Yankees, forcing them to keep troops in the Shenandoah Valley. These troops could also help Jackson fight his way out of the Valley if necessary.

On June 16, Jackson started his men on the 120-mile march to Richmond, then rode on ahead for a council of war with Lee. The timing of the offensive depended on the speed of Jackson's fabled "foot cavalry." Jackson agreed to have them in position to attack early on the morning of June 26.

Lee did not know that McClellan was also

planning an attack on a nearly identical schedule. McClellan's bridges had been built, the roads were drying, and reinforcements had arrived—Brigadier General George McCall's Pennsylvania Reserve division of 9,500 men, transferred from McDowell's army to Porter's V Corps, as well as seven regiments pulled from the defenses of Washington, D.C.

The goal of McClellan's attack, tentatively scheduled for June 26, was modest: He wanted to move a mile or so west toward Richmond and take Old Tavern, where the road north to New Bridge on the Chickahominy branched off from the Nine Mile road. It would be his first advance since the Battle of Seven Pines and would allow him to bring his siege guns a step closer to Richmond.

To cover his attack, McClellan tried on June 25 to advance the position of Major General Samuel P. Heintzelman's III Corps west from Seven Pines along the Williamsburg road. Shortly after 8:00 a.m. Major General Joseph Hooker's division led the advance, marching through wooded terrain against three Confederate brigades under Major General Benjamin Huger.

Hooker's men made some progress, but after they had fought for about two hours, McClellan, who was managing the battle by telegraph from his headquarters three miles away, recalled them, fearing they were outnumbered. He then rode to the battlefield himself, assessed the situation firsthand, and ordered the advance renewed. By nightfall, the Federals had gained about 600 yards—at a cost of 626 casualties. The Confederates had lost 441 men.

This battle, known as Oak Grove or King's School House, put McClellan within five miles of Richmond. But it would be remembered as marking the beginning of a week of almost continuous fighting that people ever afterward would refer to as the Seven Days' Battles.

CHRONOLOGY

May 31-June 1, 1862	*Battle of Seven Pines (also called Fair Oaks)*
June 12-15	*Stuart rides around McClellan's army*
June 25	*Engagement at Oak Grove (also called King's School House, The Orchards)*
June 26	*Battle of Mechanicsville (also called Ellerson's Mill, Beaver Dam Creek)*
June 27	*Battle of Gaines' Mill (also called First Cold Harbor, Chickahominy)*
June 28	*Engagement at Garnett's Farm (also called Goulding's Farm)*
June 29	*Battle of Savage's Station (also called Allen's Farm, Peach Orchard)*
June 30	*Battle of White Oak Swamp*
June 30	*Battle of Glendale (also called Frayser's Farm, Charles City Cross Roads)*
July 1	*Battle of Malvern Hill*
July 2	*McClellan withdraws to Harrison's Landing*

ORDER OF BATTLE

ARMY OF NORTHERN VIRGINIA (Confederate)

Lee

Jackson's Command

Whiting's Division
Hood's Brigade
Law's Brigade

Jackson's Division
Winder's Brigade
J. R. Jones' Brigade
Fulkerson's Brigade
Lawton's Brigade

Ewell's Division
Elzey's Brigade
Trimble's Brigade
Seymour's Brigade
Maryland Line

D. H. Hill's Division
Rodes' Brigade
G. B. Anderson's Brigade
Garland's Brigade
Colquitt's Brigade
Ripley's Brigade

Longstreet's Command

Longstreet's Division
Kemper's Brigade
R. H. Anderson's Brigade
Pickett's Brigade
Wilcox's Brigade
Pryor's Brigade
Featherston's Brigade

Huger's Division
Mahone's Brigade
Wright's Brigade
Armistead's Brigade

A. P. Hill's Division
Field's Brigade
Gregg's Brigade
J. R. Anderson's Brigade
Branch's Brigade
Archer's Brigade
Pender's Brigade

Holmes' Division
Ransom's Brigade
Daniel's Brigade
Walker's Brigade
Wise's Command

Magruder's Command

D. R. Jones' Division
Toombs' Brigade
G. T. Anderson's Brigade

McLaws' Division
Semmes' Brigade
Kershaw's Brigade

Magruder's Division
Cobb's Brigade
Griffith's Brigade

Reserve Artillery Pendleton

Cavalry Stuart

ARMY OF THE POTOMAC (Federal)

McClellan

II Corps Sumner

1st Division Richardson
Caldwell's Brigade
Meagher's Brigade
French's Brigade

2d Division Sedgwick
Sully's Brigade
Burns' Brigade
Dana's Brigade

III Corps Heintzelman

2d Division Hooker
Grover's Brigade
Sickles' Brigade
Carr's Brigade

3d Division Kearny
Robinson's Brigade
Birney's Brigade
Berry's Brigade

IV Corps Keyes

1st Division Couch
Howe's Brigade
Abercrombie's Brigade
Palmer's Brigade

2d Division Peck
Naglee's Brigade
Wessels' Brigade

V Corps Porter

1st Division Morell
Martindale's Brigade
Griffin's Brigade
Butterfield's Brigade

2d Division Sykes
Buchanan's Brigade
Chapman's Brigade
Warren's Brigade

3d Division McCall
Reynolds' Brigade
Meade's Brigade
Seymour's Brigade

VI Corps Franklin

1st Division Slocum
Taylor's Brigade
Bartlett's Brigade
Newton's Brigade

2d Division W. F. Smith
Hancock's Brigade
Brooks' Brigade
Davidson's Brigade

Artillery Reserve Hunt

Casey's Command (White House Landing)

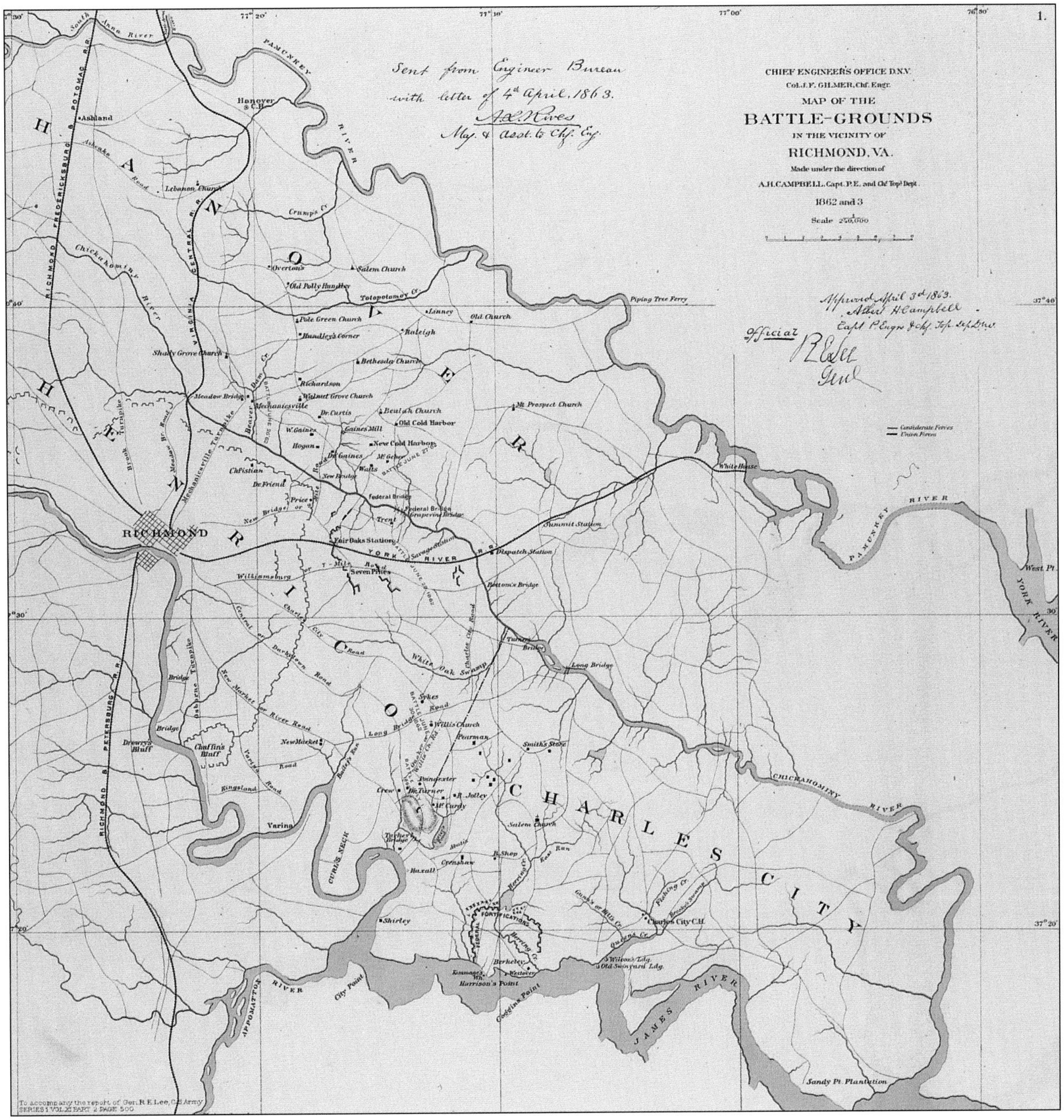

This map of the region east of Richmond was prepared by the staff of Colonel John F. Gilmer, chief engineer of the Confederate capital's defenses. The area from just north of the Chickahominy River to the north bank of the James River was the scene of heavy fighting—later called the Seven Days' Battles—as General Robert E. Lee counterattacked to halt General George B. McClellan's attempt against Richmond. Confederate fortifications are marked in red; Federal works near Seven Pines and Harrison's Landing are indicated in blue.

"Colonels and field officers! when it comes to the bayonet, lead the charge."

MAJOR GENERAL PHILIP KEARNY

DIVISION COMMANDER, ARMY OF THE POTOMAC

The dashing, financially independent Kearny lost his left arm fighting in the Mexican War, and in this photograph the stump of the amputated limb is discreetly tucked behind his back. Highly respected—Winfield Scott called him the "bravest man I ever knew"—Kearny issued this inspirational order to his division after the fighting at Fair Oaks. But the out-in-front style of battlefield leadership Kearny advocated in this directive partly contributed to his death by Confederate musketry at Chantilly on September 1, 1862.

General Orders
No. 15.
Hdqrs. Third Division, Third Corps
Camp near Richmond, June 5, 1862.

I. Brave regiments of the division! you have won for us a high reputation. The country is satisfied; your friends at home are proud of you.

After two battles and victories, purchased with much blood, you may be counted as veterans.

I appeal, then, to your experience, to your personal observation, to your high intelligence to put in practice on the battle-field the discipline you have acquired in camp. It will enable you to conquer with more certainty and less loss.

II. "Shoulder straps and chevrons!" you are marked men; you must be ever in the front.

Colonels and field officers! when it comes to the bayonet, lead the charge. At other times circulate among your men, and supervise and keep officers and men to their constituted commands; stimulate the laggard, brand the coward, direct the brave, prevent companies huddling up or mixing.

III. Marksmen! never in the fight cheapen your rifles. When you fire, make sure and hit. In wood and abatis one man in three is to fire; the others reserve their loads to repel an onset or to head a rush. It is with short rushes and this extra fire from time to time that such ground is gained; each man up in first line, none delaying; share danger alike, then the peril and loss will be small.

IV. Men! you brave individuals in the ranks, whose worth and daring, unknown perhaps to your superiors, but recognized by your comrades, influence more than others. I know that you exist; I have watched you in the fire; your merit is sure to have its recompense; your comrades at the bivouac will repeat your deeds, and it will gladden your families, and in the end will be brought before the country.

V. Color-bearers of regiments! bear them proudly in the fight, erect and defiantly, in the first line. It will cast terror into the opponents to see it sustained and carried forward. Let it be the beacon-light of each regiment. The noblest inscription on your banners are the traces of the balls.

VI. Again, noble division, I wish you success and new victories, until the cause of our sacred Union, being triumphant, you return honored to your homes.

LIEUTENANT JOHN C. BABCOCK

U.S. SECRET SERVICE

"I have had a boost," Babcock excitedly wrote to an uncle on March 4, 1862. "I have been transferred . . . to the Department of Secret Service." As one of McClellan's staff, Babcock produced "sketchings . . . of fortifications belonging to the enemy" based on the "descriptions of returned spies" and his own observations. The Secret Service, attached to McClellan's headquarters, was a loosely organized group of detectives, staff officers, spies, and scouts responsible for gathering and distributing military intelligence.

There is probably nothing for which I am in every way so well qualified to perform, as the duties that have devolved upon me during my connection with the Secret Service. I have not only found ample chances to display my qualifications as an Engineer and draughtsman, but on more than one occasion my *gymnastic* education has also been displayed. I knew as little as you did at the time I entered the S.S. of the nature of the duties I should be called upon to perform, only that they were dangerous and trustworthy. It was like taking a "leap in the dark" and knowing I had oft times to run the gauntlet between a bullet and halter, I had more fear of my incompetency for the trust, than I entertained for the rebellious sons of the South.

If I *had* the time I could not tell you now of my life and doings in the S.S., so you must wait until the close of the war when I hope to visit Harrisville at an early day. I can say however that I have won the attention and respect of General McClellan who has more than once tendered me his special thanks for my services.

I send you a photographed copy of one of my maps of the enemies country which I prepared for Gen McClellan the main points of which I obtained my own reconnoissances. He pronounces it as the finest piece of topographical work he has ever seen, and a *remarkable* work in consideration of the time and place in which it was made. He gave me his special regards for it and says it is invaluable to him, as his Engineers have proved to be very unsatisfactory in their profession. Its correctness is commented upon on all sides and is found to be correct in most every particular as fast as we advance. Nearly twohundred have been photographed for the use of the General and his officers which is a very scientific process, and is done by a photographer attached to our corps, for whom we find various uses besides the ones *inclosed.*

An actual sketch, made on the spot by one of the Special Artists of Frank Leslie's Illustrated Newspaper.
Mr. Leslie holds the copyright and reserves the exclusive right of publication.

McClellan also used aeronaut Thaddeus Lowe's U.S. Balloon Corps to produce maps and gather information about enemy dispositions and activities. This watercolor, done by Arthur Lumley for Frank Leslie's Illustrated Newspaper, shows one of Lowe's balloons straining at its mooring lines as it is pulled up the James River. High winds sometimes prevented the launch of the balloons at critical moments, and the region's lush vegetation often masked Confederate troop movements.

PRIVATE OLIVER W. NORTON

83D PENNSYLVANIA INFANTRY, BUTTERFIELD'S BRIGADE

The weapon Norton describes was an early machine gun nicknamed the "coffee-mill gun," because of its cranking mechanism. Though capable of firing 120 rounds a minute, the gun often overheated and jammed during the stress of combat, and it never found widespread favor in the Federal Ordnance Department. At Gettysburg Norton was a colorbearer for Colonel Strong Vincent's brigade and in 1913 wrote a highly regarded book, "The Attack and Defense of Little Round Top."

Our artillery and our artillerists are vastly superior to the rebels, and they are well aware of it. But of all the artillery, we have the greatest one yet in our regiment. We have a cannon drawn by one horse that one man can fire two hundred times a minute by merely turning a crank. Every revolution fires one ball. It is a curious Yankee contrivance. The cartridges are put in a hopper, carried one by one round in a cylinder, shoved into the barrel and fired. It makes a noise like the dogs of war let loose. The balls are only a size larger than our musket balls, a regular "Minie ball." Don't you think one of those coffee mills would "weed out" a *secesh* regiment about as quickly as any tools they have? I understand that every Pennsylvania regiment in the service is to have them. All the Pennsylvania regiments near here have them.

I have been quite unwell ever since the battle. I got overdone. Friday is the first day that I have felt at all like myself these two weeks. I think I shall be all right again soon.

Yesterday we had a grand review in honor of the Spanish General Prim. You have seen his name in the papers lately, I presume, in connection with the tripartite intervention in Mexico. He presented quite a contrast to the plain dress of "our George," as he rode by in his gold lace and trimmings. Well, every nation likes its own style. There are many men even in McClellan's staff who dress more showily than he does, but they don't command the respect. There is hardly a man in the army who does not know George by sight and not a man but likes him.

1861 The War For the Union. 1865
1861 Photographic War History. 1865
2510. Fort Sumner, near Fair Oaks, Va., 1862.
[FOR DESCRIPTION OF THIS VIEW SEE THE OTHER SIDE OF THIS CARD.]

Federal artillerists stand to their guns in this stereoscopic view taken by photographer James F. Gibson in June. The battery of 10-pounder Parrott rifles was posted in Redoubt No. 5, also called Fort Sumner, part of the line of earthworks constructed to defend Fair Oaks Station in the aftermath of the Battle of Seven Pines. McClellan planned to use this line of fortifications as the base for siege operations against Richmond.

PRIVATE WILLIAM J. H. BELLAMY

18th North Carolina Infantry, Branch's Brigade

During the tense lull that followed the Battle of Seven Pines, pickets of both armies maintained an aggressive stance toward their enemy counterparts. The 17-year-old Bellamy suffered a wound at Gaines' Mill and was discharged as underage shortly thereafter. He later enlisted in the Confederate navy.

We are on one side of the Chickahominy & The Yankees composed of Illinois Cavalry & Infantry directly opposite & on the other side, and when night comes, our posts being drawn into the banks of the stream are in speaking distance—

We continue to send men down daily—yesterday afternoon, we having shown ourselves as a squad on the banks of the river, a picket skirmish or *duel* began, and for awhile the contest waxed warmly. I used No. 47 freely & did my best to drop a dirty villain on a large grey or white horse, who rashly & boldly rode out in the open field & apparently requested us to do him the honor of introducing to his ears the report of our muskets. We made him acquainted with powder & lead, introducing not only to his ears the sound of our guns, but *into* his left side some where in some of the (Thoracic viscera) a piece of lead carefully moulded & of a conical shape—*who* killed him *no one knows*—I say I did, and every other man in the squad ditto—so let it remain, enveloped in mystery. Somebody killed—adding to the innumerable hosts of villains in the Yankee Paradise below,—one more. To day his carcass as also the carcass of his fine steed with feet high in air—the reflection of the sun being distinct on the iron shoes—can be seen—We hear it rumoured that the Yankees are going to make another attempt to take Richmond. They are well entrenched & slowly getting up to the City, from *their* Camps can be seen the Church spires—4 1/2 miles off. They say that they are going to eat 4th. July dinner & celebrate that day in Richmond. I'll bet my Knapsack they won't.

MAJOR GENERAL GEORGE B. MCCLELLAN

Commander, Army of the Potomac

McClellan often was supplied with —and readily accepted—incorrect information from his intelligence network about Confederate troop dispositions and strengths. The Rebel troops McClellan mentions in this telegram were Stuart's 1,200 horse soldiers on the first leg of their canter around the Federal army.

McClellan's, June 18, 1862.
The President:
I have the honor to acknowledge receipt of your dispatch of to-day. Our army is well over the Chickahominy, except the very considerable forces necessary to protect our flanks and communications. Our whole line of pickets in front runs within 6 miles of Richmond. The rebel line runs within musket-range of ours. Each has heavy support at hand. A general engagement may take place any hour. An advance by us involves a battle more or less decisive. The enemy exhibit at every point a readiness to meet us. They certainly have great numbers and extensive works. If 10,000 or 15,000 men have left Richmond to re-enforce Jackson it illustrates their strength and confidence. After to-morrow we shall fight the rebel army as soon as Providence will permit. We shall await only a favorable condition of the earth and sky and the completion of some necessary preliminaries.

Geo. B. McClellan,
Major-General.

A group of Secret Service agents, including the unit's chief, Allan Pinkerton (seated in rear, smoking a pipe), gathers at McClellan's headquarters to discuss reports. Debate continues over who was responsible for the greatly exaggerated estimates given to McClellan about the size of the Confederate forces guarding Richmond. Some historians blame Pinkerton alone. Others argue that McClellan, convinced he faced an army twice the size of his own, refused to believe realistic counts, and Pinkerton would therefore inflate his estimates to hold the general's ear.

MAJOR GENERAL JAMES LONGSTREET

DIVISION COMMANDER, ARMY OF NORTHERN VIRGINIA

With the enemy near Richmond, Rebel leaders tried to keep up the fighting spirit of their troops following Seven Pines. Longstreet's propaganda-filled address plays on the fears of Southern men with its hints at the slaughter of children and the rape of women that will ensue if Lincoln's immigrant "hirelings" are allowed to triumph.

Headquarters Right Wing,
Army before Richmond, June 17, 1862.

Soldiers: You have marched out to fight the battles of your country, and by those battles you must be rescued from the shame of slavery. Your foes have declared their purpose of bringing you to beggary; and avarice, their natural characteristic, incited them to redoubled efforts for the conquest of the South, in order that they may seize her sunny fields and happy homes. Already has the hatred of one of their great leaders attempted to make the negro your equal by declaring his freedom. They care not for the blood of babes nor carnage of innocent women which servile insurrection thus stirred up may bring upon their heads. Worse than this, the North has sent forth another infamous chief, encouraging the lust of his hirelings to the dishonor and violation of those Southern women who have so untiringly labored to clothe our soldiers in the field and nurse our sick and wounded. If ever men were called upon to defend the beloved daughters of their country, that now is our duty. Let such thoughts nerve you up to the most dreadful shock of battle; for were it certain death, death would be better than the fate that defeat would entail upon us all. But remember, though the fiery noise of battle is indeed most terrifying, and seems to threaten universal ruin, it is not so destructive as it seems, and few soldiers after all are slain. This the commanding general desires particularly to impress upon the fresh and inexperienced troops who now constitute a part of this command. Let officers and men, even under the most formidable fire, preserve a quiet demeanor and self-possessed temper. Keep cool, obey orders, and aim low. Remember while you are doing this, and driving the enemy before you, your comrades may be relied on to support you on either side, and are in turn relying upon you.

Stand well to your duty, and when these clouds break away, as they surely will, the bright sunlight of peace falling upon our free, virtuous, and happy land will be a sufficient reward for the sacrifices which we are now called upon to make.

James Longstreet,
Major-General, Commanding.

LIEUTENANT WILLIAM T. ROBINS

9th Virginia Cavalry, Stuart's Brigade

Stuart's famous ride around McClellan's army began early on the morning of June 12, when he awoke his troopers with the command: "Gentlemen, in 10 minutes every man must be in his saddle." Robins recounts the excitement present in camp as the Confederate troopers prepared for the ride that would garner them worldwide renown. Stuart cited Robins in his report of the raid for leading a "sudden dash" at a Union picket post, "infusing" the Yankees with "wholesome terror."

When the orders were issued from headquarters directing the several commands destined to form the expedition to prepare three days' rations, and the ordnance officers to issue sixty rounds of ammunition to each man, I remember the surmises and conjectures as to our destination. The officers and men were in high spirits in anticipation of a fight, and when the bugles rang out "Boots and Saddles," every man was ready. The men left behind in camp were bewailing their luck, and those forming the detail for the expedition were elated at the prospect of some excitement. "Good-bye, boys; we are going to help old Jack drive the Yanks into the Potomac," I heard one of them shout to those left behind.

On the afternoon of June 12th we went out to the Brooke turnpike,

"Soldiers: You have marched out to fight the battles of your country, and by those battles you must be rescued from the shame of slavery."

Brigadier General James Ewell Brown Stuart (above) did not determine to ride around the Federal army until his foray was under way. On June 13, he had found the position of the Union right flank, the information Lee most desired. Realizing he had surprise on his side, however, the flamboyant Stuart announced that he wanted to push on toward McClellan's rear. Despite misgivings, his subordinates assented.

preparatory to the march. The cavalry column was the 9th Virginia, commanded by Colonel W. H. F. Lee, the 1st Virginia, led by Colonel Fitz Lee, and the Jeff Davis Legion, under Colonel Martin. A section of the Stuart Horse Artillery, commanded by Captain Pelham, accompanied the expedition. The whole numbered twelve hundred men. The first night was passed in bivouac in the vicinity of Ashland, and orders were issued enforcing strict silence and forbidding the use of fires, as the success of the expedition would depend upon secrecy and celerity. On the following morning, at the break of dawn, the troopers were mounted and the march was begun without a bugle blast, and the column headed direct for Hanover Court House, distant about two hours' ride. Here we had the first sight of the enemy. A scouting party of the 5th U.S. Cavalry was in the village, but speedily decamped when our troops were ascertained to be Confederates. One prisoner was taken after a hot chase across country.

One of the troopers who rode with Stuart was Private Chesterfield S. Paytes of the 9th Virginia Cavalry (above). Paytes came through without incident. However, Union officer William Royall's pistol shots killed Paytes' commander, Captain William Latané, during a fracas near Totopotomoy Creek on June 13. Latané soon became one of the popular martyrs of the Southern cause.

PRIVATE JOHN MCCORMICK

5th U.S. Cavalry, Stoneman's Command

On June 13 McCormick and his company rode toward Hanover Court House to investigate reports that a large body of Rebel troopers had passed beyond the Union right flank. A sharp skirmish ensued near the hamlet of Haw's Shop, during which, according to Stuart, his men dispersed the Federals "in terror and confusion." In contrast, a Yankee officer commended his men for retreating "with great coolness."

My company (F) was ordered to make a reconnoissance to Hanover Court House. When we got within a half-mile of the old battleground we discovered the enemy's cavalry under Stewart drawn up in battle line, about 3,000 strong, with neither picket nor skirmishers out.

Our Lieutenant halted and ordered Serg't Mahon, with 10 men, to advance to a ravine or creek and to send your humble servant to inquire what troops they were and what their business was. To my assurance that they were rebels, and that I could distinguish the rank of their officers, the Lieutenant commanded me to obey orders.

I rode down the hill to the ravine and up the hill toward and within 75 yards of the enemy's lines, and, coming to a heavy black-oak gatepost at the roadside the hight of my breast when on horseback, I laid my Sharp's carbine on top of the post and took aim at a rebel officer who was made conspicuous by the heads of the other officers' horses being turned toward him. I blazed away and instantly a company of rebel cavalry advanced, deployed and opened fire on me and my 10 comrades beyond the ravine. Needless to say I lost no time, except while returning their fire, in joining Lieut. Lieb on top of the hill. His first question was:

"Did you ask those troops who they were?"

I looked around as I thought hard for an answer, and in the direction of the enemy saw coming at full gallop at least 100 of the 4th Va. Cav. on both sides of the road. I answered:

"Lieutenant, here they come; ask them yourself."

We got out of that scrape, but I was never sent by the Lieutenant on just a similar errand.

LIEUTENANT EDWARD H. LEIB

5TH U.S. CAVALRY, STONEMAN'S COMMAND

After the 5th's Captain William Royall was left, in his own words, "exhausted from the loss of blood from several saber wounds" at Haw's Shop, he turned his command over to Leib. Leib describes how he nearly made what would have been a costly charge into the blazing weapons of the Rebel cavalry. Fortunately for the Union troopers, the injured Royall galloped up and ordered Leib to retreat.

I still continued to retire until I reached our first pickets, stationed at a cross-road where were a few houses, known as Hall's Machine-Shop. Having heard from my scout I sent word to Captain Royall the enemy were not in sight, but repeated my first report, that I had seen two squadrons. After this I remained at the cross-roads and sent back my rear guard 1 1/2 miles on the road by which I had retired.

After remaining at the cross-roads about an hour I received an order from Captain Royall to return to camp, and withdrawing my rear guard, I cautioned the pickets that the enemy were in my rear, and took up my march toward camp. About a mile from the cross-roads I was joined by Lieutenant McLean, in command of about 30 men of Company H, Fifth Cavalry. . . . Lieutenant McLean took command, and keeping his company in front, we in this manner retired half a mile, when I was informed by pickets that the enemy were about a quarter of a mile back, advancing rapidly. I immediately sent word to Lieutenant McLean, who was in front, and also to Captain Royall, to tell them the enemy were advancing upon us. Not hearing from Lieutenant McLean I drew up in line under the brow of a hill on the side of the road, intending if my force was sufficient to charge; if not, to keep them in check with the pistol; in either event to show a bold front and conceal as long as possible the small numbers of my command. The enemy came on in a few moments in large numbers. I held them in check at least twenty minutes, emptying during that time ten saddles (the horses coming over to my command). During this time I lost no men, but had several horses wounded.

It was at this point that I felt most seriously the superiority of the enemy, who were armed with rifles and shot-guns, and had my command been furnished with carbines I would have been able to do him more injury and hold him longer in check. After I had emptied all of my pistols I drew sabers and endeavored to charge, but finding they were coming up in greatly-superior force on either flank and in front, I thought it best to fall back on Lieutenant McLean's command, which at this time was halted on the opposite side of a small bridge.

This sketch for Leslie's newspaper shows a portion of the fighting at Haw's Shop. Though this action was a small affair, Stuart's marauders added to the color of their adventure by humbling a detachment of a Regular U.S. Cavalry regiment. The 5th U.S. suffered 16 casualties and lost five guidons. Stuart's men, in the commander's words, "took possession of a number of horses, a quantity of arms and stores of every kind, [and] several officers and privates." As a final insult, what booty the Confederate cavalrymen could not take with them from the 5th's abandoned bivouac, they put to the torch.

SERGEANT GEORGE W. BEALE

9TH VIRGINIA CAVALRY, STUART'S BRIGADE

As his squadron raced through the community of Old Church in pursuit of the fleeing troopers of the 5th U.S., Beale later recounted, many women rushed "to the doors and windows and porches clapping their hands and waving their handkerchiefs in an ecstasy of patriotic joy." Beale was promoted to lieutenant in December 1862 and served in the 9th without incident until wounded while fighting near Petersburg in February 1865. He survived the injury to become a Baptist preacher after the war.

Suddenly, when past Hawe's shop and near where a body of timber on the left was bordered by our open field in the angle made by the road as it turned to the left beside the Tolopotomiy creek, we halted to make dispositions to assail the enemy in front and another body in the field to the left. It was necessary to tear down the fence in order to charge into the field, and while handling the rails here, a bullet cut an ugly gash in the flesh of a member of Company B, the first blood yet drawn on our side. The fence having been removed, a part of our squadron dashed towards the enemy in the road, and another part towards those in the field. I accompanied those who entered the field, and the squad of men at whom we were charging, broke and dashed to the right joining their comrades in the road, and formed with them a confused mass, galloping for the bridge which spanned the creek. The bridge was too narrow to admit of all crossing at once, and a number thus delayed were made prisoners as had been several before reaching the bridge.

In the gallop in the field, I did not pause on the hill and bear to the right as some of our party did, but continued with a few others, down the hill into the meadow below where the earth, made wet by recent rains, caused my mare to sink leg-deep in mire, throwing me several feet over her head. Before I could gain my feet, she had struggled out of the soft ground and, wild with excitement, dashed on into the road and joined the Yankee column at the bridge. Beautiful but foolish mare, she made no pause here and unable to get on the bridge I leaped down the bank into the river! A few minutes later, I found her on the farther side of the stream vainly attempting to ascend the steep bank, and prevented from going farther down the stream because of fallen trees. I made my way to her; saw the hopelessness of her rescue, took a pistol and haversack from the saddle and resigned Sally Payton—such was her name, to her fate.

Meanwhile, Captain Latanè's squadron had crossed the bridge and was charging up the hill beyond, the cheers of his men echoing from its wooded summit. Hastening back to where the provost-guard had the prisoners, I obtained a captured horse and with it re-crossed the bridge, and just beyond in the narrow road descending the hill, I met four or five members of Company E who were bleeding with the wounds just received. About half way up the hill, I met four men, each holding the corner of a blanket, and protruding from it behind was Captain Latanè's boot, so familiar to me from our ride together that morning. He had been instantly killed at the top of the hill

Fitzhugh Lee (above), Robert E. Lee's nephew, had a like temperament to that of his commander, Jeb Stuart—quick to laugh and fond of a good time, but nevertheless a tough fighter. Impressed with Lee's conduct during the raid, Stuart saw to it that the young colonel was promoted to brigadier general in July 1862.

where he had met a Federal squadron. . . .

It was found that the men whom we had met were commanded by a Captain W. B Royal of the 5th Regulars of the U.S. Army, a regiment of which General Robert E. Lee had been the Colonel and Fitz Lee a lieutenant. It was interesting and impressive to see a number of these men, held as prisoners, crowd around the latter officer, shake hands with him, and to hear them greet him in familiar manner as "Lieutenant." The fact that he now wore the uniform of a Confederate Colonel apparently did not extinguish their friendly feeling for him.

LIEUTENANT STEPHEN M. WELD

STAFF, BRIGADIER GENERAL FITZ-JOHN PORTER

Sent on a routine foraging expedition, Weld nearly became another prisoner of Stuart's column as it penetrated deeper behind Union lines. Despite being "worn out mentally," he made it back. Weld, a supporter of McClellan, wrote in his diary that "Little Mac" was "hampered by Stanton, whose . . . commands have . . . lengthened this war."

I went out Friday, June 13, with a light wagon and four horses and a negro driver named Sam. I am caterer for our mess now, and was going out to get some butter and eggs, etc. I went out to Hall's Mill some six miles from camp, and the place where our outpost pickets are stationed. From here, I took a road to the right, which led me to Mrs. Brockenborough's, the wife of a doctor in the rebel army. I bought 36 pounds of butter and a few onions, and turned round to come home. I should have told you before that Hall's Mill is situated at a point where four roads meet. One, the road I came on, which goes on to Hanover Court House. Another goes to Richmond, and on the prolongation of this latter road away from Richmond, I was getting my butter, etc. When I passed our pickets at Hall's Mill, they said that it was safe for me to go to Mrs. Brockenborough's as our pickets were there. As I said, I got my things all safely and turned round to go back to H.'s Mill, and from there home. When within 200 or 300 feet of the mill, I saw cavalry proceeding at a rapid rate towards Old Church, coming from the road to Hanover. At first I thought that it was all right, as the pickets had told me that our scouting parties had gone out in that direction. I thought, though, that their uniform looked rather light and so told my driver to stop while I crept up nearer them. I went into some woods on the right of the road and crept along the fence till I came within 50 or 60 feet of the rascals, and could plainly see that they were Secesh. At first, indeed, I could hardly believe that they were rebels, but thought they must be some regiment of our cavalry dressed in gray, but I remembered that we had none dressed that way. I could see and distinguish the officers by a broad gold stripe which they had on the pants and caps. The men were dressed in all kinds of clothes. Some had gray clothes, some the bluish gray, some white shirts, some red, and in fact almost all the colors of the rainbow were there. The coverings for their heads were of all sorts. Some had caps and others slouched hats, etc. A bend in the road I was on concealed the wagon from them while passing the mill, but when they had passed by the mill a few rods, there was nothing to conceal us from them. Luckily they were riding away from us, and so happened not to see us. I waited nearly an hour for them to get past us, and then turned the wagon round. I was afraid to do it before, because I thought it would attract their attention to move while they were so near. In order to turn, my man had to drive still nearer the mill where the road was broader, and this took him beyond the bend, so that he came in sight of some of them feeding their horses. They saw him, too, but made no effort to catch him. The only reason I can assign is that they took our wagon for one of the farmers' wagons belonging in the vicinity. There must have been two thousand cavalry in all, and after them three pieces of artillery. As soon as I had the wagon turned, I set the horses off on a good smart trot, expecting to see the cavalry pursuing me every moment. No one came, however, and I thought that I was all safe. I luckily knew the way to Old Church, and followed it as quickly as I could.

I was going in the direction in which the horses are faced, when I first came in sight of the cavalry. I then turned round and went in the direction of the arrow, and thought myself safe, thinking of course that the enemy would never dare come as far as Old Church. When about a quarter of a mile from Old C. I saw the rascals burning the camp of the 5th Cavalry, and the main body drawn up in line along the side of the

"The general and staff had all given me up and expected that I was a prisoner in Richmond. They all were very glad to see me."

road. I was thus cut off from our camps, as there was no other road I could take to get back. I instantly drove my horses and wagon into the woods on the right of the road, hid there in the bushes, and covered over the tracks of the wheels. I then went to the road where I could watch the rebels and not be seen. Pretty soon the main body started and went on to White House. Stragglers and pickets stayed behind, however, making it impossible for me to leave the woods. Besides, I did not know but what they might have infantry with them, and intended to occupy the place. . . . After being in the woods some little while, three men from the 5th Cavalry came in, they having been in the fight which the three companies of the 5th had with the rebels. Two of them had lost their horses. I got a negro who was by the roadside to let me know if any rebels came along, and I myself stood where I could look down the road. Soon I came where I could see a company of rebels, as I thought, coming towards me, and the negro motioned me back into the woods. These cavalry were in their shirt-sleeves and in the dust looked just like the rebels. I went back into the swamp a little way and waited there. A horse belonging to one of the 5th Cavalry neighed and drew the whole body of cavalry into the road to the wagon. I heard them talking there for more than an hour, and as it was getting pretty dark I started for home, walking through the woods. There was a private from the 5th Cavalry and my driver with me. I wandered through the woods, losing my way and expecting to meet with the enemies' pickets every minute. At about 1 o'clock in the morning I saw some of our pickets and called to them. I was in as much danger of getting shot by our own pickets as by theirs, for they are not apt to challenge when they know the enemy are near. I saw them first, and called to them, and found out the way to camp. . . . I got back to camp a little past four and glad enough I was to see it. The general and staff had all given me up and expected that I was a prisoner in Richmond. They all were very glad to see me.

CAPTAIN JOHN S. MOSBY

1st Virginia Cavalry, Stuart's Brigade

Recognizing Mosby's penchant for stealth, Stuart assigned him to do most of the advance scouting during the raid. Stuart lauded Mosby for his "distinguished service" and "shining record of daring and usefulness" during the ride around the Army of the Potomac. Mosby later gained fame as the leader of a partisan band in Virginia's Piedmont region.

Just before he gave the command to move forward he turned to me and said: "I want you to ride on some distance ahead." I answered: "All right, but I must have a guide; I don't know the road." So two cavalrymen who were familiar with the country were sent with me. That day I was riding a slow horse I had borrowed—mine had been broken down in the scout a few days before. We had not gone far before a staff officer overtook us and said the General wanted us to go faster and increase the distance between us. The reason was he did not want to run into an ambuscade. So we went on at a trot. It was important to reach the railroad before dark, and before troops could be sent there to stop us. Infantry did come on the cars that night; but we had gone. All they saw by moonlight were our tracks in the sand. As we were jogging along a mile or so ahead of the column we came upon a sutler's wagon. About a mile to the left could be seen the masts of some schooners at anchor in the river. A wagon train was loading at the wharf with supplies for the army. I sent one of the men back to tell Stuart that the woods were full of game; to hurry on. The sutler's wagon was condemned as prize of war and left in charge of my other companion. Tunstall's was still two or three miles off. I had never been there, but the road was plain and I jogged on alone. When Stuart got up to the sutler in the road he sent a squadron to burn the schooners and wagon trains. I believe this is the only instance in the war where cavalry operated on water. As I turned a bend in the road I came suddenly in sight of Tunstall's, half a mile off, and a few yards from me was another sutler's wagon, and a cavalry vedette, who had dismounted. Just then a bugle sounded, and I saw a company of cavalry, to which the vedette belonged, only a few hundred yards off. My horse was pretty well fagged out. The vedette and sutler surrendered, but I was in a quandary what to do. I thought there would be more danger in trying to run away on a slow horse than to stand still. So I concluded to play a game of bluff —I drew my sabre, turned around, and beckoned with it to imaginary followers. Fortunately, just then Lieutenant Robins, commanding the advanced guard, came in sight at a fast trot. The company of Pennsylvania (Eleventh) cavalry left in a hurry.

Shortly after the skirmish at Haw's Shop, Stuart's raiders rode into Tunstall's Station, on the Richmond & York River Railroad just five miles from McClellan's supply base at White House Landing. After capturing the shocked Union garrison, the Rebels cut the telegraph wires and began to block the track in preparation for an ambush. Confederate Adalbert Volck executed this sketch of Tunstall's Station, complete with a stereotypical depiction of a fat, befuddled foreign Yankee soldier at left.

SERGEANT GEORGE W. BEALE

9TH VIRGINIA CAVALRY, STUART'S BRIGADE

Just before the attack on Tunstall's Station, a squadron from the 1st Virginia Cavalry and one from the 9th Virginia Cavalry were sent to destroy Yankee supply ships docked at Garlick's Landing on the Pamunkey River. Beale—who incorrectly calls the landing "Gulick's" in this account—helped set fire to the ships and their attendant supply wagons. In an often-repeated occurrence during the raid, the small party of Union troops guarding the landing fled at the sight of the Rebel horsemen.

As we approached within a few miles of Tunstall's, our road was near enough to Pamunkey river to see the masts of some vessels lying at Gulick's Landing. Captain Knight with two companies was despatched to destroy the vessels, which he readily succeeded in doing, the guards of the Tenth Pennsylvania Cavalry having taken to cover at sight of his approach. This guard abandoned besides the vessels seventy-five loaded wagons on the river bank, which were burned.

As we drew near to Tunstall's Station, the signs increased of serious opposition before us. As the railroad here was the main means of communication between McClellan's army and its base of supplies at the White House, it was naturally inferred that it was under strong infantry guard at this point. Stuart consequently arranged his men in a column of platoons and we dashed into the place at a gallop. The small guard having watch here, made no resistance. The order was given as soon as we reached the station to remove the track, cut the telegraph poles and wires, throw obstructions on the road, and make ready for the coming of a train, supposed to be filled with infantry, hastening to resist us. Before their orders could be put into execution, the engine of a train, puffing its smoke, came into sight and approached, slowing down the nearer it came, and evidently preparing to stop.

LIEUTENANT JOHN E. COOKE

STAFF, BRIGADIER GENERAL J. E. B. STUART

In 1859 Cooke had marched north to quell John Brown's attack on Harpers Ferry as a member of the Richmond Howitzers, a militia unit composed of men from the city's wealthiest families. He joined Stuart's staff early in the war. The Cooke family presented a classic example of the internecine aspect of the Civil War. John E. Cooke's uncle was Union cavalry commander General Philip St. George Cooke, who was also Stuart's father-in-law. John E. Cooke's cousin and Philip Cooke's son, Colonel John R. Cooke, commanded the 27th North Carolina until wounded at Seven Pines.

Suddenly in the midst of the tumult was heard the shrill whistle of a train coming from the direction of the Chickahominy. Stuart quickly drew up his men in a line on the side of the road, and he had no sooner done so than the train came slowly round a wooded bend, and bore down. When within two hundred yards it was ordered to halt, but the command was not obeyed. The engineer crowded on all steam; the train rushed on, and then a thundering volley was opened upon the "flats" containing officers and men. The engineer was shot by Captain Farley, of Stuart's staff, and a number of the sol-

A BAND OF REBELS FIRING INTO THE CARS NE

A Federal train runs a gauntlet of fire from Stuart's dismounted cavalrymen as it steams through Tunstall's Station for White House Landing. The locomotive knocked aside the brush and logs blocking the track and continued on toward the Pamunkey, although the engineer was shot and killed. Stuart, realizing that the large infantry garrison at White House would now be alerted, got his weary troopers saddled up and moving southeastward again in the bright moonlight.

diers were wounded. The rest threw themselves upon their faces; the train rushed headlong by like some frightened monster bent upon escape, and in an instant it had disappeared.

Stuart then reflected for a single moment. The question was, should he go back and attack the White House, where enormous stores were piled up? It was tempting, and he afterwards told me he could scarcely resist it. But a considerable force of infantry was posted there; the firing had doubtless given them the alarm; and the attempt was too hazardous. The best thing for that gray column was to set their faces toward home, and "keep moving," well closed up both day and night, for the lower Chickahominy. So Stuart pushed on. Beyond the railroad appeared a world of wagons, loaded with grain and coffee—standing in the road abandoned. Quick work was made of them. They were all set on fire, and their contents destroyed. From the horse-trough of one I rescued a small volume bearing on the fly-leaf the name of a young lady of Williamsburg. I think it was a volume of poems—poetic wagon-drivers!

These wagons were only the "vaunt couriers"—the advance guard—of the main body. In a field beyond the stream thirty acres were covered with them. They were all burned. The roar of the soaring flames was like the sound of a forest on fire. How they roared and crackled! The sky overhead, when night had descended, was bloody-looking in the glare.

, VIRGINIA, JUNE 13, 1862:—SKETCHED BY MR. MEAD.—[SEE PAGE 426.]

BRIGADIER-GENERAL PHILIP S. COOKE

CAVALRY COMMANDER, ARMY OF THE POTOMAC

Cooke, a Virginian, commanded the force pursuing Stuart's raiders and became an object of ridicule in the South. "I wonder what the old renegade Virginian thinks of his dashing son-in-law?" sneered diarist Judith McGuire. "If he has a spark of proper feeling left in his obdurate heart, he must be proud of him."

If the enemy returned over the road, as was then believed he would, I should soon meet him. I had under 500 cavalry; if he had no infantry, I should need the infantry for anything like certain success. If the enemy did not return I know he had been 8 miles or more ahead ten hours before at least, so that cavalry alone could not overtake him, even if it should pursue to attack three times its strength in numbers, supported by artillery. (Mine was not horse artillery.)

I expected, then, to meet him every moment, or, if he had infantry and attacked White House depot, that General Emory and a few other troops I supposed might be there would detain him until I should fall upon him with my force of three arms. The infantry marched as fast as possible. The day proved excessively warm, and they and the artillery suffered. Near Garlick's it became certain that White House depot had not been attacked, and the enemy's motions could only be guessed. The cavalry got well ahead, with orders to halt at Tunstall's Station. Colonel Warren I authorized to halt at the first water near there. I joined the cavalry there soon after their arrival; found General Emory, and learned the enemy had been traced far southward.

LIEUTENANT JOHN E. COOKE

STAFF, BRIGADIER GENERAL J. E. B. STUART

Cooke was known in the South before the war for having written pro-secession articles that appeared in the Southern Literary Messenger. After Appomattox, he continued his writing career, publishing books related to his military experiences. Here, Cooke describes the tense situation Stuart's command faced at the flooded Chickahominy River.

At the first streak of dawn the Chickahominy was in sight, and Stuart was spurring forward *to the ford.*

It was impassable! The heavy rains had so swollen the waters that the crossing was utterly impracticable! Here we were within a few miles of McClellan's army, with an enraged enemy rushing on our track to make us rue the day we had "circumvented" them, and inflicted on them such injury and insult; here we were with a swollen and impassable stream directly in our front—the angry waters roaring around the half-submerged trunks of the trees—and expecting every instant to hear the crack of carbines from the rear-guard indicating the enemy's approach! The "situation" was not pleasing. I certainly thought that the enemy would be upon us in about an hour, and death or capture would be the sure alternative. This view was general. I found that cool and resolute officer, Colonel William H. F. Lee, on the river's bank. He had just attempted to swim the river, and nearly drowned his horse among the tangled roots and snags. I said to him:

A small portion of the immense Union supply base at White House Landing—a prize sorely tempting to Jeb Stuart—appears in this photograph. In the foreground is a group of Federal wagons like those Stuart captured and burned at Tunstall's Station. Hundreds of tents used for storage and as shelters for quartermasters and garrison troops whiten the background. Later in the month, Lee's aggressive tactics would compel McClellan to abandon this base and move his supplies to Harrison's Landing, on the James River.

"Here we were within a few miles of McClellan's army, with an enraged enemy rushing on our track to make us rue the day we had 'circumvented' them."

"What do you think of the situation, Colonel?"

"Well, Captain," was the reply, in the speaker's habitual tone of cheerful courtesy, "I think we are caught."

The men evidently shared this sentiment. The scene upon the river's bank was curious, and under other circumstances would have been laughable. The men lay about in every attitude, half-overcome with sleep, but holding their bridles, and ready to mount at the first alarm. Others sat their horses asleep, with drooping shoulders. Some gnawed crackers; others ate figs, or smoked, or yawned.

SERGEANT GEORGE W. BEALE

9TH VIRGINIA CAVALRY, STUART'S BRIGADE

On June 14 the Confederate riders arrived at the Chickahominy River. Here the high, fast-moving water and the unpredictable behavior of the horses combined to offer the most serious threat to the troopers' safe return to Richmond. Beale's father, the "Lt. Colonel of the regiment," was Richard Lee Turberville Beale. The elder Beale became a brigadier general in early 1865, serving under the command of W. H. F. "Rooney" Lee—Robert E. Lee's second son—also mentioned here.

The place of this anticipated crossing was a somewhat secluded one on a plantation, to which no public road led and was capable of being forded only when the river was low. We reached it at daylight, and Colonel W. H. F. Lee, laying aside his clothing, and descending an embankment somewhat obstructed with bushes and trees, entered the water like a bold swimmer to test the depth and force of the current. He soon returned from his venture reporting that it was impossible to get the horses over without swimming them.

Having had some experience in swimming horses in swollen streams, I offered to swim over that of my father, the Lt. Colonel of the regiment. His horse was a compact and handsome bay called Dan which swam the stream with ease, and was left tied on the farther shore. Having swam back to the side of my companions, I led my own horse—the capture of the previous day—into the river and swimming at its head landed it on the opposite shore and saw it go up out of the water. I did not deem it necessary to halter it, but turned to swim back. When I got about mid stream coming back, I heard the heavy breathing of a horse and the sound of its feet like paddles in water and looking back saw the animal I had just released following me like a dog and in danger of striking me with its hoofs. It was evident that it was intent on getting back to the other horses from which I had taken it, and I let it return.

While occupied in this endeavor to get these horses across the river, two tall pines near the water's edge had been cut down, in the vain hope that they would span the stream. Each of them in falling sprang clear of the shore and proving too short to reach the farther side were borne down the current. A long line made of bridle-reins and halters tied together had been carried by this time across and made secure to two trees, one on either side, and an attempt was made to ferry a raft of fence-rails over, capable of bearing ten or twelve men with their saddles and equipments. Only one trial of the raft was made, since as soon as it reached the centre of the stream the force of the water submerged the lower end of it, sweeping off some of its occupants' saddles, coats and boots, which were hopelessly borne away on the current.

It became manifest now that to cross twelve hundred horses and a section of artillery here was impossible, and the command was put in motion for Jones' Bridge, a mile or so farther down, where the river dividing into two streams formed an island, and greatly lessened the width of the main current.

On reaching Jones' Bridge, we found that sometime previously it had been burned and nothing but the charred piles remained.

LIEUTENANT JOHN E. COOKE

STAFF, BRIGADIER GENERAL J. E. B. STUART

Offering no clue to his own role in the affair, Cooke describes the improvisation that allowed Stuart's column to escape the pursuing Federals. Stuart, seeing that he could not ford the Chickahominy, led his men downstream to the ruins of Jones' Bridge, where they hurriedly began building a span with planks scavenged from a nearby barn. In three hours the task was completed, and the raiders crossed to safety.

The bridge had been destroyed, but the stone abutments remained some thirty or forty feet only apart, for the river here ran deep and narrow between steep banks. Between these stone sentinels, facing each other, was an "aching void" which it was necessary to fill. Stuart gave his personal superintendence to the work, he and his staff labouring with the men. A skiff was procured; this was affixed by a rope to a tree, in the mid-current just above the abutments, and thus a movable pier was secured in the middle of the stream. An old barn was then hastily torn to pieces and robbed of its timbers; these were stretched down to the boat, and up to the opposite abutment, and a foot-bridge was thus ready. Large numbers of the men immediately unsaddled their horses, took their equipments over, and then returning, drove or rode their horses into the stream, and swam them over. In this manner a considerable number crossed; but the process was much too slow. There, besides, was the artillery, which Stuart had no intention of leaving. A regular bridge must be built without a moment's delay, and to this work Stuart now applied himself with ardour.

Heavier blows resounded from the old barn; huge timbers approached, borne on brawny shoulders, and descending into the boat anchored in the middle of the stream, the men lifted them across. They were just long enough; the ends rested on the abutments, and immediately thick planks were hurried forward and laid crosswise, forming a secure footway for the cavalry and artillery horses. Standing in the boat beneath, Stuart worked with the men, and as the planks thundered down, and the bridge steadily advanced, the gay voice of the General was heard humming a song. He was singing carelessly, although at every instant an overpowering force of the enemy was looked for, and a heavy attack upon the disordered cavalry.

At last the bridge was finished; the artillery crossed amid hurrahs from the men, and then Stuart slowly moved his cavalry across the shaky footway.

LIEUTENANT WILLIAM T. ROBINS

9TH VIRGINIA CAVALRY, STUART'S BRIGADE

Once Robins torched the makeshift bridge, Stuart's cavalry was beyond the reach of the Yankees. On June 15 the exhausted troopers, many asleep in their saddles, rode into Richmond to complete a raid that would live in legend. Robins, born in Virginia's Gloucester County and a graduate of Washington College, later suffered two wounds in battle, rising to become colonel of the 24th Virginia Cavalry in 1864.

On leaving the river, General Stuart directed me to take charge of the rear-guard, and, when all had crossed, to burn the bridge. In accordance with these orders, I directed the men to collect piles of fence rails, heap them on the bridge, and set them afire. By my orders the horses had been led some distance back from the river into the brush, where they were concealed from view. The men were lounging about on the ground when the bridge fell in. I was seated under a tree on the bank of the river, and at the moment that the hissing of the burning timbers of the bridge let me know that it had fallen into the water, a rifle shot rang out from the other side, and the whistling bullet cut off a small limb over my head, which fell into my lap. The shot was probably fired by some scout who had been following us, but who was afraid to fire until the bridge was gone. With a thankful heart for his bad aim, I at once withdrew the men, and pushed on after the column.

PRIVATE DAVID HOLT

16TH MISSISSIPPI INFANTRY, TRIMBLE'S BRIGADE

On June 16, the day after Jeb Stuart's horsemen completed their ride, Stonewall Jackson's "foot cavalry" began marching east toward Richmond from the Shenandoah Valley. Jackson did not inform his troops of their destination, leading to much speculation in the ranks, as Holt relates. The veterans did become excited at the prospect of a train ride after their march over the rugged Blue Ridge Mountains.

We camped for three days near Weyer's Cave and examined it with curiosity. This was followed by orders to cook up three days' meals, and at daylight the next morning we moved on towards the eastern mountains.

Our company war council was completely nonplussed. Where in the thunder were we going? Did "Old Jack" want to convert us into a lot of

This Confederate map traces Stuart's jaunt around the Army of the Potomac. On June 12 the riders left Richmond, moving to the northwest. Later that day they took a sharp turn to the southeast and sparred with Union cavalry near Haw's Shop. They continued on a southeastward tack, firing bridges and wagon trains. After failing to stop a Federal train at Tunstall's Station, Stuart considered racing down the track to destroy McClellan's supply depot at White House Landing but judged the risk too great. Crossing the Chickahominy at Jones' Bridge, the raiders kept near the James River until they arrived in Richmond with, Stuart happily reported, "prisoners, 165 in number," and "260 horses and mules captured."

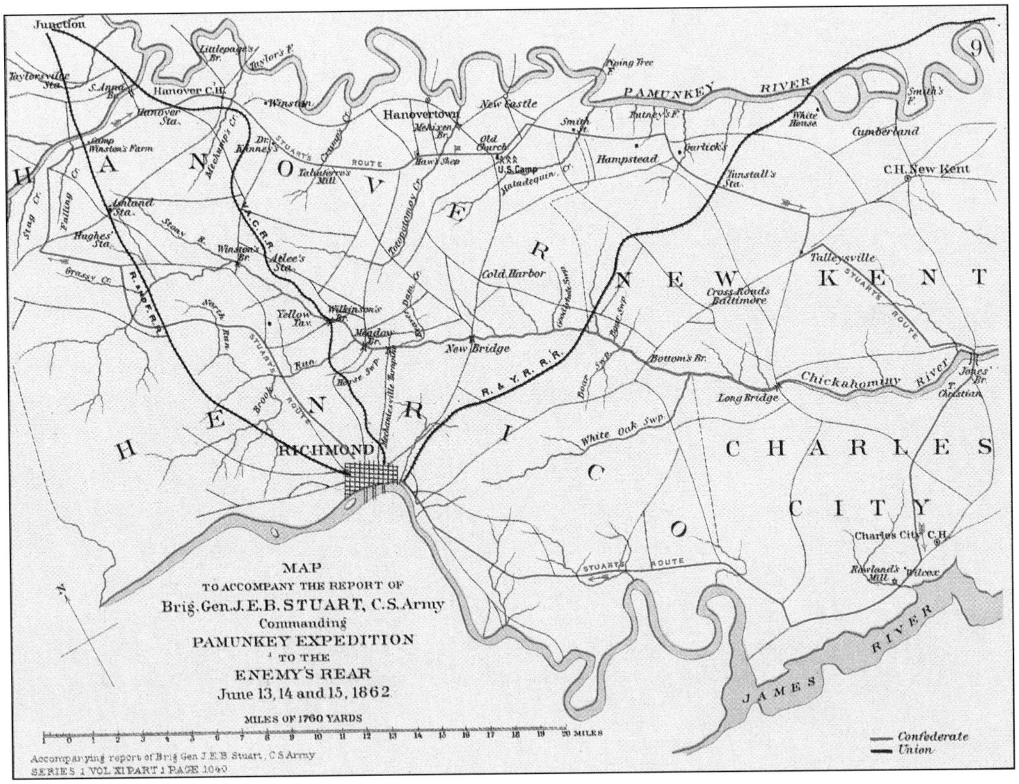

mountain timber? And how was the artillery going to climb up those hills? These were some of the questions asked [about] those orders. We followed no particular road and we seemed to be going no particular way. When we reached the mountains we took a narrow trail running up at a steep angle with a babbling brook near.

" 'Old Jack' is sending us out fishing for mountain trout," one volunteered.

"Well, what is he sending the cannon along for?" another asked.

"Why to shoot 'em if we catch 'em. Any fool can see that."

The cannon somehow went up that trail. A pioneer corps came along and by digging down banks along the trail and filling in other places, besides cutting down trees, the artillery and infantry got through. When we halted for the night, we made a small fire, boiled coffee, ate our grub, all of which had been captured, smoked and fell asleep.

When we reached the summit the next day we looked down upon a lovely valley seeing a good sized town. It was Charlottesville. Learning this, we all whooped it up. Nearing the town, we saw many railroad coaches. Some were loaded with troops. We were heading straight for the train.

CARTER S. ANDERSON

Baggage Master, Virginia Central Railroad

Jackson's men rode two major train lines to reach the vicinity of Richmond. The Orange & Alexandria Railroad ran from Charlottesville into Gordonsville, where the Virginia Central Railroad, Anderson's employer, began its eastbound path to the Confederate capital. The harrowing journey Anderson describes in this account continued for several days. At one point, John Whalley, the besotted engineer, even threw his coat into the firebox in a misguided effort to increase the train's speed.

The railroad men felt confident that we would haul no more soldiers, soon. Before noon, however, the lumbering of heavy artillery could be heard along the country roads toward Richmond, and everything wore a serious and sober aspect. Pretty soon we were ordered to prepare immediately every train. "Load them to their fullest capacity and let each train give to the preceding train thirty minutes' time. Keep trains well in hand; sound no whistle; ring no bell. Brakemen, keep a sharp look-out for trains in front and rear. *Death* to the whole crew who cause a collision!" This was indeed what might be termed a limited time card.

Our superintendent, acting under instructions from President Edmund Fontaine, who then resided at Richmond, would not assume the responsibility of running his trains any further into our unoccupied territory, but was perfectly willing to allow the Government to use the trains on its own responsibility. Since McClellan had removed the line of battle from Manasses to the Peninsula, beautiful Piedmont had been unoccupied by either army. Anywhere from the Potomac to the James, and east of the Blue Ridge to the vicinity of Richmond, the citizens would just as soon have expected a Southern army as a Northern one, and vice versa. . . .

No wonder then that our engineers hesitated to plunge their trains into such a country. The rain was pouring and it was nearly night. They did not fear for their own lives as much as for the responsibility of 2,000 soldiers, which was the average of each of the ten trains. The officers acted very nicely, and assured us that our cavalry had gone all through the country, as low as the South Anna river, and that there was not a Northern soldier west of Hanover C. H. Furthermore, they gave us two Confederate officers who rode on the pilot of the front engine.

Our ten trains of 18 to 20 cars per train, were soon placed for loading. I wish our passengers nowadays could have seen how quickly (about ten minutes) 1,500 to 2,000 men, with their heavy muskets, clumsy boots and haversacks, crawled into and on top of 20 box cars and work train flats. . . .

Conductor John H. Richardson and Engineer Martin Alley took the lead of the ten trains in this momentous occasion, and two safer men never pulled a bell cord or stepped upon a footboard. Martin looked quite serene on the "Westward Ho!" engine, with a Confederate Brigadier on either wing of his pilot. It was a war picture indeed, and as he quietly and carefully pulled his engine pin and drew his train into the curve east of Louisa, there went up a yell which seemed to fill the whole air around us. Our train came next and the signal was given to my engineer, John Whalley, to pull down in place to load. To my horror, I then discovered that John was pretty drunk, and my fireman, John Wesley, dead drunk! We needed but little steam, however, as it was mostly down grade all the way.

I hope I may never again experience such feelings as I then had. I had on board 2,000 soldiers; a train just ahead; one just in rear; overloaded; pouring rain; nearly night; engineer very much in liquor; no fireman; not a whistle allowed to be sounded; not a bell allowed to be rung!

I at once held an earnest conversation with Conductor Joshua Finks and Engineer Fendal Ragland, who were immediately behind us. No kinder-hearted man ever lived than Josh Finks. He was much older than I, and putting his arms around my trembling shoulders, said: "Carter, get on your engine and keep John from running into Richardson, and Ragland and I will keep from running into you." I gratefully acted as he suggested, and slipping upon the "Monroe" in front, tied a knot in his whistle cord. Cautioning my brakeman to keep a sharp look-out for my signals from my lamp on the engine and to use the brake on Whalley if he wanted to run too fast, I then informed Mr. Whalley that we were ready. He stepped upon the Monroe's footboard, and stooping a little to enter his cab, he tapped her open gently with his characteristic way.

I sat on the box opposite him and watched anxiously the curves as we rolled gently along toward Mineral City. Mr. Whalley told fireman John Wesley to fill her up, at the same time opening the firebox door with the toe of his boot. Wesley was so drunk that he thought the wood piled up in the tender was the firebox, and began cramming wood back and *firing the tender.* We were now approaching the 65-foot per mile down grade east of Mineral City, and as we had gotten into a pretty good swing on the level, I knew there was great danger, and asked Whalley to shut her off and get the train well in hand before he struck the grade. His eye flashed fire. He snatched the Monroe's throttle wide open and as she struck the down grade we dashed through "Rock Cut" at a desperate speed. Physically I was nothing to Whalley, but fear left my timid frame and left me strength instead. I felt I could do anything. I snatched the stick of wood out of Whalley's hand and told Mr. Whalley to shut her off. He saw that what I had made up my mind to do I would do, and reached immediately for the whistle cord, forgetting that it was *death* to pull it. The knot I had tied, however, saved his life. He at once drew her in back gear and as soon as he could possibly do so, nearly stopped the train. Looking ahead as we entered the reverse curve, I exclaimed. "Great God, Whalley, just look!" There, just ahead of us on the curve near Frederick's Hall, was what I had dreaded for the last few minutes—the *red lights on the rear of Richardon's train,* as he cautiously rolled down the grade!

Mr. Whalley realized now the situation; it sobered him. With tears rapidly rolling out of his great eyes he beckoned to me to come out to him, and drawing me close to his side, told me that when he shut off the Monroe and reversed her, it was with the full determination to throw me into the firebox, and the only thing that stopped him was the ruby glare from the rear of Richardson's train.

"I had on board 2,000 soldiers; a train just ahead; one just in rear; overloaded; pouring rain; nearly night; engineer very much in liquor; no fireman; not a whistle allowed to be sounded; not a bell allowed to be rung!"

This very narrow escape from such an awful and wholesale massacre as would inevitably have soon followed had Whalley not shut off when he did, sobered him completely; and well it might. We crept along to Frederick's Hall, and putting a brakeman to firing, I assumed his place on top of rear car, and we reached the end of our trip in good order, though drenched with rain.

LIEUTENANT HENRY KYD DOUGLAS

STAFF, MAJOR GENERAL THOMAS J. JACKSON

Douglas humorously details his secretive commander's journey from the Shenandoah Valley to meet with Lee. Jackson's surprisingly behindhand and unaggressive leadership of his 18,500 troops during the Seven Days' Battles would do much to frustrate Lee's hopes of destroying McClellan's army.

At noon the next day we detected the General as he stepped from the cars at Mechum's River. He came from the direction of Staunton. He had no instructions to give and did not trouble himself to ask the whereabouts of anybody. He had his trunk put on the train, remained about fifteen minutes, and shaking hands all round and saying good-by as earnestly as if he was off for Europe, he departed and gave no sign. Those of us left looked at each other and then gave vent to our suppressed merriment. "What the devil is he up to now?" one said, and we all thought. An inquisitive old fellow at Charlottesville thought he'd find out, and finding verbal tactics ineffectual, he bluntly asked,

"General, where *are* you going?"

"Can you keep a secret? Yes? Ah, so can I," was the answer he got. . . .

We overtook the General at Gordonsville on Saturday, where he was awaiting the arrival of the advance of his troops and put somewhat in doubt by vague rumors of threatening movements of McDowell. He was comfortably fixed in a hospitable house but was ready to go on. We only saw him at dinner, after which he took Dr. McGuire and departed, telling us to follow on Monday. Sunday we gave more to society than the sanctuary, and Monday morning, with uncovered heads, we returned the salute of white handkerchiefs waved by white hands and rode away.

At Fredericks Hall we again found traces of the General, but were informed that he had taken his departure at one o'clock the night before, without explanation and with only a courier to guide him. Our informants looked surprised because we were not amazed at such eccentricity, and we smiled at their surprise.

The next day we continued the chase, and near Beaver Dam Depot came upon the General. It was afternoon and he was in bed, and not a very refreshing or creditable sight met us. The General must have been on a rollicking frolic. His wet and muddy uniform was being dried by the fire and the appearance of his ponderous boots indicated that he might have been wading all night through mud and mire. No one seemed to know where he had been or what doing. It transpired in time that when he left Fredericks Hall so mysteriously he had gone to Richmond and to General Lee's Headquarters, and that he had returned to Beaver Dam just before we found him. He had traveled as a "Colonel" and carried a pass from General Whiting for "one officer to go to Richmond."

A Stumbling Start for Lee

On the night of June 25, after the battle at Oak Grove, McClellan sensed that something was afoot. Over the past few days he had received reports that Stonewall Jackson was coming by rail and road from the Shenandoah Valley to fall upon the rear of his right flank, held by Fitz-John Porter's V Corps on the north bank of the Chickahominy River. He was also worried about rumors that a large portion of General Pierre G. T. Beauregard's western army had arrived in Richmond from Mississippi.

McClellan, believing that the administration's failure to reinforce him with McDowell's army jeopardized his chances of capturing Richmond, grew even more cautious. Convinced that his army was vastly outnumbered and about to be attacked, he postponed his scheduled advance on Old Tavern and sent a nervous telegram to Washington announcing that if a catastrophe should occur, he would do his duty but would accept no blame. "The responsibility cannot be thrown on my shoulders," he told Secretary of War Edwin M. Stanton.

Lee, meanwhile, had a different concern. He had daringly marched the bulk of his army away from Richmond on the hunch that McClellan would hesitate to attack the city. And as the morning of June 26 wore on it became clear that he had read his opposite number correctly. John Magruder's demonstrations in the trenches before Richmond, designed to fool the Union chief into believing he faced overwhelming strength in the Rebel lines, were working. There would be no bold attempt to storm the Confederate capital.

But although Lee had accurately predicted McClellan's reluctance to attack, he was having little luck getting his own offensive under way. That morning the Confederate commander stood on a bluff looking north across the Chickahominy toward Mechanicsville, anxiously waiting for his attack to unfold.

Three Rebel divisions—D. H. Hill's and Longstreet's in front of the two bridges leading directly into Mechanicsville, and A. P. Hill's less than two miles upstream in front of Meadow Bridge—had been in position on the south bank of the Chickahominy since early morning.

Federal cannoneers man Fort Sumner, near Seven Pines, part of McClellan's three-mile-long line of earthworks that stretched from White Oak Swamp to the Chickahominy River.

They were awaiting the arrival of Stonewall Jackson's three divisions—Jackson's own, now under Brigadier General Charles S. Winder, Major General Richard S. Ewell's, and William Whiting's—which were supposed to begin turning Fitz-John Porter's right flank at 9:00 a.m. But a message sent by Jackson from Ashland, 15 miles north of Richmond, indicated that his vaunted foot cavalry was running six hours behind schedule.

At Meadow Bridge, A. P. Hill was more impatient at the delay than Lee himself. Under the plan of attack, once he heard the sound of Jackson's guns he was supposed to advance through Mechanicsville and attack the Federal force dug in beyond Beaver Dam Creek. D. H. Hill and Longstreet were then to follow the same route and join the assault. The combined Confederate forces would total at least 60,000 men, outnumbering Porter's command by almost 2 to 1.

At 36, Ambrose Powell Hill was the youngest of Lee's major generals. His Light Division was the newest and largest division in the Army of Northern Virginia, and he was eager to prove its mettle. A slender, handsome man with long, reddish brown hair and beard, in battle he liked to wear a red checked shirt under his coat. Hill was also highstrung and disputatious, traits explained in part by chronic ill health.

By 3:00 p.m., six hours had passed since Jackson had sent his message, and Hill assumed that Jackson must surely now be approaching. Without notifying Lee, who was less than two miles downstream, Hill took his division across the river, swung right, and began the offensive. He drove back the Federal pickets, routed a regiment-sized outpost in Mechanicsville, and deployed five brigades across the open plain beyond the village. Toward 5:00 p.m. Hill launched Brigadier General James J. Archer's brigade in the first of a series of piecemeal assaults on Porter's main defense line, entrenched on high ground behind Beaver Dam Creek.

Although Hill knew that the Federal line was practically invulnerable to frontal attack, he expected Jackson to arrive at any moment and outflank it. He even extended his left to make contact with Jackson so that together they could force the enemy to fall back.

At long last, shortly after 5:00 p.m., Jackson and his vanguard arrived at a crossroads called Hundley's Corner, less than three miles from Hill's northernmost brigade. Jackson's march from Ashland had been extraordinarily slow. His columns had covered only 13 miles in more than 14 hours on the road—just seven miles since 9:00 a.m.

Certainly Jackson's men were tired; in the past 40 days the majority of them had fought five battles in the Shenandoah Valley and marched more than 400 miles. Their supplies were lagging behind, leaving them hungry and dispirited. Jackson himself might have been unsure how to proceed. He did not know the boggy terrain north of Richmond, and his maps were inaccurate. He might not have fully understood Lee's orders, and he might have been confused by Lee's failure to detail a staff officer to guide him into position.

The delay was thus perhaps explicable, but nothing could account for what happened when Jackson finally arrived at Hundley's Corner. He could hear the sounds of battle from the southwest—the boom of artillery and the crackle of musketry—and all he had to do to turn the enemy flank was push forward a mile or two. Instead, without so much as sending a message to Lee, he put his men into bivouac and bedded down for the night.

So astonishing was this performance that one Confederate officer later wrote that Jackson "was not really Jackson" that day. The general was undoubtedly as exhausted as his men. During the past four days he had slept only 10 hours —and his associates knew him as a man who needed his sleep. "When he went to sleep he was the most difficult man to arouse I ever saw," wrote Dr. Hunter Maguire. "If his rest was broken for one night, he was almost certain to go to sleep upon his horse if riding the next day."

For whatever reason, Jackson went to bed early that evening while his compatriots were being slaughtered within earshot. The defenders of the unassailable Federal position at Beaver Dam Creek, George McCall's division of Pennsylvanians, were entrenched on a slope that rose from the east bank. Atop the crest were six batteries—36 guns in all—that commanded the long open plain over which the Confederates were advancing from the west. The cannon rained a deadly accurate fire on A. P. Hill's troops as they charged across the flatland toward the creek.

Lee, who had crossed the Chickahominy at about 5:00 p.m. after seeing the smoke of battle, witnessed precisely what he had made careful plans to prevent—a hopeless frontal assault. At one point, he tried to order Hill to break off the attack, but the message went awry. Seldom a man to show his emotions or assess blame—afterward, in his official report, he carefully avoided accusing Jackson of tardiness or A. P. Hill of a premature attack—he nevertheless reacted brusquely when Jefferson Davis and a large entourage of congressmen, cabinet members, and staff officers appeared unexpectedly at the edge of the battlefield.

"Mr. President," Lee said icily, "who is all this army and what is it doing here?"

"It is not my army, General," replied Davis.

"It certainly is not my army, Mr. President," retorted Lee, "and this is no place for it."

Lee ordered his other two divisions across the river and, toward sunset, sent D. H. Hill's lead brigade, under Brigadier General Roswell S. Ripley, to aid A. P. Hill's embattled troops. Ripley's four regiments assaulted the strongest Federal position of all, near Ellison's Mill on the banks of Beaver Dam Creek. The caustic D. H. Hill later wrote, "The result was, as might have been foreseen, a bloody and disastrous repulse." One regiment, the 44th Georgia, lost 335 out of 514 men sent into action.

At about 9:00 p.m. darkness ended the Battle of Mechanicsville, the second of the Seven Days' Battles. Lee, in his first major encounter, had suffered a costly failure. He had been able to bring to bear less than one-fourth of his available force and had been stopped far short of his first day's objective—a four-mile advance to New Bridge to establish a link with Magruder on the south bank of the Chickahominy. And he had lost 1,484 men killed and wounded. Fallen Confederates lay along Beaver Dam Creek, a Federal officer observed, "like flies in a bowl of sugar."

The Federals had suffered only 361 casualties. General McClellan, who had arrived at Porter's headquarters during the battle, was ecstatic. "Victory of today complete and against great odds," he wired Washington that night. "I almost begin to think we are invincible."

But for all his bravado, McClellan knew that his right flank remained vulnerable to Jackson. Thus, during the night, he ordered Porter to withdraw eastward to a second, stronger line of defense. By dawn, only a rear guard remained at Beaver Dam Creek; the rest of the V Corps was marching four miles west to another sluggish little stream, Boatswain's Swamp, about a mile southeast of a gristmill on the property of the area's largest landowner, Dr. William G. Gaines.

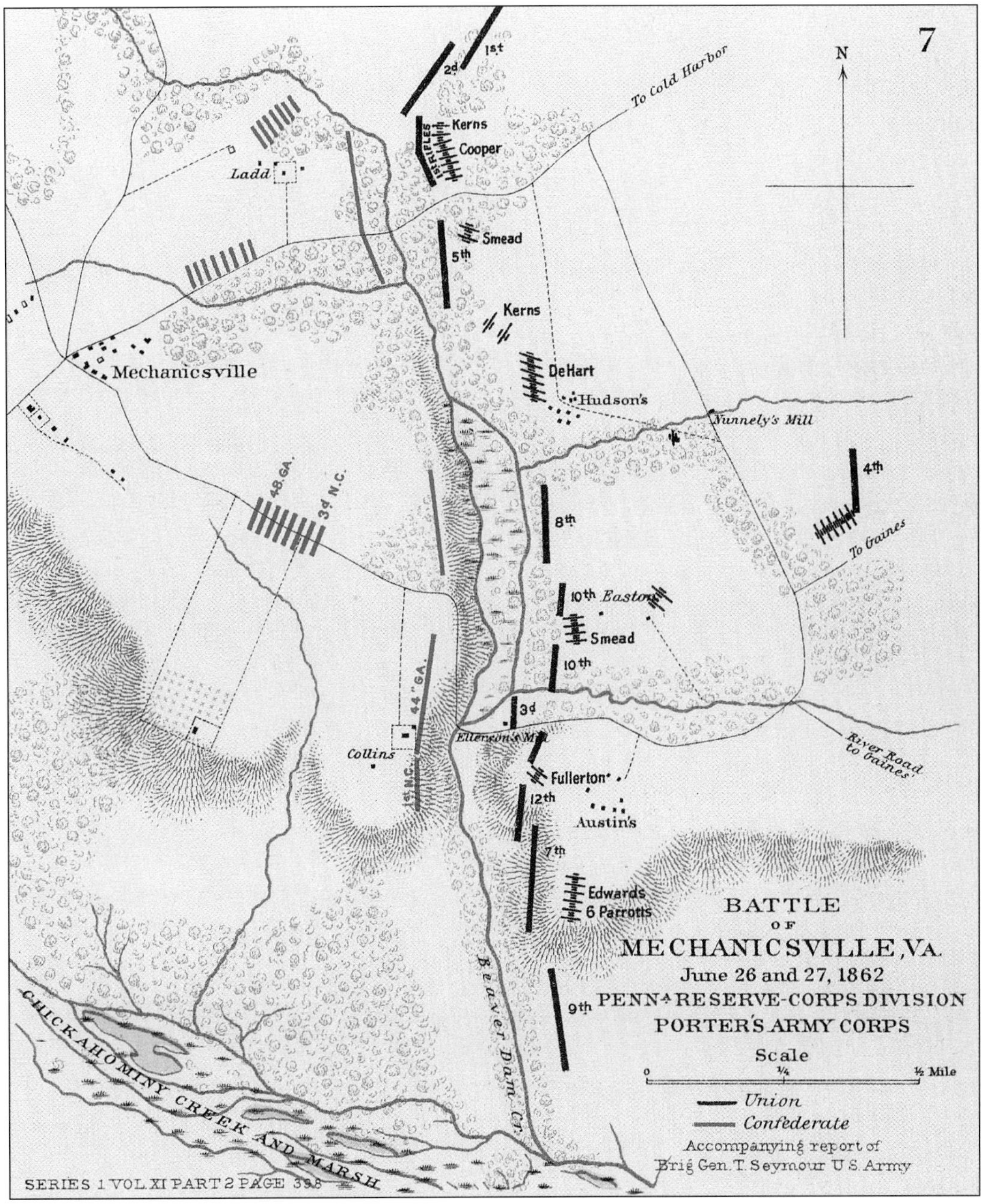

This map of the Battle of Mechanicsville, prepared for Federal brigadier general Truman Seymour, shows the positions held by elements of Major General Fitz-John Porter's V Corps. When a Confederate flanking force under Stonewall Jackson failed to arrive on the field, Major General A. P. Hill attacked the Federal earthworks across Beaver Dam Creek, only to be repulsed with heavy losses. Further Rebel assaults near Ellerson's Mill also failed. Despite the successful Federal defense, General McClellan ordered Porter to withdraw during the night.

William Waud, though not as well known as his brother Alfred, also produced many watercolors and sketches for Frank Leslie's Illustrated Newspaper and Harper's Weekly. In this sketch looking southeast toward Richmond he depicts a Union battery firing shells across the Chickahominy River to provide covering fire for the troops assembled in the left-center distance before the Mechanicsville Turnpike bridge.

PRIVATE GEORGE W. NICHOLS

61ST GEORGIA INFANTRY, LAWTON'S BRIGADE

Lawton's newly formed brigade of 3,600 men had traveled by rail from the south to Port Republic in the Shenandoah Valley. From there the men began a march to Richmond to join Stonewall Jackson's command. Nichols describes the Georgians' eastward trek, and the jeering they received from Jackson's veterans, in this account. Nichols was later wounded at Harpers Ferry in 1862 and at Winchester in 1864.

We started very early next morning and marched very hard till late in the afternoon. We stopped to camp and cook rations. Our tents were all left behind. The clouds began to collect and thunder very heavily, and the rain began to pour down in torrents, with a heavy gale of wind. It rained for very nearly two hours, and we all got as wet as we could be. Our fires were about all out. Ive Summerlin, of Company D, wrapped in his blankets, was lying down with the water ponded around him. He raised up a little and said, "Boys, it rains very well to-night." It created a big laugh. When it quit raining we renewed our fires, dried off the best we could, and finished our cooking.

We started about day next morning on a forced march, with full creeks and branches to cross. The roads were so cut up with the wagons and artillery until we could hardly get along. Some of the boys would bog so deep into the mud till when they got out their shoes would remain often ten and twelve inches below the surface. Every man had to carry his own haversack, knapsack, gun and cartridge-box. Some of the boys had white sheets, and I believe a few had feather pillows. Jackson's old soldiers, who had been following Jackson in his campaigns, made sport of us.

They would ask us what command we were wagoning for, and what train that was. Some of "our boys" cursed out the war, others shed tears (for there were a lot of *young* boys in the brigade), and said but little, while others, I suppose, prayed. We were being initiated and taking the first degree in war. We had been mustered into the Confederate service eight months, and had learned but little about the rough life of a soldier. . . .

We had to leave our baggage near Hanover Junction. We piled it up and left a guard over it. We have never seen it since.

CORPORAL RUFUS J. HOLLIS

4TH ALABAMA INFANTRY, LAW'S BRIGADE

During the lull following Seven Pines, Hollis and the other soldiers of his division had been shifted to the northwest and attached to Jackson's force as it arrived from the Shenandoah Valley. Despite Hollis' recollection of harsh fighting during the Battle of Mechanicsville, the bulk of Jackson's infantry remained unengaged on June 26, contributing to the Rebel failure to turn the Union right flank.

I never will forget how they did run to save their lives. Their pioneer corps cutting down trees across the roads so our artillery couldn't follow them. Our pioneer corps was close behind with their axes cutting up the trees as fast as the Yanks cut them down and our artillery rolled right after them shooting shot and shell into their ranks. They fell wounded and dying all around. They burned a bridge across a ravine to check us; we put our guns down, ran to an old fence, carried rails on our shoulders and filled up the ravine level and marched right on them while they were cutting down the trees across the road and Oh! how our boys did yell and pour the musket balls into [their] ranks. Our officers had issued 40 rounds of cartridges to every man that day, knowing that it was going to be one of the hardest battles of the war.

LIEUTENANT WILLIAM M. OWEN

WASHINGTON ARTILLERY OF NEW ORLEANS, D. R. JONES' DIVISION

Around 3:00 p.m. on June 26, A. P. Hill, tired of waiting for Jackson to appear, launched an attack toward Mechanicsville across the Meadow Bridge. Owen, a Cincinnati native, listened nervously to the rising crescendo of the fight and watched as wounded men and prisoners moved past him to the rear.

On the 26th of June orders were received for the Battalion to move out of its camp and halt upon the Mechanicsville road, and, everything being in readiness for action, we marched, and halted at a farm-house directly upon the turnpike. Lee was about to

Mechanicsville (above) was a sleepy collection of houses, stables, and blacksmith shops located at the intersection of the Mechanicsville Turnpike, Old Cold Harbor road, and Old Church road. A. P. Hill's charge down Old Cold Harbor road forced the Yankees to abandon the hamlet for the main Union line at Beaver Dam Creek.

"Almost instantly the crack of the rifles of the skirmishers was heard, and the gallant fellows, who but a few minutes ago were resting by the roadside, were engaged in deadly conflict."

pounce upon McClellan. Gen. A. P. Hill's division rested, stretched along the Meadow Bridge road. Longstreet's division was on the Mechanicsville road. At a dwelling on the right of the road the general officers and their staffs were congregated, their horses tied to the trees and fences.

A big movement was evidently on foot, and all were awaiting the word from Gen. Lee to begin. Some said they were waiting to hear from Jackson, who was expected from the valley to strike the enemy's right when Hill and Longstreet attack.

At 3 P.M. there was a great stir, and Hill and Longstreet mounted their horses, and staff officers dashed along the lines of the divisions, up and down the roads, carrying orders to the brigade commanders. The loud voices of the officers could be heard calling, " 'tention! 'tention! Fall in, men, fall in!"

The columns were quickly formed and moved forward, the canteens rattling and the company officers crying, "Close up! close up!"

Across the Meadow Bridge Hill's men went at a swinging pace, and into the woods on the other shore. Almost instantly the crack of the rifles of the skirmishers was heard, and the gallant fellows, who but a few minutes ago were resting by the roadside, were engaged in deadly conflict. A. P. Hill having crossed and unmasked the Mechanicsville Bridge, Longstreet and D. H. Hill followed with their fine divisions over the bridge. Longstreet turned to the right and followed along the banks of the stream. D. H. Hill went to the support of A. P. Hill, and now the artillery opened its brazen tongues and the battle had begun.

Lee had "let slip the dogs of war" upon McClellan's right, and we had it "*à l'outrance.*"

All day long the Battalion remained in the road in reserve. The boys were impatient to go ahead, but must await orders. The roar of battle continued unceasingly. Wounded men were carried by in ambulances, and many prisoners passed under guard; among the latter a goodly delegation of the Pennsylvania "Buck-tail Rangers."

Thanks to the hard-fighting command style he exhibited during the Peninsula campaign, Ambrose Powell Hill (left) received promotion from Confederate authorities to major general on May 26. Hill marked the first month of his new rank by precipitously ordering his division to attack at Mechanicsville. He later defended his action by arguing that it was better to move forward on his own than "hazard the failure of the whole plan by deferring it" any longer.

PRIVATE MARTIN T. LEDBETTER

5th Alabama Infantry, Archer's Brigade

The units of Archer's brigade, aligned along the Old Church road, moved through Mechanicsville and rushed the Union position at Beaver Dam Creek. Ledbetter expressed amazement that he had survived without a scratch, although the flag he carried was "pierced with ten bullet holes." The 5th Alabama lost 98 men killed and wounded throughout the Seven Days' Battles.

On the evening of June 25, 1862, near sunset, our brigade received orders to cook rations and be ready to march at a moment's warning. On that order we boys began to hustle, for we believed that a big battle was upon us. We could see it in the air. Before we had time to start fires even, we received orders to "fall in!" "fall in!" You could hear the order in every direction. We were directed, also, to relieve ourselves of all baggage. Well did we know that this order meant a battle. Our knapsacks, blankets, etc., were all soon tumbled into baggage wagons, and we were quickly in line with our guns glittering in the light of the setting sun, ready to march, or do anything else.

Starting on the march, our battalion was ordered to "front face!" and the various company officers made known the cause of the stir and confusion. We were told that fighting would begin on to-morrow, and that we must be "brave boys" and stand firm, be true to our country, etc. That was a solemn time to me; I will never forget it. After this another thing was done that made me more solemn than ever, and it had the same effect upon the other boys. Our commander appeared in our front, with our battle-flag in his hand, and said: "Boys, this is our flag; we have no regular color-bearer; who will volunteer to carry it? Whoever will, let him step out."

The "god of day" was now setting behind the western horizon. All nature seemed to be draped in mourning. It was only a moment, though, before I stepped out and took it. The officer told me to stand still until he made another call. He then said: "I want five men to volunteer to go with this color-bearer as guard." It was not long before the required number volunteered. I repeat, it was one of the most solemn moments of my life. I knew that to stand under it in time of battle was hazardous, but I was proud that I had the courage to take the position, for it was a place of honor. The officer in charge ordered us to take our places in line, and soon we were on the march.

We marched all night slowly, occasionally halting. The entire army seemed to be on the move. Everything indicated a great battle. We continued our march until about noon next day, when we halted and laid down by the roadside. I dropped down by my flag, and was so worn out that I was soon sound asleep. Oh, I was sleeping so good! Suddenly I was awakened from my sweet rest by some of the boys "pounding" me in the side. "Get up! Get up! There is a big battle raging, and we are getting ready to go into it." I jumped up quickly, rubbed my eyes, and was soon in place. We moved off in the direction of heavy firing. Cannon were booming and small arms could be heard distinctly. It was now after 4 o'clock P.M., and in less than one hour we had crossed the Chickahominy and were into the thickest of the engagement at Mechanicsville.

BRIGADIER GENERAL TRUMAN SEYMOUR

Brigade Commander, McCall's Division

On the Yankee left at Beaver Dam Creek Seymour's brigade of Pennsylvanians, protected by the terrain and abatis and supported by artillery, pounded the oncoming Confederates with shattering musketry volleys. The fire hit Rebel Brigadier General William Dorsey Pender's brigade particularly hard. One of Pender's aides described the "storm of shot and shells" as "deafening."

The Beaver Dam is a stream of small size, and would everywhere be passable but for its marshy edges, and, in its lower course, for a mill-race and deep ditches. The banks, which are abrupt, are covered with thick brush and woods, behind which extend broad fields. On the Mechanicsville side the crest of the slope somewhat commands, with artillery especially, the eastern side, occupied

Lieutenant Charles A. Stevens (right) of Company G, Berdan's Sharpshooters, had two close calls during the Seven Days' fighting. He was wounded at Mechanicsville but managed to stay with his command, and on June 30 he narrowly avoided capture during the fighting at Glendale. In 1864, at Cold Harbor, he was wounded again.

by our troops. From the village, which is on the main route from Richmond northward, roads diverge to Meadow Bridge, Hanover Court-House, to Cold Harbor, and along the Chickahominy, these two last intersecting the position on the Beaver Dam.

The approach of the rebel forces was announced on the morning of the 26th. Mechanicsville was then occupied by the Fifth, Colonel Simmons. A few companies of the First Rifles, Major Stone, were on picket duty near Meadow Bridge, and the Eighth Illinois Cavalry, Colonel Farnsworth, patrolled the roads toward Hanover Court-House for several miles. It was by this last route that the enemy first came down, but soon after heavy columns crossed at Meadow Bridge and above. The Bucktails made resistance, and one company, Captain Irvin, holding ground too eagerly, was surrounded and fell into the enemy's hands. . . .

As the rebels came down in great force and commenced crossing the plateau in front of our line the artillery opened upon them with excellent practice. Lieutenant Van Reed smote the head of one column so sharply with shot and shell that it broke and fled. The ground immediately in front was soon occupied by skirmishers.

Prior to the Battle of Mechanicsville McClellan (mounted, center) and his staff look over the ground bordering the Chickahominy River. One of the Rebel avenues of attack, the Mechanicsville Turnpike and its bridge over the Chickahominy, cuts through the left-middle distance of this William Waud sketch.

PRIVATE THOMAS P. SOUTHWICK

5TH NEW YORK INFANTRY, WARREN'S BRIGADE

Southwick, a 24-year-old from New York City, describes the cannonade his regiment underwent from Captain William J. Pegram's six-gun Purcell (Virginia) Artillery, parked in a field south of the Old Cold Harbor road. Although the Rebel shellfire was terrifying, the 5th reported no casualties at Mechanicsville. It did suffer heavily the following day at Gaines' Mill. Southwick mustered out in May 1863.

We had been upon the top of the hill about fifteen or twenty minutes when the firing began again and gradually approached. I kept my eyes fixed upon the open space in the direction of Cold Harbor and soon saw the pickets slowly falling back and firing in retreat; sometimes they halted to fire and finally fell back to a little rivulet where we were stationed. The artillery firing that we heard advancing now turned off and rattled furiously down through the woods and soon volleys of musketry mingled with the sound. Bye and bye I saw a single horseman appear, and another, and another, and soon several wheeled around in the open space and the sunlight flashed on the polished surface of a brass fieldpiece. It was the enemy planting his cannon and he had selected a splendid position for his battery. "See, see," I said, "they are planting their cannon." "Those are our cannon," said Sergeant Fortesque. "You don't suppose they would allow the enemy to place their piece there, do you?" "Bang!" went the loud report, down went the battalion and directly over our heads whistled the terrible engine of death. Fortesque arose out of the dust, his face pale and fixed with an anxious look. We had a battery on the right, one on the left and one on the hill in the rear and all three opened on the bold and daring enemy, who returned the first with great spirit and skill. Every gun was exceedingly well managed and every shot and shell fell with great accuracy almost in the midst of our crouching battalion. One made a peculiar kind of noise like a humming top whenever it burst. Solid shot struck the bank on which we lay and flopped spitefully around, turning end over end through the air, which was musical with the whistling shot and bursting shell. Some of the men buried their heads, others made barricades of the knapsacks, some laughed and joked, others looked serious and said nothing.

SERGEANT WILLIAM F. FULTON

5TH ALABAMA BATTALION, ARCHER'S BRIGADE

Bogged down on the western side of Ellerson's millpond, Fulton and his fellow Alabamians did their best to keep shooting while dodging Yankee fire. Confederate major E. Porter Alexander ruefully noted that the Rebel soldiers "knew too little of war to turn back, but plunged on . . . into the entanglement" of Union abatis interlacing the marshy ground. Archer's brigade suffered more than 214 casualties in the attack.

In the evening of that day we came in contact with the enemy heavily entrenched at Mechanicsville. As we came out in front in an old field they began firing on us with their artillery, and the shells passed with a whizzing sound right over our heads; it was anything but pleasant. They kept up a brisk firing but it did not retard our advance in the least. As we moved rapidly forward across the field, making for a piece of wood at the farther side where the enemy were awaiting us behind their breastworks, a battery of our artillery, commanded by Capt. Pegram and manned by a company of Marylanders, came galloping up with us and passed on to our left, the men cheering and singing, "Maryland, My Maryland." They unlimbered their pieces right out in front of the Yankee battery and commenced firing. We watched the duel as best we could as we hurried on to the timber ahead. All this was extremely exciting to me and I realized at once that we were entering upon a battle. My heart beat quick and my lips became dry, my legs felt weak and a prayer rose to my lips. We had barely entered the wood when pandemonium broke loose. The artillery redoubled its fury, the musketry of both sides began to roar like a storm, and I knew I was into it now. Strange to say the fear passed away, and I no longer realized the danger amid the excitement and I could face the bullets with perfect indifference. Reaching an old rail fence in the woods I stopped behind it, and a comrade by my side called my attention to the splinters being knocked off the rails by the minnie balls from the enemy's rifles and we both smiled, I suppose because they were doing the rails all the hurt and leaving us untouched. A great millpond full of water was directly in our front and it was impossible for us to reach the Yankees without swimming. We remained there shooting at them and they at us until night came down and then all was still.

“In a few moments I recovered my senses, and found that I was not dead.”

PRIVATE FRANCIS W. DAWSON

PURCELL (VIRGINIA) ARTILLERY, A. P. HILL'S DIVISION

A native of London, Dawson served as an unpaid volunteer in the Purcell Artillery at Mechanicsville. He witnessed the casualties caused by the cannonade of two dozen Union guns perched on the ridge east of Beaver Dam Creek. The accurate Federal counterbattery firing also damaged four of Pegram's guns.

One of Field's regiments led the advance, with two guns from our battery. We neared a narrow road between two steep banks, and were confident that we should feel the enemy there. There was a puff of smoke and the sharp crack of a rifle; the skirmishers advanced, and we threw some shells into the woods. The skirmishers kept steadily forward. They entered the woods and were lost to sight. Soon they reached the enemy's line, and the engagement began. We had now reached a point near Ellyson's Mill, at Mechanicsville, which had been strongly fortified by the enemy. They had a battery in position, and amused themselves by taking pot-shots at us. Willie Pegram, however, remained motionless in his saddle, no more concerned at the shells which were ploughing up the dust about him than if he had been lounging on the porch in Franklin Street, this beautiful evening. An officer rode hurriedly up, and then the order rang out: “Attention, Battery! Forward! Trot! March!” and with a cheer we rattled along the road and came into battery in an open field, in full view of the enemy. The guns were instantly loaded, and the firing began. The Yankees were not idle; and a shower of shot and shell enveloped us. I had not been assigned, as yet, to any particular duty in the battery, and looked on as an interested observer until accident should make a vacancy that I might fill. I tied my horse behind a corn crib, near by, and awaited developments, walking up and down in the rear of the guns to see what was going on. It was not an agreeable situation, as there was nothing to divert my attention from the manifold unpleasantnesses of the terrific fire which the enemy concentrated upon us. They had twenty-four guns in position against our single battery, and were able to enfilade our line, as well as to pound us by their direct fire. It was one of the greatest errors of the early days of the Confederacy that batteries were allowed to be knocked to pieces in detail, when, by massing a dozen batteries, the enemy could have been knocked quickly out of time and many lives saved. A solid shot bowled past me, killed one of our men, tore a leg and arm from another, and threw three horses into a bloody, struggling heap. This was my chance, and I stepped to the gun and worked away as through existence depended on my labors. For the great part of the time I acted as Number 5, bringing the ammunition from the limber to Number 2 at the piece. I felt for the first time the fierce excitement of battle. There was no thought of danger, though the men were falling rapidly on every side.

So the battle continued until about six o'clock, the men cheering wildly whenever there was any sign of weakening on the part of the enemy. I did not know what hurt me; but I found myself on the ground, hearing, as I fell, a man near me say: “That Britisher has gone up at last.” In a few moments I recovered my senses, and found that I was not dead, and that no bones appeared to be broken. The warm blood was pouring down my left leg, and on examination I saw that a piece of shell had scooped out five or six inches of the flesh below the knee, and near the femoral artery, making an ugly wound. I did not feel that I was disabled, however, and, tying a handkerchief as tightly as I could around my leg, I went back to my post, and there remained until the battery was withdrawn after sunset. Towards the end of the engagement only three men were left at the gun at which I was serving. At a second gun only four men were left. Another battery relieved us, and drew some of the enemy's fire. But I think it must have been nine o'clock when we finally left the field. The official list of casualties in our battery showed four killed and forty-three wounded, out of about seventy-five who went into the engagement. Among the killed was Lieutenant Elphinstone.

BRIGADIER GENERAL GEORGE A. MCCALL

DIVISION COMMANDER, V CORPS

The 60-year-old McCall, a respected veteran, was one of the older field officers to fight in the war. His Pennsylvanians repeatedly blunted Rebel efforts to break through at Beaver Dam Creek. Captured at Glendale, McCall was held at Libby prison until exchanged in August 1862.

At about 3 p.m. the enemy's lines were formed in my front and the skirmishers rapidly advanced, delivering their fire as they approached our lines. They were answered by my artillery and a rather general discharge of musketry.

At this moment I rode along the front of several of the regiments, and I remarked in the animated and cheerful countenances of the men the promise of that brilliant success which they so nobly achieved in the sequel. In a few moments afterward the enemy, commanded by General Robert E. Lee, boldly advanced in force under a heavy artillery fire and attacked my position from right to left. I, however, was not long in discovering that his principal effort was directed on my extreme right, whereupon I ordered Kerns' battery to that point, and at the same time moved forward Sickel's regiment (Third) to support it. Here for a long time the battle raged with great fury. The Georgians rushed with headlong energy against the Second Regiment, only to be mowed down by the steady fire of that gallant regiment, whose commander soon sent to the rear some 7 or 8 prisoners taken in the encounter.

The enemy now for a time retired from close contest on the right, but he kept up during the whole day a heavy general fire of artillery and infantry, which, with the rapid reply of the Reserves, was at times one unbroken roar of a stunning depth. After a time, however, a heavy column was launched down the road to Ellison's Mill, where a determined attack was made. I had already sent Easton's battery to General Seymour, and I now moved the Seventh Regiment down to the extreme left, apprehending that the enemy might attempt to turn that flank by crossing the stream below the mill. Here, however, the Reserves maintained their position and sustained their character for steadiness in splendid style, never losing a foot of ground during a severe struggle with some of the best troops of the enemy.

PRIVATE ALEXANDER ALCORN

BATTERY B, 1ST PENNSYLVANIA ARTILLERY, MCCALL'S DIVISION

Alcorn, a teenager from Lawrence County in western Pennsylvania, wrote this description of the Battle of Mechanicsville in a letter to his sister. She then had excerpts published in the July 26 edition of the Lawrence Journal for the benefit, she wrote, of "those who have friends in the army of the Potomac." On July 1, 1863, Alcorn was killed in action while fighting on the soil of his native state, at Gettysburg.

Our fellows, as Providence would have it, had just finished digging rifle pits the day before, so we were ready for them. The position we held was about half a mile from Mechanicsville on the bluff of Gaines Run opposite the above place. The way they came was on a level with us, but to attack us or drive us out of our entrenchments they would have to come down in a hollow or ravine. Well, on they come—now and then giving us a shot and a shell but wide of the mark. They came by brigades down the road, intending to march across a little bridge; but when they came to this bridge they found it torn up and they had to countermarch. Then we poured into them double charges

ELEVENTH STREET OPERA HOUSE.
Complimentary Benefit
TO
JOHN KERNAN,
(Who lost his Arm at the Battle of Mechanicsville, June 26th, 1862.)
By the Members of the 2d Reg. P. R. V. C.
On Monday Ev'ng, February 15th, 1864.
TICKETS 25 CENTS.

This ticket admitted the bearer to a benefit staged in February 1864 for Private John Kernan by his comrades in the 2d Pennsylvania Reserves. The proceeds were to supplement the pension he was receiving for wounds suffered at Mechanicsville.

Fight at ~~Mechanicsville~~ betwee
Beaver Creek -

of canister laying them on top of each other. This was about 7 P.M. and the sun was just disappearing, but such a sight I never wish to witness again! The groanings of the wounded, the red glare of the sun, the peal of cannon with the constant roar of musketry formed a panorama that was truly appalling. The enemy charged four different times and were as many times repulsed. You may know they were pretty close when we fired canister and 1 1/2 second fuse shell—pretty near all the time. I will relate one instance of a fellow who belonged to the 12th P.R.C. which was supporting us. The regiment had all got into the pit but one company and it had to stand out in the fire. This fellow was standing near a tree when a secesh bullet knocked the bark into his face, he lifted his gun, saying, will you shoot at me you vile rebel? at the same time firing and stooping below the smoke to see what execution he had done, then seeming satisfied that he (the rebel) was "safe" fired during the action from that place. Such acts of coolness were occurring all the time amid the hottest fire our troops have ever felt. We held the enemy

c Calls division and the rebels under . Jackson

at bay until 9 P.M. when we were ordered to fall back. Then you might have heard such exclamations: "What does this mean? What are we going to have this for? They can't whip us," &c. but it was an order from General M'Clellan and we had to obey. The Bucktails stuck to the pits until the enemy flanked them and took two companies prisoners after a hard fight, also took their colors. General M'Clellan said the Reserves done more than he wanted them to do.

Although this Alfred Waud sketch purports to show McCall's troops repulsing Stonewall Jackson's men, the Yankees were more likely engaged with one of A. P. Hill's brigades, because Jackson never did any serious fighting at Mechanicsville. The strength of the Federal position is well illustrated. To the right, Yankee cannon atop the bluff bombard Rebels hidden from view by trees and smoke. Below the artillery a Pennsylvania regiment, protected by earthworks behind the swampy ground along Beaver Dam Creek, prepares to fire a volley at the enemy.

BRIGADIER GENERAL ROSWELL S. RIPLEY

Brigade Commander, D. H. Hill's Division

At twilight Lee ordered Ripley's brigade to attack Ellerson's Mill and relieve the pressure on A. P. Hill's men. Ripley dutifully complied, but his troops were pummeled by the Union gunfire in their turn. Finally, covered by darkness and friendly artillery, the remnants of Ripley's command withdrew to safety.

Meanwhile the passage of the Chickahominy by the artillery had been impeded by the broken bridges, and night coming on and it being deemed important to attack the position at once, the advance was ordered along the whole line. General Pender's brigade and the two regiments of my own advanced rapidly on the right, while the remainder of my command moved against the front, driving back the enemy from his advanced positions and closing in upon the batteries and their heavy infantry supports, all of which poured upon our troops a heavy and incessant fire of shell, canister, and musketry. The ground was rugged and intersected by ditches and hedges and covered with abatis a short distance in front of the position to be assaulted. A mill-race, with scarped banks, and in some places waist-deep in water, ran along the front of the enemy at a distance ranging from 50 to 100 yards. To this position our troops succeeded in advancing, notwithstanding the fire of the enemy was exceedingly heavy and our loss extremely severe. . . .

Near dark Capt. A. Burnet Rhett's battery of artillery, attached to my command, succeeded in crossing the broken bridges over the Chickahominy, and was located directly in front of the enemy at about 1,200

In this Alfred Waud drawing, infantrymen of Truman Seymour's brigade crouch behind a fieldwork of logs and earth near Ellison's Mill to reload and keep up a blistering fire on the Rebels pinned down west of the waist-deep millpond. Behind the battle line a soldier tends to a stricken comrade, while a company officer stands over a row of knapsacks and blanket rolls thrown off in the heat of combat. Confederate generals Ripley and Pender had the misfortune to charge this position. Pender reported that some of his men had closed to within 150 yards of the Union works before experiencing the deadly enemy fire that shattered their assault.

yards' distance. Captain Rhett opened an effective fire, and soon relieved our infantry from the storm of shell and canister which had been poured upon them. It was soon re-enforced by another battery, and a fire was kept up on the enemy until late in the evening.

CAPTAIN GEORGE W. FLOWERS

38th North Carolina Infantry, Pender's Brigade

Flowers, who cowrote the 38th's postwar history, describes the trial by fire his regiment endured on June 26. Owing to the hilly terrain and the confusion of battle, the 38th became separated from the rest of Pender's brigade and assailed the Union position alone. During the melee, the Tarheels lost 152 men out of the 420 who had entered the fight. Flowers, who was wounded at Mechanicsville, survived a second combat injury at the Wilderness to become the regiment's lieutenant colonel.

As soon as the Thirty-eighth had gotten a little beyond Mechanicsville it was saluted with heavy shelling. A line of battle was formed and the march continued until the order was given to charge the battery that was throwing the deadly missiles. The heat was intense and the double-quick march exhausting, but the charge was kept up over the open field until the regiment reached the summit of the last elevation when a farm house, yard and garden broke the line somewhat. The Yankee batteries were upon the summit of the opposite hill with their supporting infantry in their intrenchments, and the old field pines in front cut down and piled across the stumps which were left about three feet high, forming an almost impassable barrier. The Thirty-eighth, alone and unsupported, charged down the hill, the long line of infantry playing upon it with a cross fire. On the soldiers charged, in the face of the fatal volleys, until the obstacles were reached, when the whole line stopped and began returning the fire under every disadvantage. The men were falling rapidly and it was soon seen that to take the works was impossible. Captain Thornburg and Adjutant Cowles were in front, urging the men forward. The retreat was ordered but the noise was so deafening nothing could be heard. Major Andrews reached Captain Thornburg and Adjutant Cowles and gave them the orders to retreat, after which the word was passed along the line and the retreat up the hill was begun. The enemy continuing their deadly firing. It was about sunset when the regiment reached safely the rear.

The 38th North Carolina carried this yellow-bordered battle flag at Mechanicsville. The wool-bunting color was probably issued to the regiment earlier in the spring.

Pictured above in what may be a prewar militia uniform, 29-year-old Lieutenant Oliver Perry Beam, named for the naval hero of the War of 1812, fell mortally wounded during the 38th North Carolina's harrowing charge at the Battle of Mechanicsville. He died on July 24, 1862.

The 1st North Carolina Infantry of Ripley's brigade suffered 142 casualties at Mechanicsville. The three officers above are from the regiment's Company A. Captain Tristrim L. Skinner stands flanked by Lieutenant John A. Benbury (left) and his cousin Lieutenant Lemuel C. Benbury. Only Lemuel Benbury survived the Seven Days' Battles. Skinner was mortally wounded during the charge on Ellerson's Mill, and John Benbury met the same fate a few days later at Malvern Hill.

MAJOR JOHN A. FITE

7th Tennessee Infantry, Archer's Brigade

An artillery shell struck Fite, a lawyer from Tennessee's DeKalb County, as his regiment withdrew from the banks of Beaver Dam Creek. Fite survived to be shot again at Cedar Mountain, promoted to colonel in April 1863, wounded once more at Chancellorsville, and captured at Gettysburg. Before his death in 1925, Fite wrote an unpublished memoir of his military service whimsically titled "Short and Uninteresting History of a Small and Unimportant Man."

By this time it was dark. We'd had some fierce fighting and lost a great many men, killed and wounded. When the fighting was over, about dark I suppose, the line was between a quarter and a half mile apart. The Yankees kept up an artillery duel for some time. I had squatted down and, while holding to a little pine bush, a spent canon ball came along striking the ground and bouncing and struck me and knocked me over, and knocked me senseless for awhile. In fact, I didn't know what had done it. When I came to I was very sick at my stomach but not in a particle of pain.

General Goodner came to me and told me to go back to where we had left our baggage, that he had just learned that they were going to relieve our regiment and send it back there in a few minutes. Mitchel Anderson went with me. I was terribly thirsty so Mitchel Anderson got some water out of a little pond that we had passed. I drank it and we went on back to where we had left our knap sacks. I sat down and leaned back against a little pine tree. I started once or twice to lay down but every time I did, I'd lose my breath. I then concluded I'd stay there until daylight. We were about 100 yards from our field hospital so when daylight came I concluded I'd go to the hospital, and see brother Jim and see what he could do for me. When I got up on my feet, I lost my breath, and I ran about 30 or 40 yards before I could get my breath and when I did I threw up great clots of blood.

Brother Jim saw me and so did Dr. McGuire. They both came to me and that was the first time I'd had a single pain. Jim pulled open my shirt and said, "Brother you are ruined." He and McGuire examined me and they decided that my breast bone was broken, and that some of my ribs were torn loose. I went with them to the field hospital then, they tore off a strip of a piece of domestic, about a foot wide, and they wound that around me, I don't know how many times, and put me in an ambulance and sent me back to Richmond. I did not want to go to the hospital, as nobody did.

PRIVATE CHARLES H. THURBER

5th New York Infantry, Warren's Brigade

Rousted from their bivouac south of the Chickahominy, Thurber and his comrades marched toward the sounds of fighting from Beaver Dam Creek, only to arrive after the battle had been decided. The New Yorkers soon retraced their steps as Mc-Clellan, fearful that his troops north of the Chickahominy would be overwhelmed, ordered an eastward retreat to a new defensive position near Gaines' Mill.

On Thursday, the 26th, we were ordered to pack our knapsacks and hold ourselves in readiness to march across the Chickahominy. This was about 12 o'clock. A little later than this we heard heavy firing on our extreme right, which gradually drew nearer. We remained in our camp until about four o'clock, when we were ordered to march and leave our knapsacks behind. The firing drew nearer, and nearer and we made up our minds that our fighting time had come.—We left our camp and marched on the road to Mechanicsville about a mile, to a large field where several brigades were drawn up in line of battle. We were put in position, and with beating hearts awaited the approach of the enemy; but we were doomed to [be] disappointed that night. Darkness closed the carnage for the day, and the heavy firing on our advance stopped entirely. We laid down upon our arms, with no covering but the sky, and slept soundly, dreaming of home and its associations that many of us would see no more. The night passed without alarm. At daylight we were marched back to our old camp, where we opened our knapsacks and destroyed everything that could not be carried. Many little things that had added to our comfort there, had to be thrown on a large fire. It was hard to part with them, although we were told it was the fortune of war. After destroying what would give any comfort to the rebels, we commenced falling back towards Gaine's Mills, crossed the stream and were drawn up in line of battle in a large field on the top of a hill, to the left of the mills.

Wounded soldiers crowd onto a flatbed car to await the arrival of a locomotive on the Richmond & York River Railroad near the field hospital at Savage's Station. Federal casualties from the battles along the Chickahominy were gathered from the field and transported to the station in horse-drawn ambulances. After secondary treatment, those who were able to travel made a jarring 17-mile journey by rail to White House Landing, on the Pamunkey River, where hospital steamships lay at anchor. Men too ill or severely wounded to ride on the rail cars were forced, if they stayed alive, to wait until their condition improved.

"Mother said, 'Fannie, come on.' I said, 'Mother, I can't. I might as well die here as anywhere else.' "

FANNIE GAINES TINSLEY

RESIDENT OF HANOVER COUNTY, VIRGINIA

Tinsley, whose husband served in the Confederacy's Treasury Department, was the daughter of Dr. William G. Gaines, the owner of the mill in the path of the Union soldiers retreating from Beaver Dam Creek. Eventually the advancing Rebels overtook Tinsley and her companions, and the refugees accepted an escort to a house behind Confederate lines. Their respite was brief, however, for the home's yard was soon filled with the groaning, mangled wounded of the Battle of Gaines' Mill.

We had heard the musketry all day, but did not know there was fighting going on at Mechanicsville. But the next morning, before sunrise, a Yankee officer rode up to the door and told us that we would have to get out as soon as possible, that the Union army was falling back and that they were going to make a stand there and had already planted siege guns around the house. He told us to go to the White House, so we got up, and with Dr. Curtis still as ill as he could possibly be (we did not think he would live an hour), we started. We had no way of taking Dr. Curtis except in his buggy. Father got that out and put him in it and left Mother and myself to walk through the woods, with Hattie and the little negro nurse girl, to Father's mill. This mill was about a mile from Dr. Curtis's.

When we started, I had on slippers and carried a satchel with Hattie's clothes in it. I also had a box with all my jewelry in it, but in the excitement of getting off Mother set the box down and left it at Dr. Curtis's. I also had a trunk there with my wedding presents in it and my clothes, and they were all taken. When we started out Mother thought that Dr. Curtis ought to have something to eat, so she took a live chicken (I don't know why in the world she didn't kill it) in her hand, to prepare him some soup when we should reach a short abiding place. . . .

. . . Mother and I were running through the woods and the camps. We came to the old Zouave camp and an old Irishman came out and said, "Missie, is you running?" Mother said, "Yes, and it's what you'll be doing pretty soon." Then we went on and got into an open field between the two armies—the retreating Yankees and the advancing Confederates—and the shells were bursting and blowing up the ground and going over our heads. We were facing the cannon. In this field we came to a ravine, and we got down into it all right and Mary went ahead with the baby, but when we got down there, at the mouth of this ravine there were any number of Yankees and they were all around it, looking down at us. Mother went on up the bank and I got half way up—to where there was a great big pine tree on the side of the bank. Then I felt so faint that I stopped and I leaned against the tree. Mother said, "Fannie, come on." I said, "Mother, I can't. I might as well die here as anywhere else." She looked at me and saw that I was going to faint, and said, "Goodbye, I am going. Don't you see all those Yankees looking at you?" Whereupon I did not faint, but climbed up instead. When we got out of this ravine we could not find Hattie and the nurse—they were out of sight.

We next came to the mill-dam, and up on the hill above it we saw fourteen Yankees coming down towards the dam. There was an officer with them, and he said, "Stand back and let these ladies pass." Then he stepped up to me (I still had my satchel) and said, "Let me take your satchel." I told Mother I was afraid to let him take it. She said, "Fannie, let him have it." He next offered to help me over the mill-dam. I expected to be thrown in but I let him help me. When we got across, he handed me my satchel and said, "Please tell me the way to the White House. I am going home and I never expect to fight these rebels again, I had just as soon fight the Devil as to fight them." I told him to follow the telegraph wires and they would take him straight to the White House.

. . . [Mother] went over the hill to Mr. McGhee's so she could see the yard there and see if Hattie and the nurse had gone there. Mother saw them going into Mr. McGhee's yard, then she sat down in a camp to wait for me (there was a Yankee camp on the top of the hill). While she was sitting there, one of the soldiers came up to her and told her that there was a good old man who lived up on the top of the hill and that she had better go there. Mother told him that she had known that "old man" before he did (he was our miller) and that if she was in his way she would leave. By that time I had gotten up there, so we started on. Just as we got out of the camp it was blown up.

Bridge through the Chickahominy Swamp

This Alfred Waud illustration shows one of the many causeways Union engineers constructed through the bogs lining both sides of the Chickahominy River. To make these corduroy roads, troops drove log pilings into the swampy ground, upon which they laid tree trunks that functioned as the roadbed. They then shoveled a layer of dirt onto the logs to create a less bumpy surface. After Mechanicsville, such passageways were crammed with Union troops retreating in the moonlight through the muggy, humid swamp to their new defensive line. The drawing also gives a good idea of the dense vegetation that characterized the region and hindered troop movements for both sides.

Confederate Attack at Gaines' Mill

Despite the failure of his attack at Mechanicsville, Lee had, at a stroke, wrested battlefield initiative from McClellan. The timorous Union commander abruptly abandoned all thought of resuming his offensive against Richmond with his present forces and began a retreat to the James River. For the moment, by his reckoning, the very survival of his army was at stake.

Throughout the early hours of June 27, Porter's V Corps pulled away from the blood-soaked slopes above Beaver Dam Creek and marched to a new position behind a sluggish stream called Boatswain's Swamp. One of the dusty paths the Yankees trod led past Gaines' Mill, which would soon lend its name to the largest and bloodiest of the Seven Days' Battles.

By sunrise, Porter had his troops in position on the plateau behind Boatswain's Swamp. A slope angling down to the creek bed protected the Union front, and the Federals had bolstered their position by hurriedly building breastworks of fence rails, brush, and tree limbs.

Brigadier General George Sykes' mixed division of regulars and volunteers anchored the Union right, while Brigadier General George W. Morell's division held the left. George McCall's division, which had seen hard fighting at Mechanicsville, formed in reserve. Nearly 100 Federal cannon pointed toward the north and west, ready to rip apart advancing Rebel lines. Porter had established another formidable obstacle to Lee's men, and one Confederate officer realistically asserted that his army "had no margin to spare over the size of its task."

Indeed, although Lee was eager to close on the retreating Federals, he still had to solve the problems that had plagued him at Mechanicsville—difficulty in coordinating attacks and Jackson's strange hesitation to enter battle. Lee maintained as much continuity as possible in his effort to press the retreating Porter, keeping Jackson on the left, eastward along the Old Cold Harbor road, and D. H. Hill's, A. P. Hill's, and Longstreet's divisions to Jackson's right.

As the day turned hot, Lee's men followed the Federals, looting several straggling sutlers' wagons and capturing 171 men of the 13th Pennsylvania Bucktails, who had somehow missed the withdrawal order.

A. P. Hill's division was in the van; after several sharp skirmishes with the Union rear guard, Hill pinpointed the location of the new Federal line in the early afternoon. Around 2:30 Hill, under Lee's orders, sent Brigadier General Maxcy Gregg's brigade to attack the Union center.

Gregg's men fixed bayonets and rushed toward the Union lines screaming the Rebel yell. The Union troops pitched into the enemy struggling across the boggy ground and up the plateau's slope. During one Federal counterattack the 5th New York Zouaves helped repulse Gregg's bloodied regiments at bayonet point.

The fight continued for several hours as A. P. Hill's other brigades assailed the Union line. Eventually, Longstreet's division came along Hill's right, and one of his brigades joined the fray, while Richard Ewell—the first member of Jackson's command to be heard from—pushed his Louisiana Tigers brigade in on Hill's left.

As at Mechanicsville, however, the attacks were not well synchronized, allowing the Federals to repel each brigade in turn and send them all staggering back across Boatswain's Swamp. By 4:30, after Hill had lost more than 2,000 men, Lee called off any further efforts until he could better manage his forces. Once again poor coordination and the absence of the bulk of Jackson's troops had kept the Rebels from punching through a fortified Union position.

Both sides used the lull to prepare for further fighting. McClellan had sent Brigadier General Henry W. Slocum's VI Corps division north of the river in response to Porter's appeal for reinforcements, and Porter quickly placed these troops and McCall's reserve units into weak spots in his line. Slocum's infantry, however, were to be the only troops McClellan would send to Porter until the very end of the battle. He held the majority of his army in place south of the Chickahominy, fearing a Confederate attack on his line of retreat.

Lee was once again in the dark concerning the whereabouts of Jackson, whose strange state of mind and poor staff work had caused his command to wander the maze of roads leading to the Federal right during the battle's opening stages; evening was approaching when Lee finally met up with Jackson on the Telegraph road.

The courtly commander did not berate Jackson for his tardiness, only saying, "Ah, General, I am very glad to see you, I had hoped to be with you before." Jackson made no acknowledgment of this mild chastisement but listened intently as Lee explained that an all-out attack on the entire Federal front was necessary for success.

"The fire is very heavy," Lee said to Jackson. "Do you think your men can stand it?" Jackson, his lust for battle seemingly revived, replied, "They can stand almost anything; they can stand that!" He ordered his commanders to align their troops for a frontal assault, exclaiming, "This affair must hang in suspense no longer; sweep the field with the bayonet!"

Even so, it took Jackson several hours to properly place his troops. D. H. Hill's division assumed a position on the Rebel left flank, with Ewell next over. Whiting's troops supplanted A. P. Hill's battle-worn division in the center, and Winder's men joined Longstreet's on the right. A force of about 40,000 Rebels now stood poised to attack sections of McClellan's two-and-a-quarter-mile front.

Near 7:00 p.m. the attackers stepped off, double-quicking toward Porter's 34,000 troops. Skirmish fire changed to crashing volleys as the gap between the opposing lines closed. A soldier in the 9th Alabama remembered rushing into a "perfect storm of lead . . ." that made his brigade reel back "as though pushed by a tornado."

The battle was give-and-take until John Bell Hood's Texas Brigade and Colonel Evander Law's brigade of Whiting's division rushed through the gunfire and up the slope toward the Union center. Hood dismounted to lead the attack, crying, "Forward! Forward! Charge right down on them," as his men crested the ridge and broke the Federal line. Porter's center collapsed, and his flanks followed suit.

The Confederates raced after their foes, shattering an impetuous countercharge by the 5th U.S. Cavalry. Finally, helped by the onset of darkness, two fresh Union brigades belatedly sent by McClellan halted the Rebel pursuit.

The Battle of Gaines' Mill was costly for both sides: nearly 8,000 Confederate casualties, 6,837 for the Union. But the outcome favored Lee. He had finally been able to mount a well-organized assault to defeat an element of McClellan's force. As Porter's V Corps withdrew across the bridges leading to the Chickahominy's south bank, Lee regrouped his scattered divisions and prepared to continue his pursuit of McClellan.

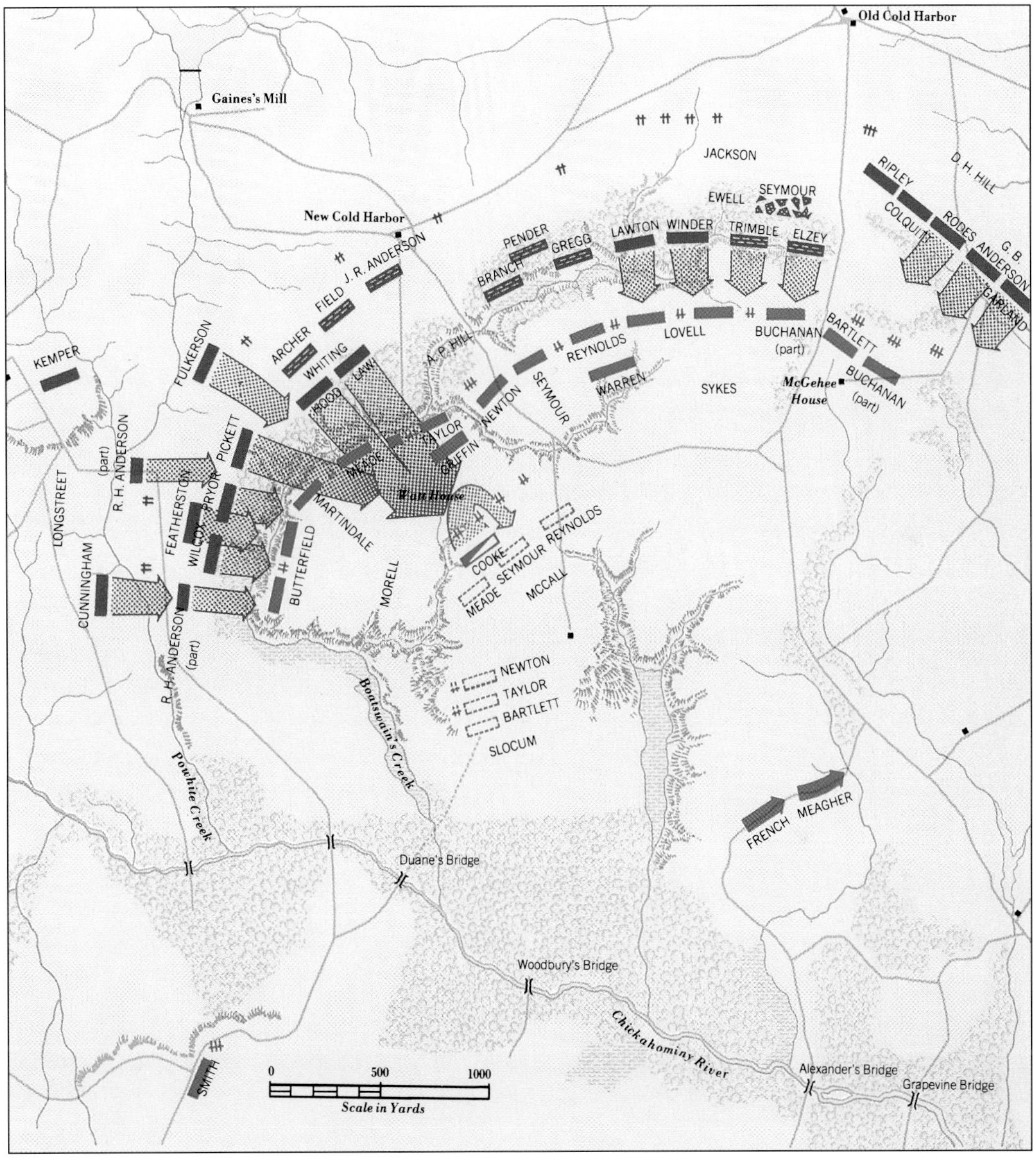

The fighting at Gaines' Mill began when A. P. Hill's division—supported by General George E. Pickett's brigade of Longstreet's division and Colonel Isaac G. Seymour's brigade of Ewell's division—attacked the point where Morell's and Sykes' divisions met at the center of the Federal line. The Rebel charges were hurled back, and Lee then waited until Jackson was in position on the Confederate left flank before ordering the final onslaught. The breakthrough came when Hood's and Law's men stormed through the Union lines in front of Porter's headquarters at the Watt house.

PRIVATE ALFRED DAVENPORT

5TH NEW YORK INFANTRY, WARREN'S BRIGADE

Crossing Boatswain's Swamp and moving uphill through thick woods, General Maxcy Gregg's brigade of South Carolinians opened the Confederate attack at Gaines' Mill. When the Rebels emerged in an open field they came under fire from the 5th New York—a regiment clad in colorful Zouave attire. Davenport, who later wrote his unit's regimental history, describes the prelude to the assault, as the Zouaves endured bombardment from both the enemy's and their own artillery.

Colonel Warren, acting brigadier, selected his ground with great care, and we ranged the sights on our pieces to reach a wood in our front; we being in an open field just below the brow of a small hill, which saved us somewhat from the artillery fire of the rebels.

We soon spied a rebel battery getting into position. The shells now began to fly rather close, and we were ordered to lie down; and immediately two of our own batteries in the rear opened upon the rebels, which put us in a bad position, as we were between the fire of all three batteries. We lay here some time, once in a while firing a few shots towards the woods as feelers at the rebel sharpshooters, who were posted in trees on our right. We could not get out of the position, so we lay there an hour and a half, the rebels firing shell and grape and canister at us all the time! The solid shot ploughed up the ground all around, and the shells were bursting above us! I tell you, we made ourselves as "flat as pancakes." One of the men had a dog, who chased after the balls; he was wounded in the leg during the fight. Our red caps and pants were too good a mark for the sharpshooters, and the battery had got an exact range of us; so Colonel Warren conducted us through a little hollow to a road running at right angles to our former position, where we were somewhat protected by a brush fence on the top of a bank by the roadside. The boys were repeatedly admonished to keep their heads down below the bank; but some of them, not heeding the advice, were killed. It seems hard to see our own men killed by our own battery! One of our captains went up to Colonel Warren, a few yards off, and told him that the battery was "killing our own men." "Can't help it," says Colonel Warren; "they are Napoleon guns and American shot, and they must *work.*"

I was peeping through the fence and saw a brigade of rebels marching by the flank and by fours, in the woods the other side of the field. I told Captain B. what I had seen, and *he* reported to Col. Warren. "Yes, Captain B., I am very much obliged to you for the information," said he, "but have I not eyes as well as you?" The captain "*sloped*," and at the instant the whole six guns poured their rounds into poor Johnny Reb trying a flank movement, and they were swept down in heaps, and those left of them were glad to get away where they came from.

Brigadier General Fitz-John Porter, whose V Corps confronted the bulk of Lee's army at Gaines' Mill, sits in a camp chair surrounded by his aides in a photograph taken near Harrison's Landing on July 16, 1862. Porter's chief of staff, Captain Frederick Locke—later a brevet brigadier general—stands in front of the tent at left. The tall officer at center is artillery brigade surgeon Charles McMillan. Porter's cook, a Mrs. Fairfax, stands at right.

CAPTAIN WILLIAM W. BLACKFORD

STAFF, BRIGADIER GENERAL J. E. B. STUART

In reserve behind D. H. Hill's division on the Confederate left, Stuart's horsemen were shelled by Yankee batteries as they waited to exploit any break in the enemy line. An engineer officer detailed to the cavalry at the start of the campaign, Blackford was characterized by Stuart as "bold in reconnaissance, fearless in danger, and remarkably cool and correct in judgement."

We were in reserve, but Stuart, with his usual enterprise, was riding everywhere, looking for chances to put in his cavalry, and with Pelham's guns he did some good service on the flanks of the enemy. He and his staff were much exposed to artillery fire but none of us was hit. Seeing some Alabama troops going into action, I found that the 5th Alabama was there and rode along the line to find my brother Eugene, who at that time commanded a company in that regiment. We were delighted to see each other and I rode with him until they got under fire and then bowed myself out. An infantry line in action is not a wholesome place for visitors, by any manner of means. As I galloped back to the General, when very near him I saw a thing that I never saw before nor have ever seen since; it was a clear view of a fragment of shell in the air just after the shell exploded. It burst close to my ear, coming from my right and almost deafening me. Turning my head in the direction the fragment flew, I saw distinctly for a considerable distance a fragment in its flight. General Stuart happened to be looking towards me at the time, and as I rode up to him he asked if I was hit, and said he was glad to hear I was not, for he was sure I had been.

While we were all sitting on our horses in a conspicuous part of the field, a battery noticed us by a round. One of the shots passed screaming a few inches over our heads. We were not so well accustomed to artillery then as we became afterwards, and most of us involuntarily ducked our heads. Capt. John Esten Cooke, while so doing, bowed a little too low, lost his balance, and fell sprawling on the ground. We were all a good deal shocked, for we did not doubt for a moment that his head had been carried off. Stuart leaned down from his saddle and in a most sympathizing voice said, "Hallo, Cooke! Are you hit?" But Cooke jumped up looking very sheepish as he dusted himself and said, "Oh, no, General; I only dodged a little too far." The reaction of feeling from the uneasiness we had felt for him, and his ludicrous appearance as he scrambled back into his saddle, still covered with dust, was perfectly irresistible, and we laughed until we could scarcely keep our seats in our saddles.

PRIVATE WILLIAM C. KENT

1ST U.S. SHARPSHOOTERS, MORELL'S DIVISION

Clad in green uniforms and armed with breech-loading Sharps rifles, the marksmen of Colonel Hiram Berdan's special unit took position with the 9th Massachusetts in advance of the main Union line. After slowing the Rebel advance near the Gaines house and millpond, the Sharpshooters retreated across Boatswain's Swamp and resumed their deadly fire on the attackers. Kent, a 21-year-old Vermonter, described the action in a letter he sent to his father at the conclusion of the campaign.

We piled our knapsacks and blankets and then formed the line of skirmishers in the edge of the woods, parallel with the valley, and then advanced down the hill, through the swamp and up the other side to the edge of the woods where we could see the approach of the rebels. There was a line of skirmishers in front of us, the Irish 9th. The enemy was by this time in possession of our camps, and began to feel their way with artillery and skirmishers. Their artillery elicited no reply, but the skirmishers soon met, and they had it all to themselves until noon, the enemy being occupied, most likely, in bringing up their men and placing them in position. About that time the artillery began to talk on both sides, and Griffin's Parrott guns did some very effective preaching. The "ninth" was now drawn in behind us, and drawn back half way up the hill on our side, where we took cover behind trees and stumps, and so watched until 3 p.m..

Then a brisk firing commenced on our right and scattered along until it came opposite to me. Tremendous volley of small arms, and the peal of heavy guns were the last things I heard before I went in. We fought pretty much on our own hook, the officers being far to the right, and the human voice was of no account. The rebels rushed down the hill in line

In April 1865 Doctor William G. Gaines' war-ravaged gristmill was photographed by John Reekie, one of Alexander Gardner's cameramen. Gaines was a prosperous farmer and an ardent secessionist whose sprawling plantation was the scene not only of the bloodiest of the Seven Days' Battles, but also of the June 1864 Battle of Cold Harbor.

of battle, but it wasn't quite so easy rushing across a swamp, waist deep in thick mud, and as they tried it we tried Sharp's rifles at eight rods, firing as fast as we could put in cartridges, the distance being so short that aim was unnecessary. We couldn't help hitting them and our vigorous fire held them in check for some minutes—minutes are hours at such a time—and they were thrown into some disorder. Meanwhile, things were not very still. The bullets came like hail, and the trees looked like nutmeg graters, but our cover was pretty good and their aim, feet too high, so that our company lost only one killed and three wounded. This couldn't last, you know, skirmishers against brigades, and they soon had a line formed on the wrong (for us) side of the swamp, and then a rush. We gave them another volley all around, and when they were six rods off, we started, keeping cover as much as possible. Just as I turned to run, a branch caught my cap and it rolled down toward the rebels. It didn't take half a wink to convince me that that cap was a goner, so far as I was concerned, and abandoning myself to that conviction, I abandoned the cap. As our line came over the brow of the hill with the brigade in full pursuit, a line of infantry who had been lying down, rose up, not twenty paces in front with guns at an aim. We couldn't get through, or around in time to escape the fire. If anyone ever saw Scylla and Charybdis, there we did. As the word "Fire" was given, we assumed a horizontal position, and as the volleys came quick and sharp, from either side, I had a most sincere desire to be somewhere else. I did feel that more consideration might have been paid to our feelings.

PRIVATE JAMES F. J. CALDWELL

1st South Carolina Infantry, Gregg's Brigade

Too eager for the fray to bother pillaging abandoned Yankee camps along their line of march, Gregg's Carolinians hit the Federal rear guard and drove the skirmishers of the 9th Massachusetts back on Porter's stronghold south of Boatswain's Swamp. The son of a South Carolina militia general, Caldwell served as a mounted orderly for his regimental commander and was promoted to lieutenant for gallantry at Gaines' Mill. He recalled the opening stages of the battle in his 1866 brigade history.

We shot down several of the enemy as they retreated across the open field; but one of them, after lying a moment, rose and attempted to follow his flying comrades. By this time the uninjured ones had passed out of sight; so this unfortunate was left to the fire of our whole line. The excitement became intense. A perfect shower of balls was hurled after him, striking up the dust before, behind, and all around him. But still he staggered on, striving but the more vigorously as the danger increased. Cries of "Kill him!" "Shoot him!" "Down with the fellow!" and others of rougher cast, resounded from every side; but shoot as we would, he succeeded in reaching a clump of pines, where we found him soon after, exhausted by fatigue and loss of blood.

It was now after two o'clock p.m. The brigade was in the two lines before described. Advancing some two or three hundred yards, we discovered the table ground to descend to a deep, wet ravine, on the opposite side of which, upon an eminence, was drawn up a line of Federal infantry. We could see an officer riding up and down it, apparently giving direction or encouragement to his men. A battery soon opened upon us, whose fire we received lying down. Their practice was pretty good, but I know of only one man who was killed in the brigade.

A native of the Abbeville District in western South Carolina, William C. Round (right) enlisted in Company B of James Orr's 1st South Carolina Rifles, a unit assigned to Maxcy Gregg's brigade. Sporting green-trimmed frock coats and trousers denoting their status as riflemen, the elite outfit was dubbed "The Pound Cake Regiment" by soldiers used to plain dress and, by implication, hardtack rations. Private Round was among the unit's 81 dead in the fight at Gaines' Mill.

SERGEANT ASHBALA F. HILL

8th Pennsylvania Reserves, Reynolds' Brigade

Initially in reserve to the right and rear of Colonel Gouverneur Warren's brigade, the men of the 8th Pennsylvania looked on as Warren's 5th New York Zouaves launched a furious bayonet charge, driving the 1st South Carolina (Orr's) Rifles back to the woods. When more of Gregg's units came forward, the Pennsylvanians were sent in, sustaining heavy losses in a vain attempt to stem the Rebel onslaught. Hill survived but was severely wounded at Antietam the following September.

In our front was a large open field, six hundred yards in width. Beyond it was a thick wood. In this field were several small hills, ridges, etc.; and about midway, running parallel with the road, was a deep depression. A regiment of zouaves (the Fifth New York) marched into this valley, a little to our right, and marched up the opposite ascent till their position remained barely concealed from any who might be beyond; there they stood in waiting. We seemed prepared to meet the approaching rebels. Now and then some field, or general officer, would ride to the brink of the bank in our rear, place his glass to his eyes, and look long and earnestly toward that frowning wood.

It was about noon, when, on an elevation beyond the wood, several flashes, accompanied by puffs of white smoke, suddenly burst forth, and in a few seconds a solid shot and a shell or two flew over our heads. Our battery replied. Another moment, and several additional rebel guns were let loose, and a number of projectiles passed two hundred feet above our heads. Our battery let off a whole volley; and we could hear the bursting of several shell in the vicinity of the rebel battery. Then the rebel battery went to work in earnest; so did ours.

A number of batteries, right and left, now opened, and were replied to by others. The fight soon became general. The artillery began to play rapidly; and shell after shell screamed over our heads, coming lower and lower every minute, and at last occasionally striking the face of the hill in our front, and ricocheting over us. They were getting the range. By and by a line of rebel skirmishers appeared at the edge of the wood, and were fired upon by the zouaves. They fell back into the deep shades of the wood; but presently a line-of-battle could be seen emerging slowly from the wood. Our brave zouaves treated them to a volley of bullets from their "Sharpe's Rifles." The rebels opened a brisk fire, and a continuous rattle of musketry was added to the roar of artillery. The zouaves stood their ground bravely. The musketry was not, however, confined to this point. Like the artillery, it was here introduced to be taken up by the forces both right and left; and it soon became general.

Colonel Hayes climbed to the top of the bank in our front, to the imminent risk of having his head suddenly carried away by a shell, and took a survey of the prospect with his glass. A moment he watched the zouaves, then he lowered his glass, and exclaimed, in admiration:—

"I tell you, boys, those fellows are fighting bravely!"

A move was made by many to climb to the top of the bank and look; but the colonel said:—

"Stay down! You musn't expose yourselves unnecessarily! It will be time enough when you are called upon."

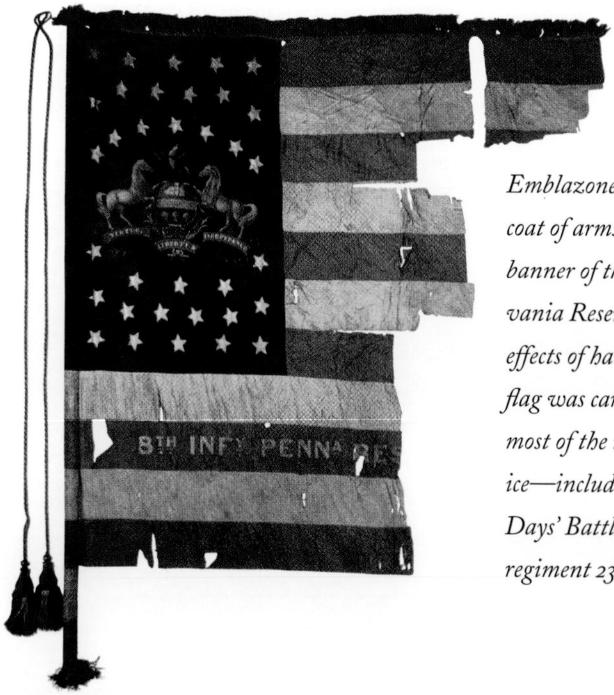

Emblazoned with the state coat of arms, the regimental banner of the 8th Pennsylvania Reserves shows the effects of hard fighting. The flag was carried through most of the unit's war service—including the Seven Days' Battles, which cost the regiment 230 casualties.

COLONEL J. FOSTER MARSHALL

1st South Carolina (Orr's) Rifles, Gregg's Brigade

A lawyer, Mexican War veteran, and 14-year state legislator, Marshall led Orr's Rifles in the opening assault at Gaines' Mill. Caught in a deadly crossfire and counterattacked by the 5th New York Zouaves, Marshall's unit lost 319 of 587 men engaged—more than any other Confederate regiment in the battle. Two months later Marshall was killed at Second Manassas.

Before giving the command to advance I called upon the regiment to remember the State from whence they came; to put their trust in God, and acquit themselves like men. At this awful moment there was not a quiver nor a pallid cheek, nor a disposition to give way on account of feeble health, when there were, as I personally know, more than 20 men who had just risen from beds of sickness to participate in the battles. There was a calmness and settled determination on the part of every man to do or die in the attempt. I gave the command, "Double-quick, march!" and as soon as we had gained the old field, "Charge bayonets," at the same time deploying the six remaining companies to the left, supporting the entire line of skirmishers.

As soon as we emerged from the pines we were met by a most destructive fire from the enemy in front and on our left, and as soon as we had cleared about 100 yards of the old field two heavy batteries on our left, about 600 yards off, poured into our ranks a deadly fire of grape and canister. . . .

My men, although now under three cross-fires, and falling thick and fast from one end of the line to the other, never once faltered. Finding no battery, they dashed on to the woods in front, where were posted seven regiments of the enemy, including the Pennsylvania Reserves. Here my men got the first chance to exchange shots. They commenced a deadly fire upon the enemy, advancing upon them as they delivered

"There were, as I personally know, more than 20 men who had just risen from beds of sickness to participate in the battles."

Two standard bearers died in the charge at Gaines' Mill bearing the flag of the 1st South Carolina Infantry (above), and all eight men of the color guard were killed or wounded. The silk banner had been embroidered and presented to the regiment by nuns of the Carmelite order in Charleston.

the fire, some of the men having it hand-to-hand, clubbing their rifles, then dispatching four or five with the bayonet; many taking deadly aim through the forks of trees. While this successful movement was going on the left wing of my regiment was about being outflanked by about 500 New York Zouaves, who came down upon my left in a desperate charge. I looked for my support, but could not see any, and then to the left of the field for the other two regiments, but could not see either of them, and thus I was left alone contending against seven regiments.

SERGEANT AUGUSTUS MEYERS

2D U.S. INFANTRY, BUCHANAN'S BRIGADE

As more of A. P. Hill's troops came forward to support the advance of Gregg's South Carolinians, the Regular Army units of General George Sykes' division were hard-pressed to hold their ground. Posted on the right flank of the New York Zouaves, the men of the 2d U.S. held the Rebels at bay until their ammunition was exhausted. At 21 Meyers was an eight-year veteran, having entered the service as a drummer boy.

We arose and in close double ranks began to fire volleys all together, to the commands of "load!" "ready!" "aim!" and "fire!" which proved to be very effective, for the Rebels retired into the woods and for a little while their firing ceased; then it recommenced in a more feeble way, when we ceased firing by company and fired at will again. While the volley firing was going on, I received what seemed like a hard blow on the right side of my head which staggered me; but I immediately guessed the cause of it and turned around to my rear-rank man, who had to fire over my shoulder, and soundly berated and threatened him. He proved to be the stupid and excitable recruit, named Davis, whom I had drilled in Washington at times. My neck and ear were blackened with powder, and it was months before I regained perfect hearing.

Loading and firing the old style muzzle loading arms was slow compared with modern arms and metallic cartridges. Before the gun could be fired, we had to take a paper cartridge out of the cartridge box, convey it to the mouth, bite off the end and pour the powder into the muzzle of the gun barrel held vertically. Then we tore off the remaining paper to free the ball and inserted that into the muzzle; the ramrod was now drawn, turned around, end for end, and the ball rammed home without any wadding; the ramrod was then drawn out, turned and restored to its place. The gun was now brought to the right hip, full cocked, a percussion cap placed on the nipple, and was then ready to aim and fire. All this required many motions and much time.

The day was intensely hot, my clothing was saturated with perspiration, the bright barrel of my gun was so heated by the fierce rays of the sun and the firing that it seemed to burn my hands and I was almost afraid to reload it without giving it time to cool off. I think we had been under fire nearly two hours, and our forty rounds of ammunition were almost exhausted when a regiment of the Pennsylvania Bucktails (so called because each soldier had a buck's tail sewed to his cap) arrived to relieve us. We were ordered to retire into the small ravine behind us, passing through the ranks of the Bucktails who advanced to take our places. We left our dead and seriously wounded behind us where they fell, unable to give them any help, crossed the little stream in the ravine and formed ranks on the other side in a field—a much shorter line than it had been but two hours before.

Colonel Joseph Howland and Lieutenant Robert P. Wilson were among 201 casualties the 16th New York Infantry sustained as it defended the extreme right flank of the Federal line. Despite their wounds, both men refused to leave the field until the fight was over. Brigade commander Colonel Joseph Bartlett characterized Wilson as "educated, brave and dashing." Of Howland he wrote, "Whatever of noble, moral, physical, and manly courage has ever been given by God to man has fallen to his lot."

PRIVATE MARTIN T. LEDBETTER

5TH ALABAMA INFANTRY, ARCHER'S BRIGADE

Although it suffered heavy casualties at Mechanicsville and now numbered fewer than 1,000 men, General Archer's brigade spearheaded the assault on the Union left at Gaines' Mill. Despite staggering losses from the volleys of the well-entrenched defenders, Archer's troops fought their way to within 20 feet of the enemy line before falling back. Ledbetter was shot down while carrying his battalion's flag.

I moved on—my color-guard was near me—until within about fifteen or twenty paces of their front line, when I looked back to see if the boys were coming; just then I was shot through my right hip. I did not know how badly I was wounded; I only knew that I was shot down. I raised on my hands like a lizzard on a fence rail and took in the situation as best I could. I soon decided if I could get up I had better do so. It seemed like death either way, but I determined to make the effort to get away. I got up, but I found I could not walk, and if I made the trip at all I would have to drag my leg. I grasped my wounded leg with my right hand and started. Just then I saw four of the boys lying down, but I could not tell whether they were all dead or not. I made my way back, dragging my leg, under a galling fire, when a minie ball struck my left wrist, and tore it up and took off my thumb at the same time. I mended my gait a little toward a deep gully. Before I reached it I looked back to see if the "Yanks" were coming, and just at that moment a ball drew a little blood from under my chin. A few more hops and I tumbled down into the deep gully. I wanted to stay there, but the boys insisted that as I was badly wounded I had better try and get to the rear or I would be captured.

That scared me up. The thought of being captured and lying in a northern prison in my condition was horrible. I could not stand the thought of such a fate. So I did not remain in the deep gully but a minute or so. Sergeant George Williams, who was afterward killed at Gettysburg, assisted me out of the gully. I had now about six hundred yards to go before I could reach the deep-cut road near the mill. I knew if I could make it there that I would be pretty safe. My route was strewn with the dead and wounded. They lay so thick that it was with great difficulty, under the withering fire of grape and canister, that I made it back to the deep-cut road. Over this entire route I dragged my hapless leg. I took shelter behind a large oak tree that stood by the roadside, in sight of Gaines's Mill. I lay down and felt pretty safe, although the shells were bursting all around me.

"Now was the critical moment when a voice of authority to guide our uncertain steps and a bold officer to lead us forward would have been worth to us a victory."

PRIVATE HENRY E. HANDERSON

10TH LOUISIANA INFANTRY, SEYMOUR'S BRIGADE

An Ohio native and a graduate of Hobart College in New York State, Handerson was a tutor for the children of a Louisiana planter at the outbreak of war. He took up arms on behalf of his adopted state, serving with the Louisiana Brigade in Stonewall Jackson's Valley campaign. At Gaines' Mill the Louisianans were repulsed by Sykes' Regulars; Handerson recalled the fight in a postwar memoir.

Soon the whistle of an occasional shell bade us prepare for action, and after some delay and apparent hesitation we formed in line of battle and advanced across an open field and through a marshy stream about knee-deep into a tangled wood which apparently covered a hill before us. Here again the direction of our advance seemed uncertain, while no enemy was visible, though the occasional whiz of a bullet assured us that the foe was not far distant. Finally obliquing somewhat to the right we ascended in rather broken order a slight ridge in the forest, when a perfect hailstorm of bullets greeted our advance. Still no enemy was to be seen, and the rattle of musketry, whiz of Minié balls and fall of the killed and wounded alone assured us that the foe was before us.

Now was the critical moment when a voice of authority to guide our uncertain steps and a bold officer to lead us forward would have been worth to us a victory. But none such appeared. Gen. Taylor was sick and absent. The gallant Col. Seymour who commanded in his absence had already fallen, while Col. Stafford who succeeded to the command by right of seniority, had not heard of his death. The line paused in natural hesitation and began firing almost at random or at the smoke which

"A moment more and he fell motionless, seemingly without a groan or struggle, and I knew that his restless career was ended."

now eddied through the trees. I peered vainly through the dense undergrowth to find some target worthy of my aim. At last, in despair of seeing the enemy in my present position, I knelt down in order to look beneath the bushes, and as I did so felt my hat (a tall felt cavalry hat picked up on the field at Middletown) tipped upon my head as I supposed by an overhanging twig. My change of position was rewarded by the sight of a man firing from behind a large pine tree, perhaps sixty yards in our front, and sighting hastily along my barrel I fired. A shower of bark from the trunk of the tree told me that I had missed my man and I hastened to reload for another trial.

Just then, a little to my left and perhaps ten paces in advance of our line, I noticed Major Wheat picking his way slowly and carefully through the dense underbrush, quiet and determined apparently, but uttering no word and followed by none of his own, or, indeed, any other command. A moment more and he fell motionless, seemingly without a groan or struggle, and I knew that his restless career was ended.

A herculean figure, standing six feet four inches tall and weighing 275 pounds, Major C. Roberdeau Wheat (left) commanded a rowdy but hard-fighting battalion nicknamed the Louisiana Tigers. His prewar adventures as a soldier of fortune included service in the Mexican War, a failed attempt to drive the Spanish from Cuba, and campaigns with Garibaldi's Italian revolutionaries. In the Battle of Gaines' Mill Wheat and his horse were felled by a Yankee volley at nearly point-blank range.

CAPTAIN JAMES COOPER NISBET

21ST GEORGIA INFANTRY, TRIMBLE'S BRIGADE

Their brigade commander dead and their formations in disarray, the Louisianans stood aside for General Isaac Trimble's brigade. Men of the 15th Alabama and 21st Georgia pierced the Federal line, overrunning Captain Hezekiah Easton's Pennsylvania battery. Nisbet recalled the charge on the guns.

We met the Louisiana Brigade coming out in good order. One said, "Boys, you are mighty good but that's h——ll in there" We got to a ridge in close rifle range to the entrenched enemy. Their three lines were firing and their artillery played on us, and over Federal heads. We were suffering terribly and should have been ordered back to get the shelter of the hill. Lieutenant Easley and six of my company had been killed and about ten men wounded.

Lieutenant Colonel Hooper came down the line, his arm broken and bleeding profusely. He said he would go back to the surgeons. He placed me in command of the regiment, saying, "Captain Waddail waives his seniority in your favor."

I hastened down the line ordering the officers to draw their companies back so as to be sheltered by the crest of the hill, and at the command, "Forward!" to advance over the hill, in double quick time to the ravine just under the enemy's first line of rifle-pits, then, to lie down. This was done, the men firing from there with better effect. Soon a charge was ordered and as we sprang forward I noticed that the enemy was retreating up the hill towards their battery. We followed closely, pouring into them a steady fire and had our innings for the loss they had inflicted on us.

The battle flag of the 16th Mississippi, one of Trimble's units, was pierced by 11 bullets and the regiment's color sergeant killed in the climactic Rebel charge at Gaines' Mill. Separated from their brigade, the Mississippians pressed through the wavering ranks of Lawton's Georgians, crossed Boatswain's Swamp, and routed the Yankee troops to their front.

The battery continued to fire until we got well up to them. A shell bursting just as it passed me, the concussion blew me up in the air six or eight feet. I turned a complete somersault but lit on my all fours as the men passed me towards the battery. As I sped through the air I thought my legs had been cut off by the shell and that the upper part of my body was flying through space. I instinctively felt for my limbs and found they were all right before I came to the ground.

We were so close to the cannon that grains of unburnt powder had stung my face and that, with the dense smoke, nearly blinded me. Fragments of that same shell wounded two of my company severely.

PRIVATE WILLIAM A. MCCLENDON

15th Alabama Infantry, Trimble's Brigade

Though dispersed in their advance through the boggy ground and wooded ravines flanking Boatswain's Swamp, Trimble's units pressed ahead alongside other Rebel formations and engaged the enemy. The troops in the left wing of the 15th Alabama were held at bay by the determined Yankees but they kept pressing for three hours, until Hood's Texas Brigade came to their support. Recently recovered from malaria, McClendon won promotion to lieutenant and commanded his company at war's end.

When we reached the top of the hill we halted, and my company, with the balance of the left wing of the Fifteenth Alabama, opened fire upon the enemy, who were down the slope on their knees about fifty yards away. We sent such a shower of buck and ball at them through the bushes and smoke that it left many of them *hors de combat*, and at the same time we received a shower of Minie-balls from them that caused several of my company to fall, while others staggered and reeled and went to the rear wounded. Those of us that were not hurt set up a yell, fell upon our knees, and loaded and fired in that position as fast as we could. Our company officers were diligent in their duties, encouraging the men by their example and ordering us to aim low that we might not over-shoot and waste our ammunition. There was so much smoke that it was only occasionally that we could see the enemy, but we knew he was there by the hissing of his bullets and the wounding or killing of a man occasionally. We could very distinctly tell when the Yankees would receive reenforcements by the increase of their bullets and their cheers, but the storm of lead that we were pouring at them prevented them from advancing any nearer than their front lines. The yelling of the Confederates and the roar of small arms and artillery was so great that I could only tell when I had fired my gun by a hard punch (kick) of the breech against my shoulder or a jar by the stock against my right cheek bone. I loaded and fired so fast that the barrel of my gun became so hot that I thought it dangerous at one time to pour powder in it, and laid it down, picked up another that had been dropped by a wounded man, and used it until mine became cooler. While I was loading, firing, and hollering, "Hurrah, boys, give it to 'em!" I would look to the right occasionally, and through the smoke would catch a glimpse of our colors fluttering in the breeze, when I would feel cheerful seeing them maintaining their position.

SERGEANT ASHBALA F. HILL

8th Pennsylvania Reserves, Reynolds' Brigade

The 8th was among the regiments held in reserve while Sykes' division met the opening Confederate attacks. Though sheltered in a sunken road, Hill's outfit still took casualties from enemy battery fire as the Rebel artillerists tended to overshoot the Union front line, their shells falling among the reserves. Captain Henry V. DeHart's battery of the 5th U.S. Artillery supported the Pennsylvanians.

Suddenly I heard an explosion a little to my right that pierced to my very brain. I naturally turned in the direction, and saw a sight that is before my eyes yet. Twenty or thirty feet from me, where the banks were not high enough to afford much protection, I saw a cloud of dust and smoke in the very midst of Company "A." I saw a man throw his hands wildly above his head, and fall backward, covered with blood. A moment he lay quivering convulsively, then he lay still—perfectly still. He was dead. Another stooped, and picked up his own arm which had been torn off by the shell as it descended, and rushed wildly toward a small hospital some distance to the rear flourishing the dismembered limb above his head, and shouting in the broad tongue:—

"Och, docther, me airm's off, me airm's off!" just as though the doctor could help it.

A percussion shell had struck fairly among the boys, killing three outright, and wounding four. It is a terrible sight to see a shell strike and explode in the midst of a body of men.

It was anything but pleasant lying in that road; the red dust was several inches deep; the heat was intense; and it was highly judicious for one to lie close to the ground, if he had any respect for the terrible missiles whose peculiar qualities were so impressively demonstrated to us, as described.

During the engagement, an officer of the battery on the bank behind us came to the edge of the bank—I verily believe he had his hands in his pockets—and with surprising coolness, said—

"Men, be kind enough to keep your heads as low as possible for a little while; I want to try a round of grape-and-canister—just one—and some of the shot may fly pretty low"; and he returned to the battery.

A moment the guns were silent. The rebel infantry, at this juncture, were pressing out from the wood in solid bodies, presenting great temptations for grape-and-canister.

Suddenly the earth shook—the hill seemed to be starting from its place as the six guns were discharged in concert; and six charges of grape-and-canister went hissing over our heads toward the wood. A moment after the battery officer reappeared at the brink of the bank, and gleefully exclaimed:

"'Twas a lucky shot, boys! 'Twould have done you good to see how they were mowed down; and how the *lucky* ones scrambled back into the woods, ha! ha!"

Recruited from Boston's Irish population, the 9th Massachusetts Infantry of General Charles Griffin's brigade was one of a number of Federal units whose regimental flags evoked their Celtic heritage. Heavily engaged at Gaines' Mill from the opening skirmish to the final collapse of the Yankee line, the 9th lost 231 men—87 of them killed or mortally wounded.

"Here on the battlefield, amid ten thousand bullets, I felt the spirit of fun awaken a new life in me."

SERGEANT WILLIAM F. FULTON

5th Alabama Battalion, Archer's Brigade

Assaulting the formidably defended center of the Yankee line, just west of Fitz-John Porter's headquarters at the Watt house, General Archer's understrength brigade was torn to pieces by the well-aimed fire of Brigadier General Daniel Butterfield's Federals. Archer was about to order a retreat when most of his men broke formation and scrambled for the rear, Fulton among them. A few companies rejoined the fight later in the day, but the demoralized brigade was unable to function as a unit.

As we were forced to fall back we had quite a long run before we could cross over the bridge and secure its protection somewhat from the fearful hail of bullets. We had to pass through the old apple orchard with its trees scattered here and there, and behind every tree were a lot of poor fellows huddled to catch breath before going farther, as most of us were completely exhausted by the charge and hardly had breath enough left to stand on our legs. As I came to an extra large tree I was minded to stop and get a little breath to bear me over the hill, and as I made a break for it I discovered about a dozen or more already there, the first fellow hugging the tree, the next hugging him, and so on down the line. There was a comic fellow in the battalion who had picked up somewhere a tall, black, beaver hat, with a tall crown and narrow brim, such as the gentry sometimes wear, and the boys called him, "Beegum." It happened that "Beegum" was on the tail end of the line behind the tree and as I came up panting for breath, some one hollered out, "Fall in behind Beegum." And here on the battlefield, amid ten thousand bullets, I felt the spirit of fun awaken a new life in me, as I threw my arms around "Beegum" about fifteen or twenty feet from that apple tree. You may rest assured that none of us hugged that tree many seconds. All we wanted was to catch one or two good breaths and then we made for the rear. As I crossed the top of the ridge and started down the other side I made a bee-line for the little branch at the bottom, fringed with weeds and bushes. As I dashed in and fell in the branch I heard a fellow groaning and moaning terribly nearby, and on looking in his direction I discovered that it was my old chum who had laughed so heartily at my plunge off the bridge when the Yankee lighted his pipe. I asked him what was the matter. "Oh I am shot plumb through." "Where?" "Right under my shoulder blade." He was evidently near death's door and I began to cut off his clothing to render what assistance I could. As I got off his jacket and through his shirt to the skin I soon saw there was no hole and no blood, but a piece of exploded bombshell had struck him under the shoulder blade and raised a great red blister, and as his shirt and coat rubbed it his imagination did the rest. When I told him there was no hole and no ball had penetrated him, he sat up and straightened himself out, and drawing a long breath he exclaimed, "Well I thought I was dying!" So I had the laugh on him.

MAJOR WILLIAM H. TOON

20th North Carolina Infantry, Garland's Brigade

Daylight was fading when D. H. Hill's brigades came into action on the far left of the Confederate line. Breasting a withering fire from four Yankee batteries posted on a hill near the McGehee farmhouse, General Samuel Garland Jr.'s five North Carolina units soon lost their alignment. But Toon's untried 20th North Carolina pressed on and captured two guns of the 3d U.S. Artillery. The charge cost the regiment 272 men, including its colonel and lieutenant colonel. When the 16th New York launched a counterattack, Toon ordered the surviving Carolinians to retreat.

We were now ordered to cross the road and prepare for action. Having passed through an open field, say about 200 yards, we reached a small piece of woods beyond which was the open ground in which the enemy had taken his position. The regiment had now the opportunity of opening fire, which was continued for half an hour, when they received orders from you to charge a battery in the field about 400 yards off and take it at all hazards.

They had advanced about half way, under a terrible fire, when by some misunderstanding the command retreated to within twenty yards of the woods. Here they were halted and the order to charge and *take* the battery repeated and understood. The regiment immediately faced about, advanced rapidly, amid a storm of grape, canister and musketry, and charged the battery with a yell. The charge was completely successful—the enemy were driven off and the battle flag of the regiment waved over their guns. One of these was turned upon their retreating columns, but the caissons having been removed, no munition could be found; a constant and rapid fire of musketry was kept up against the enemy during their retreat, and the battery was held by us, I think, a full ten minutes.

At this time, finding we were about to be flanked by a large force of the enemy and seeing no appearance of reinforcements from other regiments of the brigade, we were reluctantly compelled to abandon the guns and return to a position in the woods.

When Colonel Alfred Iverson of the 20th North Carolina was wounded, Lieutenant Colonel Franklin J. Faison (left) took command and led the regiment's charge against Lieutenant Horace J. Hayden's section of the 3d U.S. Artillery. Faison was helping to turn one of the captured cannon on the Yankee infantry supports when he was killed. "He was greatly beloved, and his memory will be cherished with veneration and pride," General Garland reported.

Photographed in June 1861 at Fort Johnston on the Atlantic coast of North Carolina, the "Confederate Grays" of Duplin County became Company C of the 20th North Carolina Infantry. The Grays were organized by 24-year-old Captain Claudius B. Denson (standing at left in the front row), commandant of a local academy called the Franklin Military Institute. The majority of the company's enlisted personnel were former cadets at the school, most of them in their teens. After 10 months of garrison duty at Fort Johnston the company traveled with the 20th to the defenses of Richmond and took part in some of the fiercest fighting at Gaines' Mill.

SERGEANT MAJOR THOMAS H. EVANS

12TH U.S. INFANTRY, BUCHANAN'S BRIGADE

Welsh-born and educated for the ministry, Evans enlisted in the army after emigrating in 1849. After 10 years of teaching recruits to read and write at a post on Governor's Island, New York, Evans was appointed sergeant major of the newly organized 12th Regiment. Gaines' Mill was his first battle.

The enemy in the woods form four deep and send in their bullets closer and closer. But still we hold on. The 14th Regiment rises, pours in a volley, and falls back in good order to the road. "Keep up your fire, men," cries our major. The 14th are halfway across the field. They halt and fire another volley.

Now comes the order to us: "Rise up!" Instantly every man is on his feet, some only to fall again and rise no more, as a fresh burst comes from the enemy. Now our gallant commander cries, "Ready, aim low, men. Fire!" Every piece is discharged in a withering volley. We pull back quickly and are halfway across the field before the enemy recover sufficiently from our volley to fire at us. Then we see another column moving up the slope to take us in flank and rear. There is too much smoke for us to distinguish who they are. Some call out that they are our own men, and hesitate. But we are soon decided, for they give us a volley.

"Step now, men, if you ever stepped." Thank God, the fence is close at hand. But great gaps have opened in our ranks. Directly in front of me six men fall in quick succession, so rapidly that I have to pause an instant to avoid trampling on them. I pass into one of the gaps, and soon we are over the road and forming behind the second fence in McGhee's orchard. The 14th have opened fire on our pursuers. We rally our shattered ranks. Every post, bush, and tree now covers a man who is blazing away as fast as he can load and fire.

PRIVATE E. FAISON HICKS

20TH NORTH CAROLINA INFANTRY, GARLAND'S BRIGADE

After driving Buchanan's brigade of Regular Army troops from their position in a sunken road, Hicks and his comrades of the 20th North Carolina continued their onslaught on the guns of the 3d U.S. Artillery. A 17-year-old student, Hicks rose to the rank of sergeant. Wounded at Chancellorsville and again at Winchester in September 1864, he finished his service in the 5th North Carolina Cavalry.

We were marching in column when the battery opened on us with shells, then we made a right wheel to face it, then advanced through a thicket to a fence that enclosed a field, and opened fire with our muskets. From there we were ordered to charge, and in order to reach the battery, we made an oblique movement to our left. The guns were located on the left, as we faced them, and in front of the house, near a road that ran in front of it. My position in line was at the intersection of the alley running from the house to the road, on the side nearer the guns. I saw our troops turn the guns, and then gave my attention to my front, and fired several shots about the house. The captured guns not firing, I looked in that direction and saw that they were abandoned, and, knowing there had been no forward movement on the part of our boys, I looked and saw our whole line had fallen back, and, the smoke having risen in my front and right, saw the enemy charge in a run towards the battery. They commanded me to halt, and, as I could not fly, I ran back and joined our lines at the charging point, at which position the regiment continued to fire.

Private Absalom H. Watson of Company C, 20th North Carolina, doing his best to affect a warlike mien, posed for this ambrotype soon after his enlistment. A former clerk, Watson was promoted to corporal but then reduced back to private in April 1862. Two months later he was among the 70 men of his unit killed in the Battle of Gaines' Mill.

LIEUTENANT E. BURD GRUBB

STAFF, GENERAL GEORGE W. TAYLOR

Dispatched by McClellan to reinforce Porter at Gaines' Mill, Henry Slocum committed the men of his division to threatened points along the Union front. Accompanied by the 20-year-old Grubb, the comte de Paris, one of two heirs to the Bourbon monarchy on McClellan's staff, guided the 4th New Jersey to support Meade's brigade on the left.

Immediately after General Slocum's aide had given orders to General Taylor to advance his brigade, and before the brigade had gotten into line of battle from the massed formation, an officer, riding very fast and coming down the line from the east, rode up to General Taylor and commenced speaking to him very rapidly in French (both of these officers whom I have mentioned spoke English perfectly well). General Taylor neither spoke nor understood French, and he turned to me and said: "Who the devil is this, and what is he talking about?" I said to him: "This is the Comte de Paris, serving on General McClellan's staff, and he has come to you by General Porter's orders, under which you are to give him one of our regiments." General Taylor said to me: "Do you know him?" I said, "Yes, sir, I do." He said: "Very well, then, give him the Fourth Regiment and go and see where he puts it and come back and report." These last few words saved me a trip to Libby Prison. We started up at once after the Fourth Regiment, where we arrived in a few jumps of our horses. The French officer was a good deal excited. He was a young man, probably about twenty-five or six years of age. I do not think that he said anything to me as we were riding, but I do remember that his horse shied at a dead man who lay in our way and very nearly threw him over his head. Arrived at the Fourth Regiment, whose Colonel Simpson, a West Point officer, was just beginning to form his line of battle. I introduced him. Colonel Simpson spoke French very well and their conversation was in French. I understood it, and heard him tell Colonel Simpson just what I had told General Taylor, and he said that if Colonel Simpson would get his regiment in columns of fours he would conduct him where he wanted to go. The regiment was put in columns of fours and went off to the left front, with Colonel Simpson, the French officer and myself riding at the head of it, Colonel Simpson on the left of us and the French officer between us. We had not gone far before I saw that we were approaching the swale that I have spoken of before, and soon we arrived at it. To my great surprise there was no more line of battle than there was in the morning, although there was a very heavy battle going on on the right, on the eastern side of this swale. My recollection is that there was not much going on on the left or western side, but I cannot say that I remember distinctly about that. At the mouth of this swale, apparently waiting for the Fourth Regiment, was the Eleventh Pennsylvania Regiment, also in columns, and also apparently under the orders of this French officer; for as soon as the Fourth came up both regiments moved off together through this swale.

LIEUTENANT WILLIAM N. WOOD

19TH VIRGINIA INFANTRY, PICKETT'S BRIGADE

To try to support Hill's and Ewell's floundering attacks, General Longstreet began his own assault on the Yankee position by ordering George Pickett's 2,200-man brigade to charge the Union left. Wood, a farmer from Chancellorsville, Virginia, recalled the dramatic assault that managed to pierce the enemy line, capture a battery, and gain the first Rebel toehold in Porter's formidable perimeter.

Going eastward we crossed Powhite creek at Gaines' Mill, filed to the right down the creek for some distance until we came to a branch that ran into the creek. Here we filed left and went up the branch and halted near its source. That ominous stillness was observable. Company A was detailed as skirmishers. I was with the regimental and brigade staff who were quietly sitting on their horses just in the rear of the Nineteenth Regiment. I heard some one remark, "Why, what is the matter with Company A?" Looking around I saw the company hesitating to advance (the first and last time) as skirmishers. Dismounting hastily and throwing my bridle reins to an orderly, jumping the branch, I was soon in their midst. "What's the matter, boys?" The response came, "We are ready to go now," and away we went, driving in the skirmish line of the enemy and nearly approaching the top of the hill, when we were ordered to return to the regiment which was at once put in motion—the brigade forming a line of battle that looked formidable. Marching steadily up the hill we received the enemy's fire before reaching the top. The smoke from their guns settled in the bottom between us, and not only concealed the enemy but shut out from view their surroundings. Unfortunately the whole line halted on top of the hill and were raked by the batteries on the south side of the river as well as from those in front. For some time the entire line seemed to hesitate. I was ordered to the left to urge an advance and ran from the right of the regiment to the left of it with the one cry, "Forward! Forward!" and returned about half way to the right when the regiment launched forth into the smoke and dust with a yell which was taken up on either side, and away we went down a steep hill, at the bottom of which was a deep ravine that separated the cleared field through which we came from the body of woods beyond. Nearly exhausted from exertion, I failed to reach the opposite bank of the ravine in attempting to jump it, and found myself at the bottom of a ten-foot ditch, and the boys climbing the hill beyond shouting and shooting like mad. By the time I got out of the ditch the three lines of the enemy's works were in our possession.

Lieutenant Henry Clay Michie (left) stands with a comrade from Company H of the 56th Virginia Infantry—a regiment in Pickett's brigade. A freshman at the University of Virginia when the war began, Michie was wounded at Gaines' Mill and at Second Manassas, and wounded and captured in Pickett's charge at Gettysburg.

PRIVATE GEORGE W. NICHOLS

61st Georgia Infantry, Lawton's Brigade

At 3,600 men and one of the largest brigades in the Army of Northern Virginia, General Lawton's six Georgia regiments were among the last of Stonewall Jackson's troops to arrive on the field. Urged on by General Ewell—afoot and shouting, "Hurrah for Georgia!"—Lawton's soldiers pushed through Gregg's South Carolinians and stormed the center of the Yankee line. Nichols, who later wrote a history of his regiment, described the grueling march to battle and the ensuing attack.

We were in the rear of Jackson's column, and marched at quick step for about four hours. We could hear the cannons booming very fast. We finally got near enough to hear the small arms, and could hear the rebel yell, and meet the wounded who were coming out of battle. We were ordered to double quick (run) for about three miles, with a few shells being thrown at us. We were all doing our best. The writer had a high fever. As we passed an old gentleman's house, one of our company said: "Old man, how far is it to hell." The old man looked like a preacher, and he replied, "My dear sir, I am afraid you will find out pretty soon." The young man was shot dead in about thirty minutes. We got up and were hurriedly formed in line and ordered to advance in a storm of grape-shot and shells.

One grape-shot broke Joe Nevill's gun and came very near breaking his neck. One shell exploded so close to Jack Collins until it addled him and partly paralyzed him for several days. We went on in line through a very thick, boggy branch where we found a great many dead and wounded yankees. Some of them were lying in the water. I was so thirsty from fever and a long march and run to the battle till my tongue was swollen. I stopped, dipped up and drank water which I knew had yankee blood in it. I am sure it was the best water to me that I ever drank. I have often thought it saved my life. We forwarded across the branch and up a little hill, stopped a minute and reformed our line. There was a terrible battle raging about three hundred yards in our front. Our line advanced in an open field, which was very smoky. We could see both the Confederate and Yankee lines. We were about two hundred yards from the Confederate line and they mistook us for Yankees coming up in the rear and fired a volley at us, and I suppose the yankees shot at us too, for we were about three hundred yards from their line.

"Forward was the order, as it floats out like the sound of a bugle upon the air and reverberates up and down the line."

PRIVATE WILLIAM A. MCCLENDON

15TH ALABAMA INFANTRY, TRIMBLE'S BRIGADE

At 4:30 p.m., following a forced march in stifling heat, General William H. C. Whiting's division arrived and swung into line behind the survivors of earlier Rebel attacks. Urged on by Lee and Longstreet, Whiting sent Evander Law's and John Hood's brigades forward in an attempt to crack the Yankee stronghold above Boatswain's Swamp. McClendon and his comrades joined Hood's 4th Texas in the charge.

About the time we got through we looked down the hill in our rear, and there came the Fourth Texas, half bent as if looking for a turkey. We greeted them with a cheer, and they responded. They marched up to our position and halted, rectified their line, fired one volley down the slant through the bushes at the Yankees, when they were ordered to cease firing, reload, and fix bayonets. The firing from the Yankees had become slack, which was an indication that they were waiting for us or preparing to advance. While these things were going on among the Texans, our officers, anticipating an order for a general charge, began to rectify our line and be ready. There was so much smoke that you could only tell an Alabamian from a Texan by a badge or the kind of a gun we carried. They were armed with short Enfield rifles with sabre bayonets, and we with smooth-bore muskets.

All being ready, the command "charge!" was given. We raised a yell and dashed down the slant pell-mell, yelling all the time, expecting a hand-to-hand encounter when we reached their line where last seen; but instead of a hand-to-hand engagement, as we expected, when we reached their line numbers of them lay dead or too badly wounded to be moved.

PRIVATE JOHN W. STEVENS

5TH TEXAS INFANTRY, HOOD'S BRIGADE

Crossing Boatswain's Swamp, Hood's forces pushed through General Arnold Elzey's brigade and swept uphill toward the Federal position. Hood swung the 4th Texas and 18th Georgia to the right of Law's brigade, while his three remaining units—including Stevens' 5th Texas—pressed ahead. Hood's men pierced the Yankee line, swept over a Rhode Island battery and captured two regiments—the 11th Pennsylvania and 4th New Jersey—not the 7th New Jersey, as Stevens wrote.

General Elzy, of the Maryland line, has been already engaged and badly cut to pieces.

They are ordered to retire. Having failed to carry the breastworks in our immediate front as they pass us to the rear, the effect upon our men is most trying to their nerves; they are literally cut to pieces. The wounded and bleeding resting upon and assisted by their friends, are slowly making their way to the rear, having left prostrate forms of more than half their number at the breastworks they failed to carry. Forward was the order, as it floats out like the sound of a bugle upon the air and reverberates up and down the line. "Fix bayonets! Charge! Give them the bayonet, my brave boys." The noble form of John B. Hood, our brigade commander, is moving here and there, up and down the line, cheering his men on. We are at the breastworks, over we go; our Texas boys are now in it to their heart's content. The enemy's line is broken, the Confederate yell resounds up and down the line, carrying dismay and demoralization to the enemy's ranks.

The battery of seven guns on that hill in our front are mowing down the Fourth Texas like grain before the scythe. "Take that battery, boys!" Like a flash of lightning the Texans moved forward upon the seven gun battery; the gunners double shot it with scrapnell and sweep our ranks at close range, cutting down our boys by the hundreds as they move toward it, but nothing daunted, with an impetuosity that cannot be portrayed by human pen, on they move, the very mouths of these death dealing machines are reached, as the dying gunner fires his last gun into our ranks and is shot down at his gun. The battery is in our hands; its destructive work ceases; the brave men, who a moment ago were working these guns, are now cold in death. The horses are all killed or badly wounded. We wheel to the left and meet the Seventh New Jersey regiment of Federals, some seven hundred or more strong. It's hilt to hilt, clubbed guns, short work the struggle is over—they surrender.

When the infantry of Brigadier General George Morell's division gave way before Hood's charge, the supporting batteries—18 guns under the command of Captain William B. Weeden—were exposed to the Confederate onslaught. With most of the battery horses dead or wounded, Weeden was able to extricate only half his field pieces, while the surviving gunners fired canister into the oncoming Rebels at point-blank range. "They were mown down in swaths as by a mighty scythe," one artillerist recalled. "But they rallied and came for us again. The desperation with which that attack was made surpassed anything I ever saw." Artist Alfred Waud's sketch shows the victorious Texans capturing two of Weeden's guns.

Photographed in Richmond soon after his promotion to brigadier general, John Bell Hood won praise throughout the Confederacy for personally leading the charge that turned the tide of battle at Gaines' Mill. Lee and Jackson credited the 4th Texas—the unit Hood had formerly commanded as colonel—with being the first to penetrate the Federal defenses. Proud of his old regiment's bravery and discipline, Hood asserted he could "double-quick the 4th Texas to the gates of hell."

PRIVATE WILLIAM A. FLETCHER

5th Texas Infantry, Hood's Brigade

When Hood ordered the charge, Fletcher's Company F troops were deployed as skirmishers to screen the left flank of the brigade's advance. While the other regiments were engaging the Yankee batteries, Fletcher and his comrades attacked the rear of the 4th New Jersey. A 23-year-old from Louisiana, Fletcher served with the Texas Brigade until March 1864, sustaining wounds at Second Manassas and Chickamauga. His marching ability hindered, he was reassigned to the 8th Texas Cavalry.

Being on down grade I felt reasonably safe while I kept up my speed, for I well knew that in favorable conditions a large percentage of the bullets would pass over. I came near falling twice on my plunge downward, as I was nearly tripped up by fallen limbs; and it seemed that the whole line was obliquely firing in my direction. When I reached the point where I had left the company I saw that they were gone, or I had headed wrong; so I jumped behind a tree for protection and scanned the surroundings for the company, and not seeing them, was satisfied that they had moved; so I moved on at quick time in the supposed direction of the company's travel. This I was correct in, for after I had gone some distance double-quicking, I ran into our orderly sergeant. I asked where the company was and he said they were mostly ahead, but badly scattered. We were then passing near a tented commissary department, which, from appearances, was well stocked with food. Just then to the right and two or three hundred yards ahead, I saw our line forming and directly to my right about seventy-five yards I saw a tall "Yankee" well bent in a long trot, and passing through the tented ground, in an effort, I suppose, to escape. I said, as I raised my gun, "Look, sergeant," and the words were not more than said when I fired—the man dropped his gun, staggered to the right and fell. The sergeant said, "You got him," and I remarked that he had quit his gun, at least.

MAJOR JOHN CHEVES HASKELL

STAFF, BRIGADIER GENERAL D. R. JONES

After bearing orders from General Longstreet to the embattled front line, the aristocratic 20-year-old South Carolinian assisted division commander William H. C. Whiting in rallying units to support his assault. Haskell then joined Law's brigade in the attack, seizing the battle flag of a wavering regiment and personally leading its charge.

"When the spurs pricked him, though I am sure he was mortally wounded, he made one of his typical rushes and had me over the breastworks."

A ball struck my saddle, grazing my leg and going into my horse, which fell to his knees. He had, up to this time, been the best horse I ever saw in battle, the only effect of the firing being to steady him, though I thought he would be utterly unmanageable. I pulled him to his feet, and—not realizing that he fell from the shot—struck my spurs into him. When the spurs pricked him, though I am sure he was mortally wounded, he made one of his typical rushes and had me over the breastworks. But he was shot dead in the act of leaping, and I was lying under him among the enemy.

A captain, I think of a New York regiment, ran up to me and grabbing the flagstaff called out to me, "You damned little rebel, surrender." I held on and jerked him to me, striking at him at the same time with my sword, which was hung to my wrist by a sword knot. He at once jumped back and fired at me with his pistol, cursing me all the time and tugging at the flagstaff. I kept jerking it back and striking at him with my sword, while at the same time struggling to get from under my dead horse, which was lying on my legs.

One ball from the pistol struck the star of my collar and burned my neck like fire, while another struck my little finger, breaking it and smashing a seal ring which I wore. Another just grazed my leg, but that one felt like a double-heated, hot iron, and made me struggle so that I found myself free from my horse and on my feet.

Our troops by this time were pouring in and the Yankees running, my opponent among them. But he was a little too late, and I caught up with him. I cut down on him with both hands, expecting to split him, as we used to read of in novels, but my sword bounced off, knocking him to his knees. He rose and turned, facing me with his pistol in his hand. I never doubted but that he was about to shoot again and ran him through. He lived only a few minutes, trying to say something. I told him that I would send his effects to his people, which was apparently what he was trying to ask.

As soon as I could, I started to re-form the men I had been leading. While I was doing this, General Hood came from my left. He was re-forming his brigade. He spoke to me, offering to help me, as I was very bloody. When I told him I was not seriously hurt, he said that he was about to charge the battery which was sweeping the level beyond the ravine, where we had just broken the enemy's first line, and suggested that I join my men to his right.

I did so, and we charged across the plateau about four or five hundred feet. When I got within a few feet of the guns, I marked a gunner fixing his lanyard into the friction primer. I made a run to cut him down before he could fire, but he was too quick. When I was not over ten feet from the muzzle the gun went off. The shot struck my right arm, crushing it and tearing it off at the shoulder. When it hit me, it seemed to knock me up in the air and spin me around two or three times, though I suppose that was imaginary, and then dashed me down with a force that knocked all the breath out of me.

When I came to, I found my arm wrapped around my sword blade in a most remarkable manner. I sat up, but almost immediately everything went dark, and I supposed I was dying. After some time I regained consciousness and unwound the fragments of my arm from my sword blade, which I got back into the scabbard. I succeeded in stuffing my arm into the breast of my coat, got to my feet and started to the rear, using the flagstaff as a support.

"Captain Whiting at once gave the order, 'Trot! March!' and as soon as we were fully under way he shouted, 'Charge!' "

PRIVATE WILLIAM H. HITCHCOCK

5th U.S. Cavalry, Cooke's Cavalry Division

After breaching the Federal position, Longstreet's brigades rushed for the Yankee batteries. General Philip S. Cooke ordered 250 troopers of the 5th Cavalry to charge the oncoming Rebels. The attack was repulsed with a loss of 55 men, including six of the unit's seven officers. Hitchcock, a printer from New York, was discharged with chronic diarrhea in 1863 but later reenlisted in the 3d Michigan Cavalry.

Just before dark, when we could tell, by the sound of the musketry fire and by the constantly advancing yells of the charging foe, that he was getting near the guns in our front, General Philip St. George Cooke, commanding the cavalry, rode to our front. I was on the right of the front line of the first squadron, and I heard his order to Captain Whiting, commanding the five companies of our regiment that were present on the field. He said, "Captain, as soon as you see the advancing line of the enemy rising the crest of the hill, charge at once, without any further orders, to enable the artillery to bring off their guns." General Cooke then rode back around the right of our squadron.

Captain Whiting turned to us and said, "Cavalry! Attention! Draw saber!" then added something to the effect, "Boys, we must charge in five minutes." Almost immediately, the bayonets of the advancing foe were seen, just beyond our cannon, probably not fifty rods from us. Captain Whiting at once gave the order, "Trot! March!" and as soon as we were fully under way he shouted, "Charge!"

We dashed forward with a wild cheer, in solid column of squadron front; but our formation was almost instantly broken by the necessity of opening to right and left to pass our guns. So furiously were our brave gunners fighting that I noticed this incident: The gun directly in my front had just been loaded; every man had fallen before it could be fired. As I bore to the right to pass this gun, I saw the man at the breech, who was evidently shot through the body, drawing himself up by the spokes of the wheel, and reaching for the lanyard, and I said, "He will fire that gun," and so kept to the right, and almost immediately felt the shock of the explosion. Then I closed in to re-form the line, but could find no one at my left, so completely had our line been shattered by the musketry fire in front and the artillery fire in our rear. I rushed on, and almost instantly my horse reared upright in front of a line of bayonets, held by a few men upon whom I had dashed. My horse came down in front of the line, and ran away partly to our rear, perfectly uncontrollable. I dropped my saber, which hung to my wrist by the saber-knot, and so fiercely tugged at my horse's bit as to cause the blood to flow from her mouth, yet could not check her. The gun I had passed, now limbered up, was being hauled off at a gallop. I could direct my horse a little to right or left, and so directed her toward the gun. As she did not attempt to leap the gun, I gained control of her, and at once turned about and started back upon my charge. After riding a short distance I paused. The firing of artillery and infantry behind and of infantry in front was terrific. None but the dead and wounded were around me.

PRIVATE COLUMBUS C. CHAMBERS

11th Mississippi Infantry, Law's Brigade

Double-quicking into line on the right of Hood's Texans, Law's troops joined the Rebel charge. Urged on by Whiting, they fought their way onto the plateau near Porter's headquarters and opened fire on the Yankee battery horses to prevent the guns from being removed. Chambers survived wartime bouts of measles and diarrhea and a bullet wound at the Battle of the Wilderness. He wrote his reminiscences of Gaines' Mill 50 years after the fight, while living in retirement in Arizona.

The head of the Texas Brigade would naturally move faster than the rear of our brigade. All were on a rush at "double-quick" to get to the proper position to form the line for the attack. Any one who has ever moved in column understands how the rear is forced to make up distance lost. During this lap both shell and solid shot were passing through our ranks. It was perfectly natural for the men to fall to the ground, some flat, some squatting. I was within ten feet of a Texan who squatted like many others. The shot struck his head squarely, taking it entirely from his shoulders, striking Dick Wilson, of the Lamar Rifles, 11th Mississippi, on his gun and blanket. It sent him whirling, but simply, addled him. He did not continue in that battle, but was killed in the Wilderness, May 5, 1864.

General Whiting, finding an open field somewhat protected from that shot and shell, formed his brigade into a hollow square, and in that position we could hear him plainly when he told us when the line was formed to move to the crest of the hill where the firing was then in progress, to "lie down and fire until the order to charge." He explained that two different attempts had been made, but had failed, and added: "When that charge is ordered, there will be no order for retreat. I will lead you, and I believe you will carry the works." I saw him wave his hat and call: "Mississippians, charge!" We did not see him after that, but with a roar, and as of one man we gave the Rebel Yell. At the foot of this hill we found solid log works with sharpened sticks and a deep ditch.

I personally was fortunate in being able to jump the ditch where the majority of the men had to jump into the ditch and get out as best they could, which of course threw them behind. The enemy fled. The second line at the top of the hill left, and the third still over the next hill, then the cavalry, made a desperate effort to check us, but failed with terrible loss, then we made for the battery. We were without officers, and every man was his own commander. A little Irishman who was with me at the last brushy run wanted to take some prisoners, but I said: "Come on, Burns, come on, and let us stop that brass band on that hill." He and I were two of the boys who shot down some of the finest horses in McClellan's army, which was to prevent the guns from being taken off. After securing the battery, we found that the field hospital was but a rifle shot in advance of us, and that but a few of the enemy were between the hospital and our advance. Then we began to form a line and saw a few officers. Our colonel, P. F. Ladell, was with us. How he got his horse there I do not know. The firing went on to our rear, and right until dark; but the old 3d Brigade, as we were known, was at the front and had kept pace with if not the lead of the Texans.

LIEUTENANT COLONEL ALEXANDER D. ADAMS

27th New York Infantry, Bartlett's Brigade

By evening Porter's left wing was in retreat, while the right maintained a semblance of order against mounting pressure. Though threatened with encirclement, Bartlett's brigade and three Regular Army batteries held the slopes of McGehee's Hill, as Adams noted in his report.

A fresh force appearing on the right, the fire of the right wing was directed obliquely against it. Soon after it was represented that we were firing on our own men, and not knowing how far the Sixteenth New York, whose constant volleys were heard on our right, might have advanced, the order was given to cease firing and re-form line of battle on the fence in rear. . . .

While this was being coolly executed the smoke lifted partially, disclosing an apparently fresh line of the enemy in front. The Twenty-seventh was at once advanced to its former position and again opened an effective fire. The small buildings offered a partial cover to a few of the men, who were enabled to fire with the utmost precision at a rest. The fire of the enemy slackened about dusk for a little, and word was again brought that our own brigade had advanced on the right so as to come within range of the fire of the Twenty-seventh. These reports coming, as before, from officers induced another order to cease firing, which, however, was speedily revoked, as the flashes of the muskets revealed the position of the enemy. Again the line opened, though the rapidly gathering gloom rendered the aim somewhat uncertain. The cessation of the firing on the right of the brigade having attracted attention it was deemed advisable to reform the line, by this time considerably thinned, on the fence in rear of the house (about 3 rods), which offered the nearest advantageous position, owing to the location of the various buildings. The appearance of a large force (apparently a brigade) on the left, marching as if to flank this brigade, who responded irregularly to the challenge of the color-bearer (and who were afterward ascertained to be the enemy), decided the propriety of this maneuver. While this was being accomplished Colonel Bartlett in person gave the order for the regiment to retire in order. On reaching the ravine from which the brigade had advanced the regiment found itself in its proper position, on the left of the column.

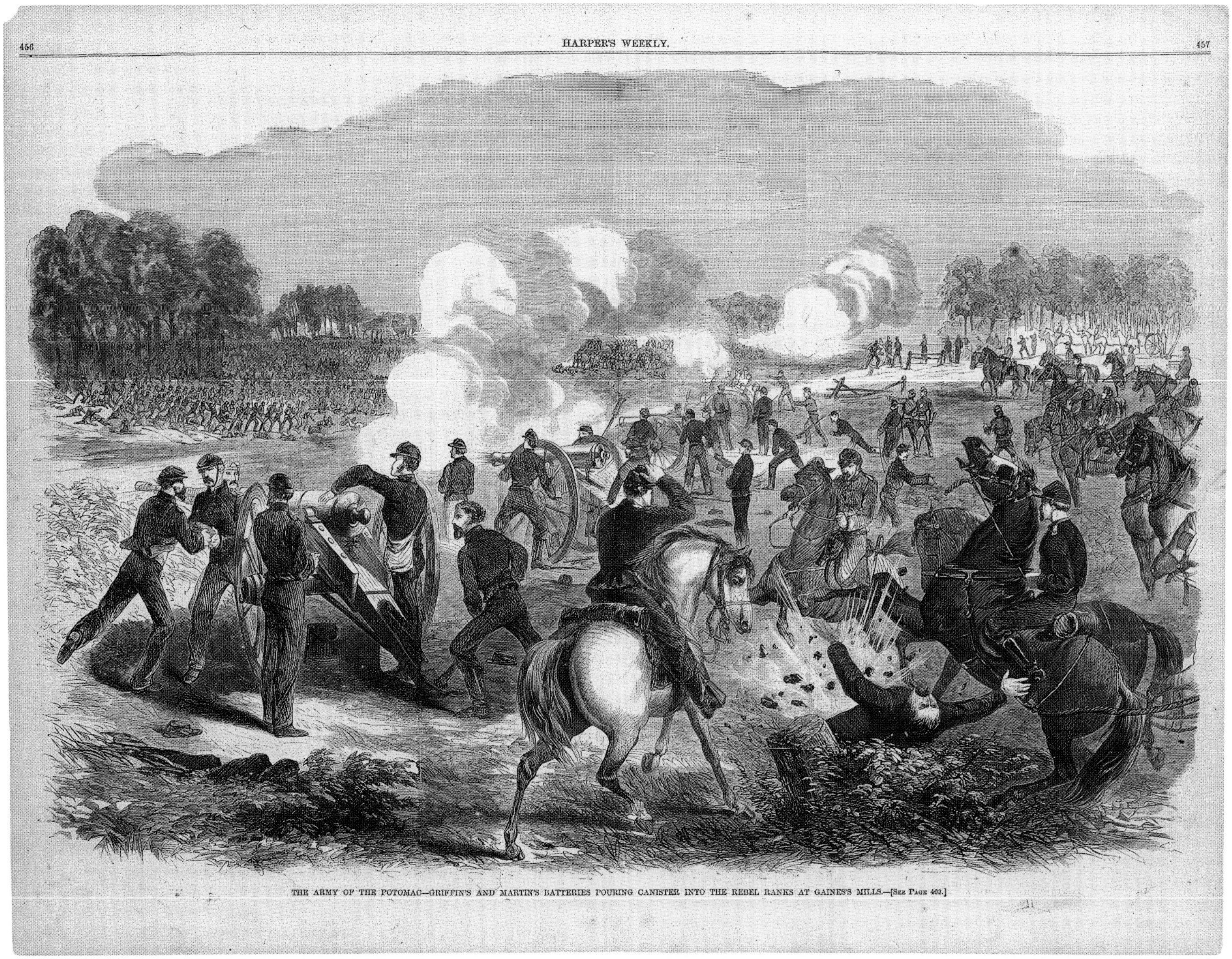

An engraving published in the July 19 issue of Harper's Weekly depicts Federal gunners of Captain Augustus P. Martin's Battery C, Massachusetts Light Artillery, firing double-shotted canister into the charging Rebel column. When the enemy was within 50 yards of the guns Martin ordered a final salvo, then hurriedly withdrew the battery.

PRIVATE ROBERT E. ESKILDSON

BATTERY L, 2D U.S. ARTILLERY, ARTILLERY RESERVE

Only 17 years old, Eskildson served alongside his father and brother in one of the Regular Army's superbly disciplined batteries of horse artillery. Captain James M. Robertson unlimbered his guns to cover the retreat of Porter's left wing and kept the Rebels at bay until his ammunition was exhausted. Only then did he withdraw from the field. Eskildson remained in the army until retiring in 1890 with the rank of sergeant.

The heaviest of the fighting early in the day was being carried on far to our right. To our left, and well in advance of our battery line, was posted a squadron of Rush's Lancers, (6th Pa. Cav., I think). As the day wore on the firing in our immediate front was constantly growing heavier up to about 4 p.m., when Stonewall Jackson's Corps made its grand charge, his right wing overlapping our left flank down to the swamp, the result of the charge in our field of action being that the battery on our right was captured almost at once, the gun-trails reversed, and put in action against our men in retreat. Gen. Porter, in whose command we were serving, fearing that our battery would also be lost, sent three orders in quick succession for us to withdraw from the fight; but our gallant commander, Maj. James M. Robertson, who had won his spurs in the Mexican War, did not think that the moment for retreat had come, and stood his ground. We opened upon Jackson's veterans with two-second fuzes, cutting them shorter as his line advanced; then with percussion shells, and in the heat of the charge we gave them canister until it was all gone, and then finished up by firing shells without fuses. These shells would explode as they left the mouth of the gun. We kept this up until our ammunition boxes were all emptied; then we "limbered to the rear" and went off the field to the rear on the gallop. Our fire was so hot and continuous that Stonewall Jackson's veterans had to hug the earth while it was going on, and before they realized it we had limbered up and were gone.

MAJOR WILLIAM S. TILTON

22D MASSACHUSETTS INFANTRY, MARTINDALE'S BRIGADE

A prominent merchant from Newburyport, Tilton was wounded and carried to the rear just as the Federal line gave way. His commanding officer, Colonel Jesse Gove, was killed while trying to re-form the crumbling formations. The battle cost the regiment 283 men, 84 of whom were killed or mortally wounded.

The noise of the musketry was not rattling, as ordinarily, but one intense metallic din. The sound of the artillery was sublime. The forces on our left began to give way by regiments. Individuals from our own first line sought shelter behind our barricade. The brave Thirteenth and Twenty-fifth New York, which had so long defended our front, were soon compelled to retreat with the rest, falling back to our breastworks. The First Michigan did the same. Before many of the troops had fallen back to our breastworks I shouted to our men to rise and fire by file. Some fired one, some six rounds, but they were much embarrassed by the difficulty of distinguishing friend from foe, so

While the 22d Massachusetts was passing through Manhattan en route to the front, a committee of New York City ladies presented the regiment with this silk national color. The flag was briefly seized by a Confederate in a hand-to-hand grapple at Gaines' Mill, but it was snatched back and saved by Color Corporal Louis Crone.

closely were the former pursued by the latter.

At this juncture I was shot through the right shoulder, went to the rear, and was ordered to the hospital by Surgeon Prince. While the surgeon was examining my wound the house was surrounded by Confederates; so our whole line must have given way. Soon after I left the field the house was penetrated many times by shells from our own batteries. After this I can say nothing, as I saw no more of the action, unless it may be to recite the reports of some of my captains.

Marshall S. Pike (above), drum major of the 22d Massachusetts' regimental band, was among 117 soldiers in the unit reported as missing in action after the Battle of Gaines' Mill. Taken prisoner while assisting the wounded, Pike was confined at Richmond until September 7, when he was paroled and sent north for mustering out.

PRIVATE OLIVER W. NORTON

83D PENNSYLVANIA INFANTRY, BUTTERFIELD'S BRIGADE

When the regiments to its right gave way, the 83d was briefly surrounded by the enemy. It managed to fight its way clear with heavy losses, including its commanding officer, Colonel John W. McLane. The day before the fight Norton, the regimental bugler, had returned to duty, following a spell of dysentery. He was later a lieutenant in the 8th U.S. Colored Troops, as pictured here.

Suddenly I saw two men on the bank in front of us gesticulating violently and pointing to our rear, but the roar of battle drowned their voices. The order was given to face about. We did so and tried to form in line, but while the line was forming, a bullet laid low the head, the stay, the trust of our regiment—our brave colonel, and before we knew what had happened the major shared his fate. We were then without a field officer, but the boys bore up bravely. They rallied round the flag and we advanced up the hill to find ourselves alone. It appears that the enemy broke through our lines off on our right, and word was sent to us on the left to fall back. Those in the rear of us received the order but the aide sent to us was shot before he reached us and so we got no orders. Henry and Denison were shot about the same time as the colonel. I left them together under a tree. I returned to the fight, and our boys were dropping on all sides of me. I was blazing away at the rascals not ten rods off when a ball struck my gun just above the lower band as I was capping it, and cut it in two. The ball flew in pieces and part went by my head to the right and three pieces struck just below my left collar bone. The deepest one was not over half an inch, and stopping to open my coat I pulled them out and snatched a gun from Ames in Company H as he fell dead. Before I had fired this at all a ball clipped off a piece of the stock, and an instant

"He said: 'Where is the Fourth?' I said: 'Gone to Richmond, sir.' . . . He turned to me and said: 'Young man, this is no place for levity.' I said: 'They are captured, every man of them.' "

after, another struck the seam of my canteen and entered my left groin. I pulled it out, and, more maddened than ever, I rushed in again. A few minutes after, another ball took six inches off the muzzle of this gun. I snatched another from a wounded man under a tree, and, as I was loading kneeling by the side of the road, a ball cut my rammer in two as I was turning it over my head. Another gun was easier got than a rammer so I threw that away and picked up a fourth one. Here in the road a buckshot struck me in the left eyebrow, making the third slight scratch I received in the action. It exceeded all I ever dreamed of, it was almost a miracle.

LIEUTENANT E. BURD GRUBB
Staff, General George W. Taylor

Detached from their brigade by General Porter's French aide, part of the 2d New Jersey and all of the 4th New Jersey moved into the front line, where both were enveloped by the Rebel breakthrough. Of some 680 men in the 4th, only 83 escaped death or capture; more than 400 were taken prisoner. The unfortunate Yankees were later paraded through the streets of Richmond to the taunts and jeers of the inhabitants.

The last I saw of the French officer and Colonel Simpson and the right of that regiment was a swarm of grey-coated soldiers, with their rifles in their hands, within no more than thirty yards from us, and with General Taylor's words in my ears to "Come back and report," I lay flat down on my horse, put both spurs to him and did so. I rode up the line until I came to some wounded soldiers of the Third Regiment, and right here I saw Colonel Tucker, of the Second Regiment, carried out of the woods and put on a stretcher and then shot dead after he was on the stretcher. I asked some of the Third men where General Taylor was, and they said "With the Third Regiment," of which regiment he had been colonel before he was promoted. I dismounted and tied my horse to a little mulberry tree at the edge of the woods, and to which tree General Taylor's horse was also tied—which tree is still alive, or was so within the last four years, as I saw it. I then went up through the woods about one hundred and fifty yards and came upon the line of battle and soon found General Taylor, parading up and down the line like a wounded lion, and in the midst of one of the most terrible battles I ever saw.

As soon as I came close to him and he saw me he said: "Where is the Fourth?" I said: "Gone to Richmond, sir." I shall never forget how the old fellow's eyes glared, as with his sword in his hand he turned to me and said: "Young man, this is no place for levity." I said: "They are captured, every man of them." He said: "My God, My God," and fairly wrung his hands.

PRIVATE ALFRED DAVENPORT
5th New York Infantry, Warren's Brigade

Inspired by Sergeant John Berrian—who carried the colors forward after learning that his brother had fallen—the 5th New York Zouaves charged and scattered the leading units of Gregg's South Carolina brigade, but the Zouaves were ultimately forced from the field with the rest of Porter's command. Before retreating, Lieutenant Colonel Hiram Duryea had his men count off to ensure perfect alignment.

Our regiment had lost many men, and began to waver; Sergeant Varian seeing it (he carried the colors), walked, without flinching, right ahead of the regiment about thirty paces! Col. Duryea called to him to return, but he did not heed it. As soon as we saw that brave action, with one accord we gave a great shout, charged through the woods, completely scattering the rebels, and driving them in every direction. Some of them had thrown away their arms and were trying to climb up a bank; but their supports were coming up, and we had been fighting for nearly three hours. We (Duryea's Zouaves) were the last to leave the field of Gaines' Mill, covering the retreat. We went through some awful moments in this last fight: we were obliged to form again near night, in order to cover the retreat. Some of our troops were running, others falling back. Soon there was nothing in front of us but Stonewall Jackson's hordes. We were on a little knoll; there were about 150 of us (Duryea's Zouaves) who stood it out; we were supporting a battery, all ready to skedaddle at a moment's notice. As far as we could see through the smoke the rebels covered the hard-fought field, on which Union and rebel soldiers alike lay *together* in their last sleep.

The battery was firing its rounds as if life depended on it—which, in fact, it did; the shell and bullets of the enemy were flying like a storm over us; I lost my knapsack: we every one of us expected to sacrifice our lives or be taken prisoners,—"a fate worse than death."

A captain in the Swedish army, Baron Ernst Maltais Peter von Vegesack (above) came to America to fight for the Union cause. Assigned to Butterfield's staff, Vegesack displayed what the general called "courage, gallantry and coolness" in the Battle of Gaines' Mill. He was later awarded the Medal of Honor for his service there.

PRIVATE WILLIAM H. OSBORNE

29th Massachusetts Infantry, Meagher's Brigade

The arrival of Brigadier General Thomas F. Meagher's Irish Brigade combined with the oncoming of darkness to save Porter's corps from possible annihilation. After crossing the Chickahominy, Meagher's troops came into line and covered the Federal retreat, recrossing the river the next day. A Medal of Honor recipient for gallantry at Malvern Hill, Osborne described the action in his 1877 regimental history.

When our men reached the summit of the hill, the enemy had crossed over the field, and was seen forming on a long ridge nearly opposite our position. The smoke had now risen to the tops of the trees, and beneath this pall lay the ground, formerly a grass-field, but now a dusty plain, where the principal part of the fighting had taken place; the Confederate and Federal dead, wounded and dead horses, knapsacks, muskets, clothing, wrecked caissons and cannon, were scattered in wild confusion over this space, while here and there were the wounded of both armies, crawling and staggering towards their respective lines to escape capture. It was a scene that presented at a glance all the ruin of a terrible battle; but, fortunately, the advancing troops had but a moment to contemplate it. The brigades were at once hurried down the hillside toward the enemy's new line; several of the

Presented in January 1862 to the commanding officer of the newly organized 29th Massachusetts, this state flag was carried into action at Gaines' Mill by Sergeant Horace Jenks. The unit had been attached to the Irish Brigade just before the battle, despite the fact that few of its members were of Irish heritage.

field-officers of Porter's corps going along with them, and uttering words of encouragement. Among these officers was General Butterfield, who was without a command. Catching sight of the State flag carried by the Twenty-ninth Regiment,—it was the only Pine-tree flag then on the field,—he went dashing up to the color-sergeant, and cried out, "Give me the white flag of Massachusetts, and I'll lead you against the enemy." The Sergeant (Horace A. Jenks of Company E) tightened his grasp on the colors and gave a look of inquiry to the Lieutenant-Colonel of the regiment, who was but a few feet distant. That officer quietly replied, "Keep your colors!" which he did, carrying them bravely forward in the face of a bitter fire.

"I called sternly upon them to surrender, which it seemed they were desirous of doing and laid down their arms."

CAPTAIN EUGENE BLACKFORD

5TH ALABAMA INFANTRY, RODES' BRIGADE

The 5th Alabama was the only one of General Robert E. Rodes' five regiments to fight through the Federal position, losing nearly as many men as the other four units combined. The Virginia-born Blackford, whose brother William was serving on Jeb Stuart's staff, recalled the final Rebel advance past the McGehee house and into the valley of the Chickahominy.

As we were running towards the enemy by the flank, it became necessary to pass in front of a battery which threw spherical case at us most horribly—I had been talking with the comdg officer of the company in my rear, Lt. Ramsay, a gallant fellow, and left him to obey an order to hurry up. As I did so I heard a whizzing sound, and looking around saw my comrades headless trunk in the act of falling. His head had been severed from the body completely. Just after this they made us halt tho' the glare of the sun was awful, and the enemy's battery still very active. Notwithstanding these circumstances the men discovered that the house around which we were standing was a sutler's shop, from which the Yankees had not succeeded in taking anything. Of course its contents were speedily distributed. I obtained a bottle of what seemed to me most delicious claret thru' the attention of one of my men. I thought I had never seen anything so refreshing after the extreme heat & dust. In those days, too, I always carried a Sharps carbine besides my heavy sabre, very foolishly, too, as tho' I bagged a man or two occasionally, my time could have been better employed in caring for my men, and making them shoot. Not long after this we advanced thru some woods in which the enemy made a most infernal noise by firing their guns and we neither saw them or heard of the bullets. A very gratifying result. After passing to the edge of the wood we were halted to await orders. No one knew what to do, firing was going on all around us, and there was so much smoke about us that we could distinguish nothing. I had offered to go forward and reconnoitre, and so crept forward in the broomsedge on my hands & knees to the left of the hill in our front. Here raising my head I had a grand view. Far in front & on both flanks the enemy were in motion towards the rear, just in our front some 100 yards or more stood a Yankee line, and on their right a battery the men all alert watching the woods where we lay. With this intelligence I hastened back, but ere I joined it the line advanced and met me; there followed a wild yell and charge, and the usual result. The enemy fled in every direction. On our right I noticed the Zouaves whom our men seemed to single out for the field was covered with their dead. By this time it was past sundown, and in the excitement of the chase I ran down a steep hill to sieze some pieces of artillery left there in the flight. When at the bottom I looked back I saw that but 5 men had followed me, and to my dismay what appeared to be the head of a Yankee column came out of the woods. I called sternly upon them to surrender, which it seemed they were desirous of doing and laid down their arms.

Savage's Station to Glendale

Late on the night of June 27 McClellan met with his top generals and informed them of a momentous decision: The Army of the Potomac would abandon its entrenchments before Richmond and its supply depot at White House Landing and move south to a new position on the James River, where a flotilla of Federal gunboats could provide protection. McClellan was careful to label this movement of men and matériel a "change of base." But eventually his soldiers would figure out that the term was a euphemism for retreat.

The commander of the Army of the Potomac was rattled. Ostentatious demonstrations of strength orchestrated by Magruder in the fortifications east of Richmond had fed McClellan's worst fears. He felt confirmed in accepting the wildly inaccurate reports he had been receiving from Allan Pinkerton's Secret Service operatives that Lee had 200,000 troops to put in against the Federals. McClellan now was certain that the Confederate attacks north of the Chickahominy had only been jabs preparatory to a knockout blow that would come south of the river.

Given what he believed, McClellan could have much more easily taken his troops to safety whence they had come—back down the Peninsula toward Yorktown. But there would have been no way to avoid calling that a retreat. Moreover, establishing a base on the James, some 20 miles from Richmond, left open the possibility of resuming the offensive from the south.

Early on the morning of June 28, the Federals began withdrawing. Long columns of men, horses, guns, and wagons streamed eastward on the Williamsburg road, then south to the two bridges over White Oak Swamp. According to McClellan's plan, two of his five corps would take the lead in the movement and establish a defensive position on Malvern Hill, on the north bank of the James. The other three corps would hold position to slow Lee's pursuit, then would retreat in their turn.

Lee awoke at his camp north of the Chickahominy on June 28 to find the Yankees gone. He decided that McClellan must have retreated eastward along the river's north bank to defend his supply line. But when Jeb Stuart led a cavalry force to White House Landing, he found that the supply depot there had been abandoned and mountains of goods set on fire.

By late afternoon, clouds of dust swirling skyward along the Williamsburg road made it clear the Federals were pulling out. Their immediate threat to Richmond had evaporated. Elated at the success of his strategy and the deliverance of the Confederate capital, Lee now determined to catch and destroy McClellan's army. But which way were the Federals retreating?

Not until early the next morning, June 29, did Lee get an answer. A reconnaissance confirmed that McClellan had abandoned his westernmost fortifications, near Fair Oaks. And Ewell's troops, guarding Bottom's Bridge four miles to the east, reported no enemy activity. Since McClellan would most likely have taken that route if he were retreating across the Peninsula, he must be heading south.

Lee hastily mapped a new plan, under which his entire command would take part in the pursuit. From their positions near the Gaines' Mill battlefield, Longstreet and A. P. Hill would cross the Chickahominy at New Bridge and, in cooperation with Huger, knife southeastward to intercept McClellan below White Oak Swamp. Meanwhile, Magruder was to advance eastward from Richmond against the Federal rear along the line of the Richmond & York River Railroad. He would be aided by Jackson, who was to cross the Chickahominy at Grapevine Bridge and link up with Magruder's left. If all went well, Lee's forces would trap much of the Federal army.

Coming from the Gaines' Mill battlefield, A. P. Hill and Longstreet had the greatest distance to travel. Thus, it would be up to Magruder and his force of 14,000 men marching east from Richmond parallel to the rail line on the Williamsburg road to bring the Federal rear guard to bay.

About three miles east of Fair Oaks Magruder came up against a strong Federal defensive position. Drawn up in battle lines around the railroad depot at Savage's Station were 40 artillery pieces and nearly half of McClellan's army: Heintzelman's III Corps, Sumner's II Corps, and half of Franklin's VI Corps.

Greatly outnumbered, Magruder's force waited for help. Their position was almost due south of the Grapevine Bridge, where Jackson was supposed to cross the Chickahominy with 18,000 men. But Jackson was late again, for the third time in the past four days. While Magruder waited, the Federals used the respite to set ablaze huge piles of supplies that they could not carry away.

At about 5:00 p.m. Magruder brought up a 32-pounder naval gun mounted on an armored railroad flatcar. This novel contrivance had recently been put together at Lee's behest to

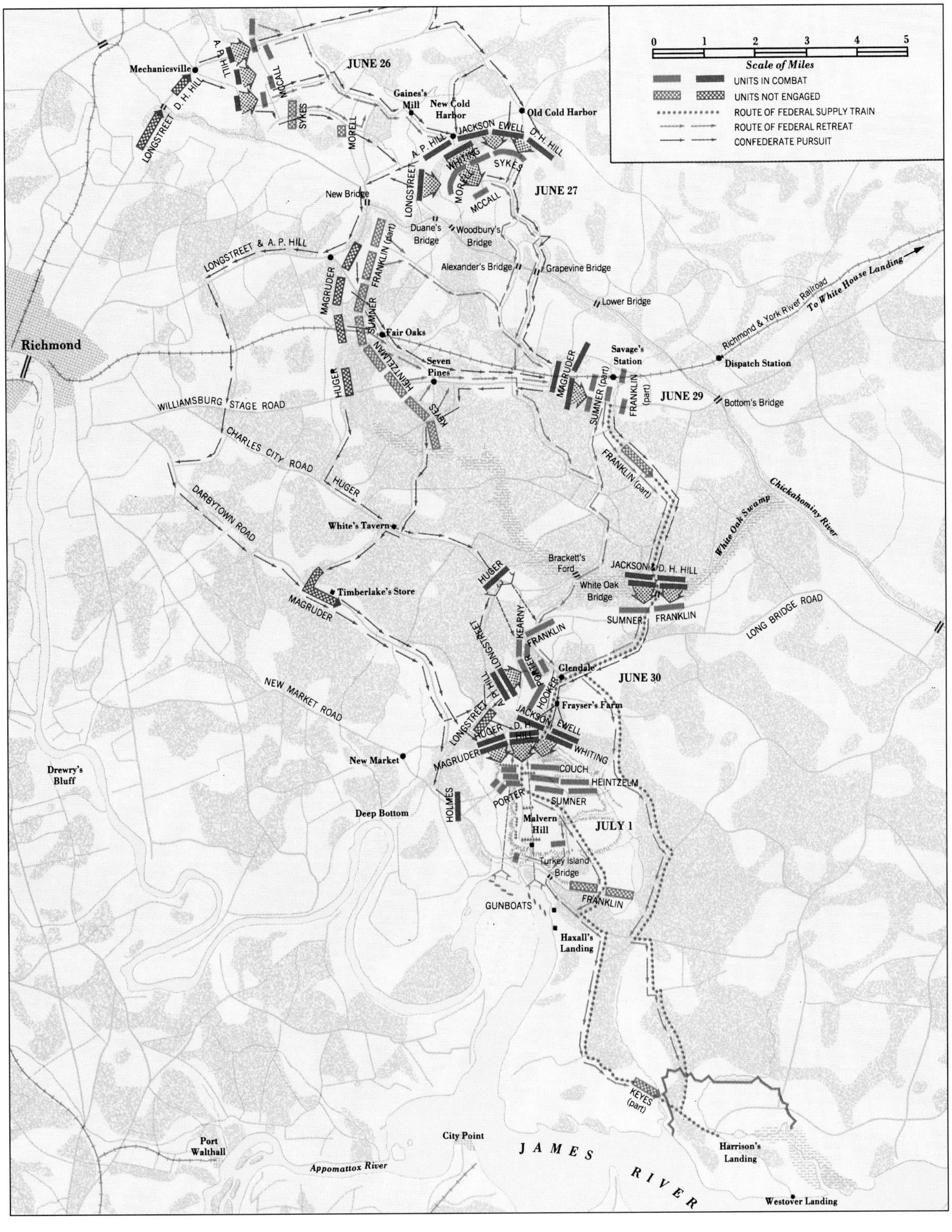

Following the Confederate victory at Gaines' Mill, McClellan was compelled to retreat south across the Chickahominy River bridges. Convinced that he was outnumbered, the alarmed Union commander abandoned his supply base at White House Landing on the Pamunkey River and withdrew his entire army southward to a new base on the James River. To cover the army's retreat, McClellan's troops fought off fierce Confederate attacks at Savage's Station on June 29 and at White Oak Swamp and nearby Glendale on the following day. By July 1, the Army of the Potomac found itself with its back to the James River on a promontory called Malvern Hill.

counter the expected threat of McClellan's siege guns. The gun's rifled barrel projected through an opening in the car's protective shield of iron. A locomotive pushed it into range, and for the first time in the history of warfare a piece of railroad artillery opened fire.

But the lone gun's effect against massed enemy artillery was minimal. Magruder, left with no alternatives, finally attacked with infantry but could gain no ground against the effective Yankee gunnery. He took heavy losses, including one brigadier general, Richard Griffith, mortally wounded.

The fighting ended at dark and the Federals resumed their retreat, leaving behind, at McClellan's order, about 2,500 sick and wounded soldiers, along with enough surgeons, attendants, and medical supplies to care for them. Jackson never did reach the battlefield; he had spent the entire day rebuilding the Grapevine Bridge, even though he had been told of a usable ford nearby.

The success of the Union rear guard's delaying action at Savage's Station had been just what McClellan wanted. By midmorning on June 30 the Army of the Potomac was safely across White Oak Swamp. But McClellan knew he had to protect the line of retreat for one more day to enable his supply trains to reach the James.

Meanwhile, Major General Erasmus D. Keyes' IV Corps and Porter's V Corps had reached Malvern Hill, with the army's remaining three corps, consisting of seven divisions, still en route. McClellan posted two divisions under William Franklin at White Oak Swamp. He deployed the other five, three miles south of the swamp on either side of a crucial crossroads village called Glendale.

The crossroads, situated halfway between White Oak Swamp and Malvern Hill, was vulnerable to an attack from the west. It also constituted a dangerous bottleneck for the converging Federal routes of retreat. Near a farm named after its original owners, the Frayser family, the two routes from White Oak Swamp funneled into the Willis Church road, which led to the James. Here Lee hoped to cut the Federal army in two.

June 30 was a critical day for the Confederates. Jackson crossed the Chickahominy before dawn on the rebuilt Grapevine Bridge and met with Lee at Savage's Station. Lee ordered him to take over the direct pursuit of McClellan's rear guard. But Jackson wasted precious time rounding up Union stragglers and leftover supplies. It was nearly noon before he reached the ruins of the bridge over White Oak Swamp, which the Federals had burned less than two hours before.

About half a mile across the swamp, Jackson could see the Union rear guard resting on a hill. He deployed his artillery along a ridge and opened fire at about 2:00 p.m. Then, with skirmishers from D. H. Hill's division and a regiment of cavalry, Jackson forded the marshy creek for a personal reconnaissance. But the rear guard, two divisions under Brigadier Generals Israel B. Richardson and William F. Smith, and six batteries of artillery, returned the fire, forcing Jackson to hightail it back across the creek.

Jackson's situation was a difficult one; the Federal fire was so hot that it repeatedly drove away the soldiers he sent forward to rebuild the White Oak Swamp bridge. The hero of the Valley campaign now once again lapsed into the lethargy that had afflicted him since his arrival on the Peninsula four days before. Around 3:00 p.m., while the Federal artillery boomed back and forth, he lay down under a tree and went to sleep, ignoring—as he had at the Grapevine Bridge—reports from a cavalry officer of a cow crossing suitable for fording some 400 yards downstream.

Jackson was not the only Confederate general to be stymied that afternoon. Several miles to the southwest, Benjamin Huger's division of 9,000 men was one of the two Rebel columns aimed at the Glendale crossroads, where McClellan's slow-moving mass of wagons was funneling into the Willis Church road. Huger was slanting southeast on the Charles City road while, less than two miles to his right, the larger column of Longstreet and A. P. Hill—with Magruder scheduled to follow in reserve—was proceeding down the Darbytown road. When Huger reached Glendale, the sound of his artillery firing was to be the signal for both columns to attack.

Before noon, when Huger's lead brigade was about two miles northwest of Glendale, it ran into an obstruction of felled trees on the road. Commanding the lead brigade was Brigadier General William "Little Billy" Mahone. When Mahone saw the trees, he made a snap decision. Instead of instructing his men to remove the logs, he had them hack a new path through the woods that bordered the road. Up ahead, the Yankees of Slocum's division redoubled their own efforts with the ax. While Mahone's Rebels worked away at cutting a swath through the woods, Slocum's men felled more trees to extend the depth of the obstruction on the road.

By 2:00 p.m. the Confederates had managed to win this battle of the axes, carving a mile-long bypass and emerging onto the road beyond the obstructions. But now Huger encountered a more serious obstacle. Deployed across the road on a rise about a mile short of Glendale was Slocum's division. Huger moved a battery into position and opened fire. The Federal guns answered. Huger's men took a few casualties, then withdrew to the woods. Though Huger outnumbered the Federals facing him by 3 to 2, he was finished fighting for the day.

Not far to the south, Lee, accompanying the column of Longstreet and A. P. Hill, was also only a little more than a mile from the Glendale crossroads. With 18,000 men, Lee had swung left from the Darbytown road onto Long Bridge road and was approaching Glendale from the southwest. He was ready to attack the Federals as soon as he heard Huger's guns go into action.

When Huger's brief cannonade was heard at 2:30 p.m., Longstreet ordered his own batteries to fire in acknowledgment. The Confederate exchange triggered a response from the Federal batteries on Long Bridge road. Longstreet sent forward a brigade, which got into a brisk firefight with a Federal force. But Lee, having heard nothing more from Huger, decided to delay a general assault.

Meanwhile, a fourth column of Confederates was converging on the retreating Federals about three miles farther to the south. This force consisted of 6,000 troops under Major General Theophilus H. Holmes, who had brought his men across the James River on pontoon bridges at Drewry's Bluff.

Lee was not counting on the 57-year-old Holmes for any hard fighting, but he hoped that Holmes could get within artillery range of McClellan's column and do some damage. An opportunity arose at 4:00 p.m., when Holmes got word that Federal wagon trains were streaming up Malvern Hill on the Willis Church road.

Malvern Hill was less than three miles east of Holmes' position on the River road, and he started forward with six pieces of artillery. On the way, he met Lee, who had received a similar report and ridden south to see for himself. Lee ordered Holmes to bring up his infantry in support of his guns, then headed north to rejoin Longstreet and A. P. Hill.

As Holmes' infantrymen hurried forward on the dirt road, their shuffling feet raised clouds of dust. This sign was visible to the Federals on Malvern Hill, where Fitz-John Porter had deployed his V Corps and part of the army's Artillery Reserve. A few minutes later, at 4:30 p.m., when Holmes had his half-dozen guns in position about 800 yards from the train of wagons on Malvern Hill, havoc suddenly descended on them. Shells from no fewer than 30 guns poured down on the Confederates.

Even more terrifying were the salvos from the Federal gunboats on the James River a half mile south of Holmes' column. A signal officer atop a farmhouse on the southern edge of Malvern Hill directed the fire of the gunboats. The shells were 100-pounders. The Confederates, hearing the heavy black objects whoosh down, called them "lampposts."

Holmes withdrew. Lee's four-pronged pursuit was now reduced to the single column of Longstreet and A. P. Hill on Long Bridge road. The sixth day of fighting was slipping away, along with McClellan's supply wagons. Lee did not know it, but the wagons Holmes had tried to attack constituted the end of the Federal train. There now remained on the line of retreat only the seven divisions of Federal infantry—the two at White Oak Swamp and the five at Glendale.

At 5:00 p.m., in the hope that Huger on his left and Jackson up at the swamp would hear the commotion and join in, Lee ordered an assault on Long Bridge road. Longstreet went in first, his battle lines splashing across the swampy ground and moving uphill toward Frayser's Farm and the crossroads.

The Federal flanks were firmly anchored by Brigadier General Philip Kearny's division on the right and Hooker's on the left. But the brunt of the Confederate attack was felt by the center, held by George McCall's division of Pennsylvania Reserves. The division was understrength, numbering fewer than 6,000 men. Battered at Mechanicsville and Gaines' Mill, the troops had slept only a few hours in the past three days.

For a time, McCall's men staved off Longstreet's charge. But the Confederate pressure finally proved too much for one regiment. The men of the 4th Pennsylvania Reserves broke and ran up the hill toward their own artillery. Following on their heels, the 11th Alabama captured the Federal guns in hand-to-hand fighting. Now the 55th and 60th Virginia regiments of A. P. Hill's division stormed the Federal center to exploit the breakthrough. McCall's division collapsed and the commander himself was taken prisoner.

In the meantime, fresh Federal troops from Brigadier General John Sedgewick's and Richardson's divisions were joining the fray. With Hooker holding on the left, Kearny was able to halt Hill's breakthrough and even mount a counterattack.

For a time it seemed that Kearny would regain all the lost ground. But then A. P. Hill turned the tide with an inspiring display of bravery. Hill rode to the front of the battle line, where one of Longstreet's regiments was about to give way. The general seized their flag and tried to lead them forward. When the men hesitated, Hill shouted, "Damn you, if you will not follow me, I'll die alone!" and spurred his horse forward. Galvanized by Hill's courage, the soldiers charged, repulsing Kearny's counterattack.

As night fell, the desperate, back-and-forth fighting sputtered out. In the battle that would be known as Glendale, or Frayser's Farm, the Federals suffered 2,853 casualties. Lee had gained a strip of shell-torn woods and some artillery pieces, but he had lost more than 3,300 men. More important, an opportunity to cut off McClellan's retreat had slipped through his fingers.

STEPHEN R. MALLORY

Confederate Secretary of the Navy

Mallory made the decision to construct the ironclad Virginia, which had helped slow McClellan's march up the Peninsula toward Richmond. Following Gaines' Mill, Mallory, traveling as part of President Davis' party, ventured from the Rebel capital to gloat at the Yankees' retreat and browse through the abandoned Union camps.

I was out all day yesterday on the field of battle. The enemy had abandoned his works during the night, and with his whole remaining force was endeavoring to reach the James river. We had 50,000 men in pursuit of him. Just at 6 o'clock our advance overtook a portion of his rear guard and a fight of about two hours ensued, the result of which we as yet do not know; but the firing was very brisk on both sides. His intrenched camps occupied a larger space than the entire city of Richmond, and he fled leaving all his tents standing, but destroying a vast quantity of stores. I rode through his abandoned works, which were very strong, and which terror alone could have induced the abandonment; for we could only have taken them by the loss of thirty thousand men. Overcoats, blankets, flannel sheets, soda crackers, nuts, gingerbread, bayonets, broken guns, empty bottles & tins, tin cups, boots, books, newspapers, &c were scattered over the Camps & roads for miles.

This morning we sent a baloon up far in the rear of their late postion, but could see nothing of them & my belief is that McClellan is pushing towards the forks on confluence of the James & Chickahominy rivers, there to intrench himself, receive provisions from his vessels and await reinforcements from Halleck's army.—Our troops will, I trust, push him to a general engagement in which case we hope to capture or kill the principle portion of his army.—Thus has this boastful & bullying horde of barbarians been driven from its strong-hold before Richmond. They are today twenty-two miles off at least, in full retreat, with 50000 men in pursuit. Prisoners from them represent their army as demoralized & sick of the fight. Wheat of La & many others are killed.—This day & tomorrow will be eventful. If we crush out McClellan completely the backbone of this campaign will be broken & crimination & recrimination will be the order among the papers & politicians of the Yankee thieves. As it is, even thus far, our success has been great & glorious. Our men fought like heros. In fact, nothing less than a separate & distinct resolve of each man to take a foeman by the throat and drag him to the earth could have won us the battles we have gained; for we took from them position after position, battery after battery, against all odds & in spite of every loss.

CAPTAIN ROBERT E. PARK

12th Alabama Infantry, Rodes' Brigade

Although McClellan had withdrawn, Stonewall Jackson's corps remained north of the Chickahominy and endured Union artillery fire such as that described here. General D. H. Hill had his uniform ripped by a shell fragment during one of these exchanges. Park was captured later in 1862, paroled, and wounded at Gettysburg. At Winchester in 1864 he was wounded and captured, and ended the war a prisoner.

The next day, an extremely hot one, while we were in line of battle in the blazing sun, I witnessed a piece of recklessness, or, heroism, if you choose to call it so, on the part of Captain L'Etondal, of Company A, from Mobile. The Twelfth Alabama was stretched out, and the men were lying prone upon the ground, enduring the sun's rays, and suffering greatly from the heat. Suddenly their attention was drawn to a novel sight, perhaps never a similar one was seen in any battle. At the end of Company A an umbrella was stretched over the prostrate form of Captain Jules L'Etondal. Soon the notice of the enemy's artillery was attracted by the umbrella, and they began aiming their Napoleon guns at that portion of the regiment, and the balls began to strike in dangerous proximity to it, and to the brave men near it. The men of the other companies began to call aloud, "shut down that umbrella," "close it up, you old fool." The cries had no influence upon L'Etondal, or his company, and when, some of the other companies, indignant at his willingness to expose his comrades to the fire of the enemy, by his efforts to protect himself from the blazing rays of the burning sun, called to him that they would come and shut up the umbrella if he didn't do it, and a few rose and started toward the cap-

"They said Jackson was coming & they wanted to be off on the first Boat."

tain as if to carry out their threat, some of his company rose to meet them, and swore that he should keep the umbrella raised over head, if he wanted to, and it was none of their d——d business. This state of affairs continued for some little time, but L'Etondal kept up his shade, and was totally oblivious to the commands and entreaties of the men, and his own company humored him, laughing at his persistence. When we were ordered to move forward, the captain, with his two hundred and fifty pounds of avoirdupois, streaming with perspiration, continued to hold aloft his umbrella.

LIEUTENANT BENJAMIN F. ASHENFELTER

6th Pennsylvania Reserves, Seymour's Brigade

The easy time had by Ashenfelter's regiment—guard duty at White House Landing —came to an end when trainloads of wounded from Gaines' Mill streamed into the depot, bringing predictions of impending disaster at the hands of Jackson. Ashenfelter, a shoemaker, wrote this letter after he arrived at Harrison's Landing on July 1.

I had not Dinner that Day But I was about to have a good supper. When I was about half Done eating Col Buttler told me to take 20 men & go up to the Boats double quick he said there was trouble ahead. I went. The train had just arrived from the army with sick & wounded soldiers. They had awful stories to tell. They said Jackson was coming & they wanted to be off on the first Boat.

Some of the Officers was very Rough with the Poor fellows. But they acomplished no Good By it. I tried another Plan & Met with Sucsess. I Persuaded them to go with me to White House Hospital only a 1/2 mile off & they would be safe. Well cared for & Shipped next Day. In this way I got 195 Poor fellows to go with me. (They was well cared for & shipped on Saturday) By the time I got them quartered away it was Midnight. I went to the Boats again and tried to get another Squad to go Down But they was all too sick to walk that far in. The Medical Director said he would Put them on the Boat that Night. Saturday all was in motion. Vessal after vessal was being towed Down the River whilst hundreds of wagons was going Down By land. By 2 o'clock the Harbour was Cleared of almost every vessal But there was hundreds of People on the Bank all wanting to know how they was to get away No one could tell. at 4 the Boats was at the Warf to take us on Board. at 7 we was ready to sail. The torch was applied to all Combustible material some time previous and the sight By this time was one long to be Remembered By Me.

KATHARINE P. WORMELEY

Volunteer Nurse, U.S. Sanitary Commission

Wormeley, safely aboard a steamship, remained calm during the flight from White House Landing and even seemed amused by the chaos ashore. Her attitude may have been inspired by her belief that this evacuation had not been forced by Rebel arms, but was, as she put it, another "masterly strategic movement of McClellan's."

As for what is going on with the army to-day, it would be simple folly to attempt to give you any account of it. The wildest and most contradictory rumors are afloat. We lie at the wharf, and all around us are people eager to tell absurd and exaggerated stories. I make it a rule to believe nothing that I do not pick up from Captain Sawtelle. Yesterday there was an impression that Stonewall Jackson was coming down upon us to destroy this depot; and that has hastened the removal which was already prepared.

Stripped of all exaggeration, I suppose the truth is this: General Porter, being flanked in immense force, has wheeled round and back. He crossed the Chickahominy at four o'clock this morning. The whole army is now across that river; the enemy are in part on this side of it. We may now go into Richmond on the left,—Burnside co-operating. In that case this base of supplies will be more available up the James River. Meantime Colonel Ingalls and Captain Sawtelle are sending forward supplies in trains and army-wagons as fast as possible. The troops have six days' rations in their knapsacks. The enemy evidently hope to ruin us by seizing this station,—hitherto the sole source of supply to our army. Instead of which, everything has been sent away; the few things that remain are lying on the wharves, ready to go on board a few vessels at the last moment. The "Elm City" is waiting for the Ninety-third New York Regiment, which is stationed here on guard-duty. We

Soldiers enjoy the facilities of the Michigan Soldier's Relief, one of the many agencies set up by civilians of the various states at White House Landing. Such facilities provided troops with "home-style" cooked food, tailoring services, and perhaps most important, conversation with attentive females. During the landing's evacuation, dozens of civilian workers frantically sought space on overcrowded vessels.

have had our steam up all day, ready to be off at a moment's notice; and *even as I write* comes the order to start, the enemy having got the railroad. And so rapidly have we gone, that between writing the words "Elm City" and "railroad" we are off!

Such a jolly panic! Men rushing and tearing down to the wharves,—these precious civilians and sutlers and "scalawags!" The enemy are in force three miles from us; they have seized the railroad, and cut the telegraph. We privately hope to get a glimpse of them as we go down the river; it would be something to say that we had *seen* the Confederate army of Richmond!

We have just enjoyed the fun of seeing the last of the shore-people rushing on board schooners and steamers,—the former all yelling for "a tow." I never laughed more than to see the "contrabands" race down from the quarters and shovel into barges,—the men into one, the women into another. The "Canonicus" stayed behind to carry off Colonel Ingalls and Captain Sawtelle, who are highly pleased with the way the whole thing has been done,—as well they may be, for it reflects the greatest credit upon them.

All our army is now across the Chickahominy: General Porter crossed at four this morning; only General Stoneman and the cavalry are this side of the river. The order which finally moved us was in consequence of a message from General Stoneman to General Casey, which came by mounted messenger while Mr. Olmsted was with the latter. It said: "I hold the enemy in check at Tunstall's (three miles from White House, on the railway), and shall for a short time. I shall then retreat by White House." Then the great gun of the "Sebago" boomed out, and we all slipped our moorings. The gunboats were in line of battle; we passed between them and the shore; the men were beat to quarters, and standing at their guns,—the great ferocious guns!

We had scarcely turned the first bend of the river before we heard explosions, and saw the smoke and fire of the last things burning,—such as locomotives, cars, a few tents, whiskey, etc. Before leaving, we saw clouds of dust, and General Stoneman's baggage-train came trotting in; and at the same moment a *corral* of invalid horses and mules, kept here by the Quartermaster's Department, seven hundred of them, were let loose and driven towards Cumberland. The last I saw of the White House, General Casey was sitting on the piazza, and the signal-men on the roof were waving the pretty signals, which were being answered by the gunboats.

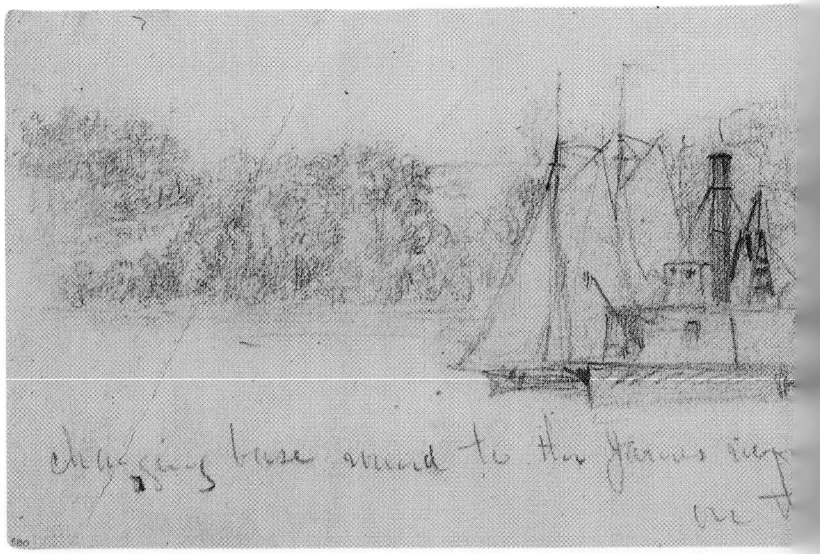

CHAPLAIN ARTHUR FULLER

16th Massachusetts Infantry, Grover's Brigade

Fuller's commanding officer had sent him to White House Landing to ensure the safe evacuation of the regimental baggage. After completing this task, the exhausted cleric witnessed the nightmarish orgy of destruction of leftover supplies and equipment. Plagued with ill health, Fuller resigned from the army at Fredericksburg on December 10, 1862, but stayed with his regiment one more day and was struck dead by a Rebel bullet.

Then ensued a destruction of all stores and buildings, which was fearful, yet grand to contemplate. All supplies were put on board schooners and transport steamers, which were sent down stream. This was done calmly by the military authorities, but with great energy. A vast deal, however, of public property could not be saved. Soon a large encampment of tents was in flames. Two long trains of railroad-cars were burned, with their contents. Every now and then an explosion took place which filled the air with fragments and towering columns of smoke and flame. A huge storehouse of bacon sent volumes of black smoke upward. The stores chiefly abandoned were sutlers' stores, belonging to a class who excite less sympathy than any other in the army when they suffer loss. One sutler abandoned a storehouse containing four thousand dollars worth of goods; another of one thousand dollars in value. The "boys" revelled in these, as all things were free that day, and men procured a good dinner or clothing outfit "without money and without price." As they sorely needed one good meal and to be reclothed, and the sutlers could well afford the supply from their profits, the sight was, upon the whole, a pleasant one. All this time the White House, belonging to the rebel Colonel Lee, stood unharmed. It is a modern structure, and it is a shame that any such house should stand on the site of what once was the home of Washington, to shelter rebels and haters of the country for which he lived and suffered. Few of us grieved when this property of a rebel officer was in flames,

Federal ships carrying supplies taken from White House Landing travel east down the Pamunkey River, heading for the York River and then the Chesapeake Bay. From there the vessels would travel around the tip of the Peninsula and up the James River to McClellan's new supply base at Harrison's Landing. The side-wheel steamship in the foreground tows two heavily laden barges in addition to assisting the two-masted sloop tied to its starboard side. Alfred Waud mimicked McClellan's euphemistic terminology when he titled this illustration "Changing base round to the James River. . . ."

"The old theories and pictures of the judgment-day seemed glowingly actualized and painted anew on the twofold canvas of earth and sky."

also, as by its destruction nothing which Washington ever touched or looked upon was consumed.

Meanwhile the old scows, filled with bulky stores, were burned, some wagons which could not be removed were burned or rolled over the bank and broken, while old muskets, rebel relics from Fair Oaks, shovels, pickaxes, etc., were committed to the bosom of the Pamunkey, to be concealed there in that muddy stream. Horses careered wildly about, terrified contrabands brought over boats, while the incendiaries, with a good purpose, applied the torch on every side. Surgeons were detailed to destroy such of the hospital stores as could not be removed, which they did effectually. The scene was soon grander, wilder, more brilliant than I have ever witnessed before. The very clouds caught the lurid glow, and reflected in radiant hues the sad, fearful splendor below. Bursting bombs made noise like the shock of thunder-clouds, and scattered fragments about till earth and sky seemed mingled in one awful conflagration. The old theories and pictures of the judgment-day seemed glowingly actualized and painted anew on the twofold canvas of earth and sky. That scene it was a sorrowful but great privilege to witness! Since it must have been done, I am glad to have had such an experience. An artist was sketching it, so that some faint idea will be given of it to the public by a sketch other than this of words. O the desolation, the waste of war!

COLONEL WILLIAM T. MARTIN

JEFF DAVIS LEGION, MISSISSIPPI CAVALRY, STUART'S BRIGADE

When Martin's troopers reached White House Landing on June 29, they found the "White House" in ruins. This former home of George Washington's wife, Martha, had been burned against orders by a misguided Union soldier. By 1865 Martin was a major general commanding a cavalry division.

I joined the brigade at Dispatch Station, and moved with it the same afternoon to the vicinity of Tunstall's Station. Here the artillery of the brigade drove back a squadron of the enemy's cavalry. We bivouacked at this point and next day advanced to the White House.

Captain Avery, Jeff. Davis Legion, and Lieutenant Murray, Fourth Cavalry, with their companies, were dismounted and, with two pieces of the Horse Artillery, sent forward to engage a large gunboat lying off the White House. The boat was compelled to retire, and the brigade took possession of the place, with the large and valuable stores abandoned by the enemy in his precipitous flight.

The preceding night large fires were seen in the direction of the White House. This place was now a scene of desolation; the house was wantonly burned, with its contents. Many of the shade trees were felled and all the fencing had disappeared. This once beautiful estate, made more interesting by associations connected with the great leader of the first Revolution, George Washington, now utterly despoiled, forcibly reminded us that we were contending against a foe respecting nothing, sparing nothing.

Scattered over the fields were abandoned wagons and ambulances, mules, tents, commissary and quartermaster's stores. Hundreds of bonfires had been made by the enemy of whatever was combustible; still an immense amount of property was left uninjured. My command was supplied with abundant rations for three days and the horses with forage from the enemy's supplies.

CAPTAIN WILLIAM W. BLACKFORD

STAFF, BRIGADIER GENERAL J. E. B. STUART

Blackford and the rest of Stuart's horsemen delighted in the foodstuffs and delicacies they found in the wreckage of the Union supply base. Another of Stuart's men—Mississippian John S. Foster—though regretful of the "awfull destruction" he witnessed, happily stated that he and his comrades were able to fill their haversacks "with good things" overlooked by the Yankee forces during their flight.

Escorted only by Col. W. H. F. Lee's regiment, General Stuart and staff went in to take possession. The destruction had been great, but yet vast quantities of things remained which had either been overlooked in the hurry of the evacuation or had failed to burn. It was a curious thing to see the evidences of the luxury in which the Federal army indulged at that period of the war. Their sutler's shops were on the most elaborate scale—quantities of barrels of sugar, lemons by the millions, cases of wine, beer and other liquors of every description, confectionery, canned meats, and fruits and vegetables, and great quantities of ice, all still in excellent condition. The eggs were packed in barrels of salt, and where they had been exposed to fire, the salt was fused into a solid cake with the eggs, deliciously roasted, distributed throughout the mass; it was only necessary to split off a block and then pick out the eggs, like the meat of a nut.

There was a place where embalming was done and several bodies were under treatment, presenting a ghastly spectacle. These were no doubt officers killed in recent engagements, but there was no record of who they were. Before he was aware there was liquor within reach, some of Colonel Lee's men began to get drunk and many of them had bottles stowed away in their clothes; so Colonel Lee caused a report to be started that the enemy had poisoned all the liquor, leaving it there for us as a trap, and that one man had just died in great agony from the effects. As the report extended along the column, bottles of champagne and beer and whiskey went sailing through the air, exploding as they fell like little bomb-shells; while the expression of agony on the tipsy faces of those who had indulged too freely, as they held their hands to their stomachs, was ludicrous in the extreme.

For several days since the fighting began, we had been living on salt meat and crackers and were well prepared to appreciate the luxuries before us as we spread the delicacies we had collected for a lunch out upon the grass under the trees near the river. Great buckets of iced lemonade to begin with to quench our thirst, for the day was intensely hot; pickled oysters, eggs roasted in blocks of salt, canned beef and ham, French rolls, cakes and confectionery of all sorts, and last but not least, boxes of delicious Havana cigars, and coffee. No one but a soldier can appreciate the pleasures of such a repast.

PRIVATE ROLAND E. BOWEN

15TH MASSACHUSETTS INFANTRY, SULLY'S BRIGADE

Bowen described the Seven Days' Battles as a "Hellish tumult . . . going on . . . continually." In this letter, he told of his regiment's June 28 retreat to Savage's Station. On June 29 the 15th took part in the battle there, during which Bowen saw a "Damned old" Rebel battery get "knocked . . . all to pieces in about two minits" by Union gunners.

Well a little before noon the rebs found out where we were chopping and they opened on us with shell; they got the exact range, we had to stop our work and lay down or get behind trees the best we could. The dirt flew in all directions for 30 or 40 minits and all was quiet, we give them as good as they sent I guess, any how we made considerable racket if nothing more. Some of Smiths men got hurt but I think none of the 15th, some say one was wounded in our Reg. Well we went on and finished the *pit.* About sundown we started for camp and lo and behold every Reg we passed was packing up. I says, what's up, *don't know* was the universal answer. Now I began to open my eyes for it was evident we were not a going to advance so of course a retreat was in contemplation. Said I, guess the rebels didn't cheer for *nothing* last night. As soon as we got to camp we had orders to leave every thing we did not actualy need and pack up forthwith. Its quite singular but its a fact, in less that 30 minits it was whispered around that McCall & Porter had been driven back and the enemies scouts had torn up the rail-road, and we had got to make tracks for the James river as the only means of escape. Well what things the boys thought they could not carry were distroyed. About 9 our tents were struck. (I supose you know what kind of a tent we have, what is called a shelter tent, each man carrying his own, then two, four or six build together). For some reason unknown to me we did not go with the Brigade but went direct for the rail-road and down to Savages Station. When we moved off not a loud word was spoken. I occasionaly heard a low whisper. It was about 4 miles down to the Station, we arrived there about 11 at night. The Col (George Ward) had no further orders so we went into the field beside the R.R. and lay down to sleep and dream of the next days operations.

CAPTAIN EUGENE BLACKFORD

5TH ALABAMA INFANTRY, RODES' BRIGADE

In conjunction with the Army of the Potomac's retreat to the James River, McClellan ordered that all goods "not indispensable to the safety or maintenance of the troops must be abandoned and destroyed." Although much was destroyed, Blackford's infantrymen and the other soldiers of D. H. Hill's division found a wealth of Union supplies and equipment as they pressed along to Savage's Station. One of the Alabamians' more curious finds was a dehydrated potato-and-bean stew.

Every where were countless arms, equipments, and stores of every sort. Never was an army so magnificently equipped as this. Their appliances were so elaborate that really our men could not devise the uses of many of them. I remember well that night we were very hungry, and busied ourselves making an elaborate supper of plunder taken in the field. Among other conquests some one produced a substance resembling "grits" or small hominy, which we proceeded to boil in a kettle, this being half-filled & set to boil, very soon it began to swell untill the vessel was filled and also several others. Afterwards I carried it always in my haversack to make soup. One spoonful would expand until it made a quart of thick gruel. As far as we could judge it was composed of irish potatoes, beans &c skillfully prepared, then granulated. We also found vast quantities of dessicated vegetables in tin cans, which were a great treat to our famished fellows. My pen is unable to tell of the wonderful equipment of this Army—of its perfect military stores, the lavish manner in which the individual soldiers were equipped. All this was made the more striking from the great & necessary differance existing in our Army. All along the route of McClellan's army, were strewn ambulances of the most elegant patterns: light one-horse carriages something like an ambulance, made to carry the personal effects of the Field Officers, and these worthies themselves when they were weary.

PRIVATE EUGENE SULLIVAN

42D NEW YORK INFANTRY, DANA'S BRIGADE

The 42d was nicknamed the Tammany Regiment, because the Tammany Society, a New York City Democratic political organization, had raised and outfitted it. The regiment took heavy casualties in its first action, the 1861 Battle of Ball's Bluff. Sullivan was captured there but exchanged shortly thereafter. Here, he describes the 42d's efforts to destroy the Grapevine Bridge over the Chickahominy River.

We crossed Grapevine Bridge to the north side, where the regiment was halted, the other regiments of the brigade continuing the march. Three companies of the regiment—E, K, and I—were detailed to destroy the bridge which had done such good service in time of need.

While the three companies, under command of Capt. Wm. O'Shea, were working like beavers, in the river and on both banks, destroying the bridge, the other seven companies, under command of Col. Edmond C. Charles, were drawn up in line of battle on the high ground, a short distance in rear, in support. It did not take the three companies long to destroy the work which had taken the entire regiment days and nights of hard labor to construct.

Before the destruction was consummated, the enemy discovered what we were doing, and opened fire upon us with artillery. While the fire of the enemy's artillery was somewhat harassing to our support, it had no effect whatever on the men working in the river, and only made them work with renewed energy, the orders being to destroy the bridge, so that the enemy could not use it.

As our men were about to sever the last link, one of Gen. McClellan's Aids—at least we supposed him to be—came dashing to us on a spirited horse, which he forced into the river, asking in a loud and commanding voice: "Who is in command here?" Now, Capt. O'Shea enjoyed a most decided impediment in his speech when excited. Eying the officer sharply, the Captain said: "I-I-I-am in c-c-co-com-comand." The officer, looking at O'Shea, asked: "Can I get a few pieces of artillery across here?" O'Shea looked at him in amazement that he should ask such a question, having seen for himself the condition of the bridge, and the impossibility of getting artillery across, and it made the Captain rather angry, yet amused him, too, and he stuttered: "I-I am in com-com-command here to s-s-see that this br-br-bridge is p-p-prop-prop-properly destroyed; b-b-but you c-c-can get artillery across if it be f-f-fly-fly-flying artillery, and ca-ca-can travel on wings." Giving Capt. O'Shea a look of scorn the officer turned, and rode back in the direction whence he came, and in a little while afterward Grapevine Bridge was a thing of the past.

On June 2 a detachment from the 15th New York Engineers built Duane's Bridge (above), one of several critical Union spans over the Chickahominy. Late on June 27 and throughout the next day these crossings were packed with the retreating troops of the Union V and VI Corps. After the troops had safely crossed to the river's south bank, they destroyed the bridges in order to slow the Confederate pursuit.

MAJOR GENERAL GEORGE B. MCCLELLAN

Commander, Army of the Potomac

After Gaines' Mill McClellan, bent on ducking responsibility for his defeat, sent this telegram to the president. A stunned telegraph officer in Washington removed the last two inflammatory sentences before passing it on, likely saving Little Mac from severe censure by the administration. On the same day, McClellan also wrote bitterly to his wife, Mary Ellen, "I thank my friends in Washn for our repulse."

Headquarters Army of the Potomac
Savage Station, June 28-12-20 A.M.

I now know the full history of the day. On this side of the river (the right bank) we repulsed several strong attacks. On the left bank our men did all that men could do, all that soldiers could accomplish, but they were overwhelmed by vastly superior numbers, even after I brought my last reserves into action. The loss on both sides is terrible. I believe it will prove to be the most desperate battle of the war.

The sad remnants of my men have behaved as men. Those battalions who fought most bravely and suffered most are still in the best order. My regulars were superb, and I count upon what are left to turn another battle, in company with their gallant comrades of the volunteers. Had I 20,000 or even 10,000 fresh troops to use to-morrow I could take Richmond, but I have not a man in reserve and shall be glad to cover my retreat and save the materiel and *personnel* of the army. . . .

. . . I again repeat that I am not responsible for this, and I say it with the earnestness of a general who feels in his heart the loss of every brave man who has been needlessly sacrificed to-day. I still hope to retrieve our fortunes, but to do this the Government must view the matter in the same earnest light that I do. You must send me very large reenforcements and send them at once. I shall draw back to this side of Chickahominy, and think I can withdraw all our material. Please understand that in this battle we have lost nothing but men, and those the best we have.

In addition to what I have already said, I only wish to say to the President that I think he is wrong in regarding me as ungenerous when I said that my force was too weak. I merely intimated a truth which today has been too plainly proved. If, at this instant, I could dispose of 10,000 fresh men, I could gain a victory to-morrow. I know that a few thousand more men would have changed this battle from a defeat to a victory. As it is, the Government must not and cannot hold me responsible for the result.

I feel too earnestly to-night. I have seen too many dead and wounded comrades to feel otherwise than that the Government has not sustained this army. If you do not do so now the game is lost.

If I save the army now, I tell you plainly that I owe no thanks to you or any other persons in Washington.

You have done your best to sacrifice this army.

COLONEL WILLIAM W. AVERELL

3d Pennsylvania Cavalry, III Corps

Between June 27 and the Battle of Malvern Hill, the 3d picketed roads, guarded the rear of the III Corps, and slowed the enemy's crossing of the Chickahominy. Averell reported that his men held Jones' Bridge until June 30, only retreating when "attacked . . . in force with artillery." He records that McClellan repeated his belief that the movement to the James had been necessary to save the army and, thereby, the Union.

At daylight on the 29th, Captain White's squadron, with two hundred infantry and two guns, was sent to picket and hold Jones's Bridge on the Chickahominy. About 9 A.M. my scouts reported a regiment of the enemy's cavalry advancing in column about a mile away. Some woodland intervened. Between this and my position was an open field a quarter of a mile across. A picket was quickly posted at the higher edge of the wood, with orders to fire upon the enemy when he should come within range and then turn and run away, thus inviting pursuit! On my position two guns were already placed to enfilade the road, and a few squadrons held in readiness to charge. The enemy came, was fired upon, and the picket fled, followed by the enemy in hot pursuit. Upon arriving within two hundred yards of our position, the picket quitted the road through the gaps in the fences made for that purpose, thus unmasking the enemy's column; the two guns of Major West fired two rounds, and two squadrons, led by Captains Walsh and Russell, of the Third Pennsylvania, were let loose upon the enemy, and over sixty of his officers and men were left on the ground, whilst the survivors fled in great disorder toward Richmond. The command was the First North Carolina and Third Virginia Cavalry, led by Colonel Lawrence Baker, a comrade of mine in the old army. The Third Pennsylvania lost one man killed and five wounded.

After this affair I galloped back to see General McClellan, and found him near a house south of White Oak Swamp Bridge. Near him were groups of a hundred officers eagerly but quietly discussing our progress and situation. So soon as McClellan descried me, he came with the Prince de Joinville to the fence where I dismounted. After telling him all I knew and had learned from prisoners and scouts, I ventured to suggest that the roads were tolerably clear toward Richmond, and that we might go there. The Prince seemed to exhibit a favorable interest in my suggestion, but the General, recognizing its weakness, said promptly, "The roads will be full enough tomorrow"; and then earnestly, "Averell, if any army can save this country, it will be the Army of the Potomac, and it must be saved for that purpose."

CAPTAIN WILLIAM G. LEDUC

Assistant Quartermaster, Dana's Brigade

Though merely a captain, LeDuc was charged with the responsibility of shepherding the II Corps' immense supply train to Harrison's Landing. The capable LeDuc had to cope with problems posed by poor communication within the army's bureaucracy, ignorance of the region's geography, poor roads and the quagmire of White Oak Swamp, and the churlish behavior of some fellow officers.

To army headquarters I went, and saw Adjutant General Seth Williams. "I am sent by General Sumner," I told him, "to ask where I may take the transportation of the second corps, and when I may start."

"Our destination is the James River—by what roads I know not," he answered. "Better you see the chief quartermaster, General Van Vliet."

To him I went, and he knew nothing of the roads, and directed me

South of the Grapevine Bridge, in the vicinity of the Trent house, soldiers of the VI Corps scurry toward Savage's Station as smoke rises from torched commissary stores. To the far right, a battery awaits harassing Rebel cavalry. The infantrymen at right center are from the 16th New York, identifiable by their white straw hats.

"I know nothing of your power to arrest, but I know that this bridge has to be kept clear to save the lives of soldiers."

to see the chief engineer, and he told me he had no map of the country, and knew nothing of the roads.

I reported to General Sumner, and said: "I will have to find a road, or make a road. The transportation is all ready. Shall I start them?"

"Not by my order. Get that from the Adjutant General, Seth Williams."

To him again I went, and by this time the engineer had heard of a narrow road through the woods leading south across White Oak Swamp, and advised that I take that road, on which teams were already moving. This road led by Savage Station, where immense piles of army supplies were stacked up to be fired, to prevent their falling into the hands of the enemy. I ordered my men to take on all they could carry of boxes of hard bread, and other supplies, and, finding the road leading south, pushed everything forward, and, before sundown, was well into this thicket of woods and brush.

The transportation of some of the troops that had been fighting on the north side of the Chickahominy was ahead of me, and made the delay that gave the opportunity to load some of my teams with supplies that were not receipted. The halting of a single wagon for any purpose checked the entire movement. There was no such thing as passing unless a new road was cut around the obstruction. The weather was damp. Soon a drizzle commenced which emphasized the darkness. After a halt longer than usual, I became impatient, and pushed my horse through the brush. Reaching the head of the train, I found a team halted, and the driver on the wagon asleep. I had to shake him violently to wake him, and he said he had run into something, and having been up and without sleep for two nights, he could not keep awake to find out what was the trouble.

I shaved some light bark from a tree, and, with some other light stuff made a fire on the ground, near the wagon that was fast. . . .

The light of my fire disclosed the difficulty and enabled the driver of the artillery wagon to back off, and resume the road. The trains being again in motion, I went forward until the swamp was reached just at break of day. I saw an artillery caisson to which four horses were attached, and the driver could get the discouraged team to move only a few yards at a time through mud which was up to the axle. I saw it would be impossible to get my train through that swamp, and ordered the wagon masters to park their wagons in an open field, which inclined toward the swamp, as fast as they came up, and to feed the animals. Then I rode back to a camp of engineers we had passed, and had the sentry wake the officer in command, and of him I asked questions about the swamp.

He had been sent, he told me, to build a bridge over the stream, so that the artillery could cross safely. His wagon of tools was down by the stream, and in it were axes to the use of which I could help myself. He said his men had been up so much of nights, and so pushed, that he must let them have some sleep and breakfast; after which he would bring them down to work; that a general in command of troops was camped on the other side of the creek, and that a good stone road was covered by trees that had been felled to obstruct it.

I rode back, struggled through the swamp, crossed the stream, and found the camp of the general (General Morrell, I think), who was wakened with difficulty to listen to my request for a detail of five hundred men, and my explanation of the necessity for the detail. He ordered it, and it was made immediately. We made short work of that quarter of a mile of big timber, and I soon had the transportation moving at as fast a gait as possible. The sticky places were the bridge, and the *débouché* on the south side, where the holes cut in the soft ground soon caused a stoppage. But I would not allow any halt to the movement across the bridge, and found it necessary sometimes to break the trains, greatly to the discontent of the officer in charge. A finely equipped train passing over was stopped by a leading team sticking in a mud hole. I ordered the teamster to pull to one side, and clear the bridge. A lieutenant on the other side hallooed to the driver to keep his place, not to break the train. I pricked up the mules with my sword, and compelled obedience to my order. When the lieutenant got across he was noisy with anger, and said: "This is General McClellan's headquarters train, and I am a provost marshall, and I arrest you."

I said: "I care nothing for a headquarters train, or any other train. I know nothing of your power to arrest, but I know that this bridge has to

In this illustration by Alfred Waud, a burning Federal supply train, its load of munitions critically overheating, is sent sliding off the Richmond & York River Railroad bridge over the Chickahominy. A Union soldier who witnessed such a scene told a relative: "A long train of cars were fired. . . . You ought to have seen the smoke from the ammunition and hear the Shells burst when they got hot." This same infantryman also helped toss ammunition into a stream, but as he and his mates concluded, "this was mighty hard work," so they simply set fire to the remainder.

be kept clear to save the lives of soldiers of the second corps, who are bringing up the rear. If you have any right to arrest me, you can't do it, but I will promise to report in arrest to the Commander-in-chief within twenty-four hours, and I promise further to give you a good, old fashioned, country licking the first time I meet you after I get clear of this more important duty. Now you get out of the way, and get out quick!" And he went.

I heard vociferous laughter, and looking round saw, seated on the grass a little way off, my engineer friend, (Alexander, I think his name was,) who had ridden with me after sweet potatoes, sitting near his grazing horse, laughing immoderately. I rode up to him, and said: "Something seems to have touched your funny bone—what is it?"

"Why," he replied, "I was sent here to keep this bridge clear, and to see you doing my duty so well tickles me."

CAPTAIN G. CAMPBELL BROWN

STAFF, MAJOR GENERAL RICHARD S. EWELL

Brown recalls the blazing Union train's plummeting into the Chickahominy (above) and the confusion caused by the destruction of Union supplies at Savage's Station. Later in 1862 Brown helped save Ewell's life when he aided the general after his wounding at the Battle of Brawner's Farm. And in May 1863 he became Ewell's stepson when Ewell married Lizinka Brown, the captain's widowed mother.

About noon we reached a point opposite the immense depot of stores that McClellan had had at Savage Station, and saw the dense column of smoke rising from their burning. Soon afterwards the head of our Column reached & crossed the R.Rd. at the Bottom's Bridge road—and we halted, throwing out a company or two of the M'd. Line [1st Maryland] as skirmishers. They soon became engaged in a skirmish with a small party of Cav'y who held the Bridge. The R.Rd bridge over the Chickahominy (York River R.R'd.) was already destroyed, so as to indicate plainly that McClellan had given up that line of retreat. While our troops lay here, mostly in the woods along the road, I was sent off with an order & Turner soon after with another, for Trimble (I think). At any rate we met in search of the same party just as the most fearful explosion took place that I ever heard, sounding like the simultaneous discharge of many guns—and the woods between us & the river were filled with falling shells. Our first idea was that the enemy intended to force a passage of the river and had concentrated batteries and opened fire for that purpose. Turner rode on with his message while I started to find Gen'l E. & tell him of the batteries' falling short. But I met him coming full gallop & in a minute saw a dense white column of smoke unlike that from guns, showing an explosion. Pretty soon, just as we had got out into the open in sight of the bridge, we heard a roaring in the direction of Savage Station, growing momentarily louder & clearer—then an Engine & train came full speed towards the bridge, loaded with bursting shells, powder barrels &c. The troops on the road were hurried away for fear that the train might possibly leap the gap in the bridge—but instead of doing so it went down with a grand crash, thirty miles an hour, into the river. It was one of the grandest sights I ever looked at.

It is hard to realize the value of all the stores destroyed by McClellan. As I passed a house that day, I asked for a drink of water. The man brought it to me, but said I had better not drink as the Yankees had somehow poisoned his spring—though he couldn't find anything in it. I tasted the water—it was not poisoned, but impregnated with two or three different medicines. I saw the Spring—a bold, clear stream. Riding a mile further & crossing a good-sized branch, or small creek, I came to a Federal Hospl & a well down which they had emptied an immense quantity of drugs and hospl stores—and the mystery of the Spring was at once explained. I saw the owner afterwards & learned that in less than two days the water was good again.

Wounded Union soldiers from the Battle of Gaines' Mill lie in the yard of one of the buildings clustered about Savage's Station. In the foreground, a straw-hatted officer from the 16th New York examines a comrade's leg wound; other injured men from that regiment—also wearing straw hats—can be seen in the background. This distinguishing headgear had been a gift from the wife of the 16th's colonel to help prevent sunstroke. A member of the 16th named Cyrus Stone noted, however, that many of his comrades had been shot in the head at Gaines' Mill and thought that the enemy "must have aimed at our hats." Most of the men in this picture were captured by the Confederates after being left behind during the Union retreat.

"When the tremendous explosion came, all eyes turned in that direction and we beheld a dense black column of smoke shoot up in the air perhaps a thousand feet."

PRIVATE JAMES C. MILLER

2D DELAWARE INFANTRY, FRENCH'S BRIGADE

A resident of Chester County, Pennsylvania, Miller had crossed into Delaware to enlist. At Gaines' Mill, his regiment's first battle, Miller remembered rushing past a "New York Fire Zouave" who had been shot in the chest and imagining that he had felt a bullet strike him in the same place. In this account, he describes the huge smoke cloud that arose from the Union munitions blown up at Savage's Station.

Our division covered the retreat. But I must tell of the blowing up of the railroad bridge across the Chickahominy and the destruction of an immense quantity of stores. There seemed to be a pile of the latter as long as a city block and as high as a two-story house. It was all burned, and when the bridge was blown up, we were about a mile distant from it. The sight was most grand.

When the tremendous explosion came, all eyes turned in that direction and we beheld a dense black column of smoke shoot up in the air perhaps a thousand feet. The top spread out like an immense mushroom, whitish gray on the top, shaded darker underneath, with a stem reaching to the ground. There it hung and kept its shape for several minutes, then gradually dissolved and floated away.

After dark we lay on the field until about midnight, when we started to march rapidly. In the morning we arrived at White Oak Swamp, crossed it, and halted along the side of the road that crossed the swamp.

PRIVATE JOHN G. SONDERMAN

1ST MINNESOTA INFANTRY, SULLY'S BRIGADE

The first major effort by the Confederates to hinder the Union retreat came on June 29, when an outnumbered force of 5,000 Rebel troops led by "Prince John" Magruder clashed with the Union rear guard west of Savage's Station. Sonderman's regiment lost 10 men killed or mortally wounded. After the final Confederate assault had been turned back, the Minnesotans resumed their march at 9:00 p.m., moving over moonlit roads toward the bridges spanning White Oak Swamp.

On the afternoon of June 28 we were ordered to pack up everything but shelter tents and at nightfall these were struck and we lay on the ground without covering. The trains had been going to the South all day, and at dark the sick and disabled were also sent away, and at early daylight the morning of June 29, leaving our picket line, we marched in the rear of the army.

The roads were blocked with masses of moving troops, impeded farther along by trains and artillery, and in the dense mist of morning very slow progress was made. We had advanced about three miles when, at 9 o'clock a.m., our picket was forced back, followed by the enemy under the active and alert Magruder. This force attacked at once, as we formed near the peach orchard on Allen's farm. The fighting was sharp for a brief time, though the attack mainly fell on troops just to the right of our regiment, and but little of the enemy's fire, save from artillery, reached us. After several repulses the enemy fell back and our army proceeded on its way.

Moving on, we reached Savage Station about 1 o'clock p.m., and were massed with a considerable body of the Second Corps near the road leading across White Oak Swamp. The remainder of the army had passed on, and a large amount of material at the railroad bridge was being destroyed. When the bridge with engines and trains upon it, was blown up, an immense body of dense smoke arose, assuming perfectly symmetrical and continually changing forms and colors, beautiful and

Arthur Lumley drew this view of the Battle of Savage's Station. In the center foreground, II Corps commander Major General Edwin V. Sumner sits astride his horse, observing the fighting on the horizon and relaying orders through the staff officers clustered about him. Sumner's troops mounted a defense that held the Confederates at bay, allowing the bulk of the Union army to cross White Oak Swamp. Lumley also included in this sketch a burning Union supply train on the Richmond & York River Railroad. The train's boxcars were full of ordnance, and periodically a shell would flare skyward and explode—dramatic fireworks labeled "rockets" by the artist and shown in the sky.

grand to the view, in whatever form it took, like the changes in a kaleidoscope, and observed by all for several minutes before it was dissipated.

About 4 o'clock the rebels ran down the railroad a heavy gun mounted upon a flat-car and protected by railroad iron, and opened on our troops. This was followed closely by infantry and other artillery. The 1st Minn. and Gen. Burn's Brigade of our division were ordered to the point of attack, and soon drove off the enemy. But Confederate infantry at once appeared on another road farther to the left, and we were sent to that point, being joined by the other regiments of our brigade. The 1st Minn. here formed the extreme left of the line, and resisted the heaviest attack, which was made with artillery at canister range, and with infantry extending beyond our left flank, which was in great danger of being turned. The attack here was most persistent and severe, and as we got the enemy's fire diagonally from its extended right, as well as from the front, our loss was considerable.

PRIVATE ROBERT A. STILES

Richmond (Virginia) Howitzers, Griffith's Brigade

Called forward to support the infantry near Savage's Station, Stiles' unit was pounded by Union counterbattery fire. The admiration Stiles expresses here at his comrades' cool performance was soon tempered by the horror he felt upon seeing his brigade commander, Brigadier General Richard Griffith, collapse with a mortal wound from "half a shell from a three-inch rifled gun lodged in his body."

We then crossed over to the York River Railroad, upon which we had what our men called our "railroad gun," a siege piece, mounted on a flat-car with an engine back of it, the front of the car being protected by rails of track iron fastened upon an incline, the mouth of the gun projecting a little as from an embrasure. As it puffed up, a number of Federal batteries, invisible to us, opened upon it and upon the troops, and General Magruder sent an order for our guns to cross the railroad by the bridge hard by and come into battery in the smooth, hard field beyond.

We executed this dashing feat in gallant style, our captain riding ahead, the pieces in a wild gallop and the men on a wild run following. Again we seemed to be in full sight of an unseen enemy, for the bridge was raked and swept by a fearful storm of shot and shell. I distinctly remember the shells bursting in my very face, and the bridge must have been struck repeatedly, the great splinters hurtling past and cutting the air like flashes of lightning, yet no one was hurt. Once across, we were ordered, "Forward into battery, left oblique, march!" which elaborate movement was executed by the men as if on drill. I could not refrain from glancing around, and was amazed to see every piece, limber, caisson and man in the exact mathematical position in which each belonged, and every man seemed to have struck the very attitude required by the drill-book. And there we all stood, raked by a terrific fire, to which we could not reply, being really a second line, the first—consisting of infantry alone—having passed into the dense, forbidding forest in front, feeling for the enemy.

COLONEL JAMES D. NANCE

3d South Carolina Infantry, Kershaw's Brigade

Deployed south of the railroad, the 3d advanced eastward toward Savage's Station, blundering through heavy brush into shattering Yankee volleys. In two hours of battle, the regiment lost 136 of its 467 men. Nance, a graduate of the South Carolina Military Academy, was killed at the Battle of the Wilderness in 1864.

We had not advanced much farther before we came up with the enemy near Savage Station and were halted. My regiment, when halted, held a position in a slight hollow in an open field, with its right flank resting on a wood of thick underbrush and forest timber, and its left resting on the right of Colonel Kennedy's regiment, whose left rested on the York River Railroad. The ground gradually ascended in our front for about 60 yards, where began a wood, whose line ran nearly parallel to our line of battle. This woods had a depth of about 400 yards. The first part, although of heavy timber, was rather open and not filled or obstructed by the thick underbrush, which alone was found in the last part of the wood. These bushes were of dense thickness, and continued to an open field 400 yards in front of our line of battle. The ground of these woods was slightly undulating. In the position I held my men were so well protected from the fire and shells of the enemy that they effected no injury to my command before the advance was made.

After some firing between the skirmishers and artillery of the contending parties we received the command forward and immediately thereafter the command to charge. The commands were obeyed with alacrity and great enthusiasm. My regiment dashed up the ascent in front through the woods, yelling as they went, and into the thick undergrowth, in which it was impossible to discover either friend or foe over 20 yards. We were not aware of the exact position of the enemy until we received his galling fire at a distance of 25 or 30 yards after we had proceeded some distance in the thick undergrowth already described. The fire checked us for a moment, but we pressed on slowly, returning the enemy's fire and making him yield gradually, when I ordered a charge, and pushed him out of the wood and some distance across the open field beyond. We had scarcely emerged from the woods before I heard, to my surprise, the command, "Cease firing." I immediately went to the right of the regiment, where I heard an officer giving this

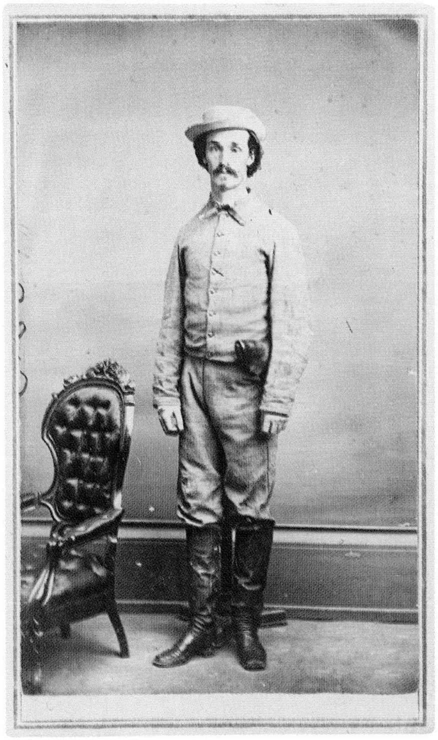

Mortally wounded at Savage's Station, Private A. B. Reading (left) of the 21st Mississippi was one of the 151 casualties incurred by his regiment during the Seven Days' Battles. The 19-year-old student, a resident of Vicksburg, Mississippi, enlisted in May 1861 and died of his wounds on July 4, 1862. This photograph was taken at a Vicksburg gallery known as the Palace of Art.

command, of whom I inquired by what authority he spake. He replied that it came from the right, and that he understood we were firing on our friends. Remembering the caution that had been given early in the day for all "line officers to repeat the commands," and knowing the impossibility of otherwise hearing the commands, recollecting that the brigadier-general was on our right as we entered the woods, and thinking a body of troops moving on our right—whose character I could not with certainty determine, on account of the approaching darkness and smoke of battle—might be our people moving on the enemy's flank, I ordered the regiment to cease firing.

We had scarcely ceased to fire before the enemy, either re-enforced or encouraged by the example of some of their men who fired upon us as they retreated, rallied on a hill opposite us and renewed the attack with great vigor. Suspecting the command to cease firing was either a ruse or an error, I withdrew a short distance in the underbrush, and reformed my line as best I could under an extremely severe fire. By the time this was accomplished the enemy had almost traversed the field and reached the edge of the undergrowth from which we had driven them. As they advanced they poured a deadly and incessant fire into my line. I met them again, pushing my line almost to the edge of the undergrowth, when, besides the fire in my front, I was subjected to a threatening fire upon my right flank. In this emergency, without, so far as I could discover, supports either on my right or left flank, I deemed it prudent to retire, which I did, moving by the right flank.

PRIVATE D. AUGUSTUS DICKERT

3d South Carolina Infantry, Kershaw's Brigade

Wounded as his regiment advanced through a woods he described as "dark as night," Dickert was eventually carried to a rear-area hospital. But he later hobbled to a resting place under a tree, driven outside, he explained, by the "oppressive . . . peculiar odor of human blood, mingling with the setting smoke of the . . . battlefield." Dickert recovered, continued to serve with the 3d, and was promoted to lieutenant. In 1899, he wrote and published a book, "History of Kershaw's Brigade."

The men became woefully tangled and disorganized, and in some places losing the organizations entirely, but under all these difficulties they steadily pressed to the front. When near the outer edge of the thicket, we could see the enemy lying down in some young growth of pines, with their batteries in the fort. The graping was simply dreadful, cutting and breaking through the bushes and striking against trees. I had not gone far into the thicket before I was struck by a minnie ball in the chest, which sent me reeling to the ground momentarily unconscious. Our men lost all semblance of a line, being scattered over a space of perhaps 50 yards, and those in front were in as much danger from friend as from foe. While I lay in a semi-unconscious state, I received another bullet in my thigh which I had every reason to believe came from some one in the rear. But I roused myself, and staggering to my feet made my way as well as I could out of the thicket. When I reached the place from whence we had first made the charge, our drummer was beating the assembly or long roll with all his might, and men collecting around General Kershaw and Colonel Nance. Here I first learned of the repulse. The balls were still flying overhead, but some of our batteries had got in position and were giving the enemy a raking fire. Nor was the railroad battery idle, for I could see the great black, grim monster puffing out heaps of gray smoke, then the red flash, then the report, sending the engine and car back along the track with a fearful recoil.

Built at Lee's request, this flatcar-mounted, 32-pounder banded naval rifle was used at Savage's Station; it had little impact on the fighting but elicited comments from soldiers of both armies. One Rebel stated that the "great siege cannon . . . was one of the most novel batteries of the war." This photograph was taken in 1865, after Union troops had captured the gun near Walthall's Station, Virginia.

Private Alfred Caldwell (left) served in the nattily uniformed 72d Pennsylvania, a regiment known as Baxter's Zouaves in honor of Colonel DeWitt Baxter, its organizer. The 72d fought throughout the day on June 29, first sparring with the enemy near Orchard Station, then retreating eastward to the main Yankee line at Savage's Station. At some point during the nearly continuous combat, the youthful Caldwell fell with a mortal wound.

PRIVATE ISAAC M. BURTON

5th Vermont Infantry, Brooks' Brigade

The Green Mountain State regiments of Brooks' brigade were approaching the bridge over White Oak Swamp when a courier from Sumner ordered them to retrace their steps to Savage's Station. In the ensuing fray, Rebel fire caused 25 casualties among the 59 men in Burton's Company E. Burton himself suffered; he wrote, "I carried my broken arm to Harrison's Landing, leaving my dead brother on the field."

We had passed Savage's Station, where cords upon cords of hard-tack and bacon were given to the flames, and were nearing White Oak Swamp when the column halted. Aids passed rapidly back and forth, and that nameless feeling, foreboding a general engagement, pervaded the ranks. Sure enough, General Brooks, mounted on "Old Baldy," countermarched the brigade to Savage's Station, where we were deployed in line of battle, supported by the Second, Third, Fourth and Sixth Vermont volunteers, composing our brigade (Brooks'). The order came, "Fix bayonets!" and with unloaded muskets we were ordered forward. We passed the Station, and the brigade swept forward in line of battle, column of brigade, and we entered the woods. Everything was quiet; not a shot was heard—nothing but the low, quiet, nervous commands of the officers—and we began to ask ourselves if there had not been another mistake, and there were after all to be no uninvited guests present. But we soon got an introduction to them.

The first intimation we received that we were expected was when we saw a big butternut-colored chap step from behind a tree and deliberately fire, and, then "git." Poor Bolster—my right-hand man—caught it through the head, and then the fight became general. With unloaded muskets we left the woods and entered a clearing, to find ourselves confronted by a rebel battery, supported by a line of infantry. Here the line was halted and dressed, under a perfect storm of canister and musket-balls, and ordered to "load and fire at will!"

Good God! As I remember it now, I cannot help wondering why we did not fix bayonets and, with an old-fashioned Vermont hurrah, take that battery. But the order was, "Commence firing!" and we did, with no thought of but to "stop that battery." Men tore savagely at their cartridges and cursed because their guns were foul and it took longer than usual to ram the charge home. But the fire of the battery began to slacken. The rebel supports moved up, and the whole line broke into flame and smoke. If anything, the din increased; but the hiss of the minie was not so offensive as the howl and whir of canister.

A few moments apparently, but in reality an hour, passed; and as I looked around I saw, not the solid line of familiar faces, but here and there a little group of men, black as powder and dirt could make them, still tearing cartridges and nervously ramming them home, while scattered on the ground lay more than were in line.

PRIVATE LEVI J. FRITZ

53d Pennsylvania Infantry, French's Brigade

Before the war Fritz had been a printer for the Montgomery Ledger, a newspaper back home. From the army he sent letters to the paper eloquently recounting the experiences of his regiment. This dispatch describes the 53d's role in the Battle of Savage's Station. Fritz mistakenly refers to White Oak Swamp as the Chickahominy.

While this brilliant victory was being won in our front, we lay quietly in the woods, undisturbed save by the enemy's shells and grape, that sometimes seemed to take a notion to rake us. About 6 o'clock, P.M., we made a charge through the woods to the railroad but failed to start up a rebel. Coming back again—it was now twilight—we found that the army was again moving off. Finally all had

In 1869 Julian Scott, a former Union drummer boy who had served during the Seven Days' campaign, painted this rich and vibrant scene of Brigadier General William T. H. Brooks' Vermont Brigade defending a crossing point at White Oak Swamp during the early evening of June 29. At right, a gun crew strains to push its field piece to safety, while Brigadier General William Smith, Brooks' division commander, sits atop his mount at center, gesturing with his sword.

gone and we were left once more alone with the skulking enemy and the deep shadows of night around us. We were the last of the Mohicans. We waited until midnight on the battle field of Savage's Station, when we quietly took up our line of march. Quickly we go forward over muddy roads and through black and ominous looking woods, not knowing what moment the rebels in numbers strong, would open a devastating and deadly fire upon our devoted, brave, but little band. Still we gallantly forwarded on under the lead of our vigilant Colonel, who proved himself as able to conduct a dangerous retreat, as he was to heroically lead the advance in the strife of contending armies. The road was filled with stragglers from the main column, that the fatigues of the hasty march had forced to fall back and linger along the road. Most of these worn out men were asleep when we came along. We waked them up, and told them to hurry along with us, as we were the rear guard and behind us were nothing but desperate foes and death. These arguments were irresistible, and they crowded in our ranks and pressed upon our flanks to the number of thousands. All the time we were moving over the road as fast as we could possibly could; we did not know at what fatal moment the rebels would attack and endeavor to completely cut us off from our friends in the front. Day was just breaking as we came in sight of the Chickahominy. Waiting for an hour or more until a number of teams and a crowd of stragglers had passed over the bridge, we finally filed across. We had barely landed on the other side, and we had not time to form the regiment in line and see whether all were present, ere the 53d were ordered to cut away and burn the bridge across the stream. The boys set to work and in a few hours the bright lurid flames of the burning bridge timbers were shooting upwards toward the blue clouded heavens. This being done, our regiment, with the rest of the brigade, moved back about half a mile on the highlands, a very airy and beautiful place for a camp, known as Nelson's Farm. Here we rested for several hours. The men were enjoying what they so much needed, a goodly dose of the "sweet restorer, balmy sleep," when the rebels opened upon us, from batteries on the other side of the stream, a sweeping and deadly fire of shot, shell and grape. The cannonading was, in its commencement, fearful. They appeared to do no point blank firing, but threw their shots indiscriminately. The air was filled with exploding shells, and the ugly fizzing of shot was heard all about one. The earth was torn up, and mud, dirt and dust thrown up, and things looked as if a certain black horned cloven foot was indeed loose. For awhile it seemed as if there would be a general panic and stampede. Their was a large number of teams on the ground, and these, in endeavoring to get to the rear and out of danger, came very nearly throwing the soldiers into a panic, but thanks to the coolness of our officers, and the sound, sober second thought of the men, this was prevented; and the different regiments formed in splendid style, and were soon put in position to support our batteries or to resist movements on our flanks. While the infantry was forming, a battery was got in position and returned the fire of the enemy. The cannonading was the most terrific we ever heard. The earth trembled, the heavens were clouded with the cannon's smoke, and we inhaled the gunpowdery air. Our regiment was lying flat on the ground on the gentle declivity of a hill,—shot and shell were falling around and in our ranks.

PRIVATE ERHARD FUTTERER

20TH NEW YORK INFANTRY, DAVIDSON'S BRIGADE

On June 30 the 20th New York endured a pounding from Jackson's artillery that scattered and demoralized the regiment. Futterer, like most members of the 20th, was a German immigrant, an artist born in Baden in 1833. He escaped harm in this action, but in September at Antietam a Rebel bullet through his jaw put him out of the war.

The Confederates accidentally fired on a Union hospital at Savage's Station, causing a surgeon to come forward under a white flag to request a halt to the shooting. Frank Schell sketched this incident, noting the "flashy" attire of the Rebel officer (at left).

From 10:30 a.m. until noon, our side of the swamp was very peaceful. It was so peaceful that General Smith decided to take a bath. At high noon, just as he was relaxed in the tub, Jackson opened fire with all his cannons simultaneously and without warning. The earth shook! Shell after shell came down on us like rain; trees were uprooted, wagons smashed, tents destroyed; groups of men died on the spot where they sipped their last cup of coffee! Mule teams, watering at the edge of the swamp, ran helter-skelter trampling surprised, relaxed, and unprepared soldiers. Finding cover was the only thought in everyone's mind. Smith's bath was abruptly ended as a shell exploded inside the farmhouse. He was unharmed; but, the owner, who stayed to protect his chickens from being ravaged by the Yankees, had his leg shattered, and he bled to death! Captain Hazard was, instantly, killed as a shell demolished one of his batteries.

Our brigade was ordered to withdraw down the road. All of our regiments moved except us. We were in the foremost advanced position and did not hear the order. Momentarily, the cannons ceased firing and, finding ourselves alone, we shouted, "Sergeant, what are our orders?" He replied, "I have none; I cannot find Colonel Weiss!" A voice came from the far right side of the line, "Weiss wants you over with Hancock's brigade." This was followed by a contradictory notice, "Weiss is gone! Find Colonel Shack; he will know what to do!" We rose from our prone positions. At that instant, and again without warning, Jackson's cannons poured shells directly at us. One shell burst in the middle of our line and the men split. Half of them ran toward Hancock and the other half went toward Shack, plunging into the ravine as they did so. I was with the latter group.

Those who went into the ravine were engulfed waste deep in the mud. Some lost their muskets as they tore loose; others were lacerated by broken branches or sprained their ankles. Those who tore loose ran toward General Caldwell's brigade. When he saw them coming toward him without muskets, he was furious. He gave an order to his 5th New Hampshire Regiment, "Boys, stand firm! Raise your bayonets! Run those skulkers through!" Our men kept coming, shouting in German that they were joining Colonel Shack. The New Englanders, not understanding German, stood as ordered, and bayoneted the first group which met their line. Shack, hearing the Germans' cry, gave a quick translation to General Caldwell, who immediately rescinded the order. The General was mortified!

LIEUTENANT RUFUS KING JR.

Battery A, 4th U.S. Artillery, Richardson's Division

King had an uneven war record. In 1861 the West Point graduate helped organize the Iron Brigade, and at White Oak Swamp he took command of the 4th's Batteries A and C after their captain had been hit, for which he was later awarded the Medal of Honor. But during Second Manassas he was accused of drunkenness and disobeying orders, and he saw no more active duty before resigning his commission in 1863.

We commenced firing between 1 and 2 o'clock p.m., firing very rapidly and drawing the entire fire of the enemy's batteries upon us, no other battery being in position. The enemy was completely covered by a thick wood, and the only indication we had of their position was from the smoke of their guns. Their fire was very rapid and very precise, most of their shot and shell striking within 20 feet of the battery and a perfect shower of grape passing through the battery. Were it not for the splendid position we had, few of us would have left the battle-field that day without a serious wound. The brow of the hill forming a natural breastwork, our guns, just pointing over the top of the hill, were in a manner sheltered, and most of the solid shot fired by the enemy struck the brow of the hill and ricochetted harmlessly over our heads. The men stood to their guns nobly, working

Union guns duel with Stonewall Jackson's artillery on June 30 in this sketch by Alfred Waud. Captain Romeyn B. Ayres, chief of artillery for the 2d Division, VI Corps—mounted at left—directs Federal artillery crews. The Confederate fire was so intense that one New Hampshire Yankee wrote, "Hell seemed to have opened upon us." The Federal guns were soon forced to withdraw, allowing a Rebel cavalry reconnaissance to pick its way across the morass of White Oak Swamp.

"The men stood to their guns nobly, working them as coolly as if it was an ordinary practice."

them as coolly as if it was an ordinary practice, the chiefs of pieces sighting their guns themselves and relieving the cannoneers from their arduous duties by performing them themselves. Captain Hazzard behaved in the most gallant manner, encouraging the men and cheering them when they appeared fatigued, also superintended the entire fire of the battery, frequently changing the direction of the guns and sighting them himself. At one piece, where three of the horses of the limber had been shot and the harness entangled by their fall, and two of the drivers shot through the legs and feet, being unable to disentangle them themselves, Captain Hazzard performed the deed himself, also carrying ammunition to one piece where the cannoneers were entirely tired out, and taking turns with myself in performing the duties of No. 1.

About half an hour after we had been in action Captain Hazzard was standing by one of the limbers, superintending the taking out of the ammunition, when a shell burst in the battery, a fragment striking Captain Hazzard in the leg, breaking the bone, and wounding him severely. He was immediately carried off the field and sent to the rear. Great praise is due to Captain Hazzard for the soldierly conduct he displayed in this engagement. The command of the battery then devolved upon me, and I continued firing until I had expended all my ammunition.

General Meagher stood by one of the pieces, and, exposed to the hottest of the fire, assisted the men in running the gun forward. Upon my telling him how near out of ammunition I was, he kindly volunteered to ride to General Richardson and have ammunition sent to me as soon as possible; but before the ammunition could reach me I had expended every shot in my chests, and had to fall back into a hollow where my battery was protected from the murderous fire of the enemy, and there I refilled my ammunition chests.

PRIVATE ALBERT MAXFIELD

11th Maine Infantry, Naglee's Brigade

During the Peninsula campaign, the 11th's regimental band was sent back to Maine, leaving their instruments hanging from apple trees about their camp, and Maxfield noted that the musicians "tooted . . . no more" for the regiment. At White Oak Swamp, the 11th was serenaded instead by booming artillery pieces and whistling, shrieking, and exploding Confederate projectiles raining down on their bivouac.

We were lying in the edge of the woods that bordered the great cleared field in which the troops and trains were massed, and perhaps had an advantage in all being wide awake. At any rate we were not a bit demoralized. Scarcely a man started to his feet, all waiting for the word of command. It came quickly, and from the mouth of General Naglee himself, who riding up to us and seeing our immovability while the troops around us were in evident confusion, could not restrain his delight at our coolness, but cried out "Fall in, my Yankee squad," for the Eleventh was few in numbers now. We fell in, and as he proudly led us across the big field to a new position, we stiffened our necks and neither dodged or bowed to the storm of iron beating down upon us. We had made a hit, and we knew it.

Taking up a position behind the rails of a torn-down fence, the Eleventh lay listening to Jackson's cannon and watching Hazzard's battery as it swept the White Oak Swamp Bridge with a storm of grape and cannister that kept even Jackson at bay. The cannoneers fell one by one—were thinned out until the officers not yet killed or wounded dismounted and took their places at the guns. It was whispered that their ammunition was giving out—was most gone—a few rounds more and the last shell would be fired, and then Jackson and his 35,000 men would pour across the bridge and up the heights to learn what sort of stuff we were made of.

But this was not to be. Just as we were gathering ourselves together for the apparently fast coming struggle, there came a yell from the rear, a sound of desperately galloping horses, and with slashing whips Pettits' battery came tearing on at the top of their horses' speed, General Naglee leading them into position. Ours, as did all the regiments massed in the big field, rose and cheered Naglee and the artillerymen as they swept by. Inside of a minute from their first appearance, they were in position, unlimbered, and were sweeping the bridge with grape and cannister.

CAPTAIN BERNARD J. REID

63D PENNSYLVANIA INFANTRY, ROBINSON'S BRIGADE

While the artillery tempest raged over White Oak Swamp, Reid and the other weary soldiers of McClellan's army trickled toward Malvern Hill, unaware that a Rebel column composed of A. P. Hill's and Longstreet's divisions was preparing to strike at them near the crossroads hamlet of Glendale.

The swamp was passed by the brigade at a bridge two miles below, after dark, and we rested on our arms in the high ground beyond till daybreak, when we moved on to the intersecting of our road with the Charles City. Here the brigade was massed in column, while scouts and skirmishers were thrown out, up and across the Charles City Road, feeling for the enemy's approach on our right flank. We rested two or three hours without any tidings of the foe, and then moved on towards Malvern and were posted in a large clover and oats field to the right of our road and on the near side of the Newmarket Road. The day was clear and beautiful and the men, unslinging their knapsacks, pitched their shelter tents for the sake of the shade they afforded, and after the fatigues and marches of the last few days and nights, most of them made a bed on the luxurious verdure beneath, to seek a few hours of much-needed sleep and rest. There had been considerable cannonading early in the day in the direction of White Oak swamp, where we were holding the enemy, but towards noon all became still and calm as any rustic scene could be in time of peace. It was the death-like stillness preceding the tornado, so quiet it seemed that being bi-monthly muster day, the Sixty-third was regularly mustered, as though we were secure in permanent camp or barracks. Scarcely was the ceremony over when there arose symptoms of break in the unusual calm, and early in the afternoon an occasional cannon shot was heard.

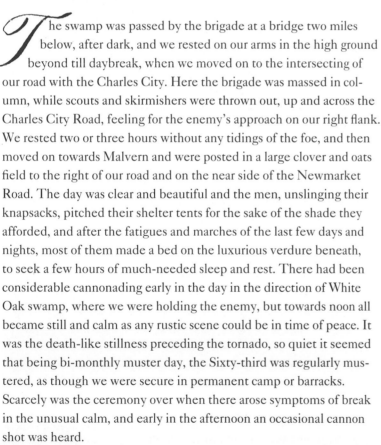

PRIVATE DAVID E. JOHNSTON

7TH VIRGINIA INFANTRY, KEMPER'S BRIGADE

Jackson's and Major General Benjamin Huger's infantry were to have begun the Battle of Glendale but never got started. Lee then ordered Longstreet to attack, and "Old Pete" sent forward three brigades, including Brigadier General James L. Kemper's. This account is from "Story of a Confederate Boy in the Civil War," Johnston's recollections.

Pushing ahead early the next day, Monday, June 30, the enemy was encountered about noon. The skirmishers were soon engaged, but the advance of our troops did not begin until about 4 o'clock P.M., and after we had suffered for two or more hours from a severe shelling. While under this severe fire and in line in the woods, in a swamp amidst brambles and vines, a shell from one of the enemy's guns burst immediately in our front and only a few feet away, scattering the fragments and shrapnel in our midst, one of which struck a man close by me, burying itself in a testament in his breast pocket, which thus saved his life.

From the firing we had every reason to believe that the enemy was close at hand in large numbers, seemingly not distant more than half a mile. The advance of our forces was through a dense wood, tangled underbrush filled with brambles, and partly covered by water, with no possibility of keeping the men up to their places, the stronger ones pushing through over the obstacles, while many of the weaker, unable to keep pace, were left behind. Kemper's brigade was leading and his advance soon became a charge, the enemy being posted on the farther side of an open field. Some of the line officers implored the regimental commander to halt long enough to get the men in order and close the ranks, but the officer cried out: "Forward! Forward!" and on rushed the men, every man his own general, which they usually were in making such a charge.

In a fierce battle a man's courage is severely tested. Here our regiment is in battle line on the edge of a wood; less than a quarter of a mile in front is another wood, sheltering the enemy; between the opposing forces is an open field; the regiment is advancing and the lines move out into the clear sunlight. Men will hurriedly reason with themselves: "The enemy is posted in that timber across the field; before we move many yards he will open on us with shot and shell; this is perhaps my last day on earth." So each man reasons, but every face is sternly set to the front and not a man falters. The shell and shot blow dozens to gory fragments, but the line does not halt, the living saying to themselves: "The fire will presently change to cannister, then I shall certainly be struck." The prediction is being verified, gaps are opened through the ranks, only to be closed again; the regiment has lost its adhesion and marching step, its lines are no longer perfect, but the movement is still onward. From knowledge of methods in battle, our men suppose the infantry is in support of the battery. We have escaped shell and cannister, but when we meet the musketry fire we shall be killed. There is no hanging back, no thought but to push ahead. The leaden hail now comes and the lines are further disordered; the left wing has lost its front by quite a distance, but the push is forward, men grip their guns, their eyes flash, and with a yell, on to the battery they rush, bayonetting the cannoneers at their posts. The Federal infantry supports give way precipitately—then follows that famous bone-searching rebel yell of triumph.

The crossed bayonets on the flag of the 60th Virginia Infantry (above) signify the hand-to-hand fighting the regiment experienced at Glendale. After the battle the regiment's commander reported that a number of his men had suffered bayonet wounds.

The brigade, led by the brave General Kemper, met a shower of shot, shell, cannister and storm of leaden bullets; it never faltered, rushed upon the Union battery—Randol's Pennsylvania—routing its infantry supports. Here Ensign Mays planted the colors of the 7th regiment on the Union guns. They were ours, won, however, at fearful cost. The failure promptly to support our brigade—the enemy flanking us on both wings—caused General Kemper to order the retirement of the brigade, now suffering severe loss from the fire of these flanking columns, which in turn were themselves flanked and defeated by the troops coming to our support. Such is the fearful game of war with men of the same valor and blood.

COLONEL WILLIAM E. STARKE

60th Virginia Infantry, Field's Brigade

Sent to add strength to Longstreet's stalled attack, Starke's regiment drove down the Long Bridge road, running head-on into Lieutenant Alanson Randol's Union battery. Here, a bloody melee ensued as both sides fought for control of Randol's six guns. Wounded in the left hand during the fight, Starke temporarily relinquished command of the 60th to his major. On September 17, 1862, at Antietam Starke was hit by three bullets during the morning fighting and died later that day.

The regiment advanced at double-quick nearly two miles to the brow of the hill, where a battery of eight guns, Randall's Penn Battery, was posted, which had been taken from the enemy and by them recaptured before we reached the ground.

We were immediately formed into line of battle, the Fifty-fifth Virginia on our right, and ordered to retake the battery. Delivering a few volleys the regiment moved forward, charged the enemy, drove them into and through the woods for a considerable distance, killing, wounding, and taking many of them prisoners, and recapturing the battery. On reaching the wood, however, the enemy poured a heavy fire into our line, upon which the command was given to charge bayonets. This command was obeyed with great alacrity, and very many of the enemy fell before the formidable weapon. After driving them for half a mile beyond this point the brigade was ordered to halt, where we remained for half a hour, it being then quite dark. The enemy not again appearing, the regiment was ordered to return to the battery, and there remain until the pieces were carried off the field.

"I met him just as he was coming out of the fight and he was weeping like a child at the destruction of his brave, noble men."

MAJOR THOMAS J. GOREE

STAFF, MAJOR GENERAL JAMES LONGSTREET

On July 21 Goree wrote a letter to his mother about the Seven Days' Battles. In this excerpt he describes the attack led by Colonel Micah Jenkins' brigade at Glendale. Goree told his mother that "Jenkins is a great friend of mine and he is a favorite with the army. . . . He is only 27 years of age & is a perfect model of a Christian hero." Jenkins was mortally wounded by friendly fire at the Wilderness on May 6, 1864.

The So. Ca. Brigade under the gallant Col. Jenkins commenced the attack. Kemper was on the right of Jenkins, Wilcox on the left, & Pickett's, Pryor, & Featherston still to the left. One of A. P. Hill's (Branch's Brigade) was ordered as a support to Kemper & Jenkins. Kemper's (which used to be Genl. Longstreet's old brigade) charged & took a battery. The enemy then brought up reinforcements and Branch failing to support Kemper, the battery was retaken and many of the old brigade captured with it. Jenkins in the meantime had taken a battery and still kept forward. His advance at this time was the most desperate I ever knew. A few hundred yards to the left of the battery he took was one that Wilcox was trying to take. Just in Jenkins' front was a very large force of the enemy's infantry which he immediately engaged, when this battery on his left commenced on him with grape and canister. Thus he advanced in the face of a terrible musketry fire at the same time infiladed by artillery. Notwithstanding, he pushed on, charged the enemy and drove them from their position with terrible slaughter. He then brought up Branch's Brigade to hold the position. But as soon as they reached the place and saw how far in advance it was & the number of the enemy a half mile farther on, they turned & fled. Being left so far in advance unsupported, Jenkins fell back from the position & went to the assistance of Wilcox. The enemy did not return to the position he left. Wilcox during this time had been fighting desperately. He had taken a battery, but it had been retaken, but when Jenkins came in, they made another charge and held it. . . .

. . . The So. Carolina Brigade (Jenkins') lost more than half & the Ala. Brigade (Wilcox) lost at least one half. The 11th Ala. (Col. Syd Moore's Reg.) out of 10 officers commanding companies lost 8 killed & two wounded. The Palmetto Sharpshooters (Col. Jenkins' Regt.) out of 375 men, lost 44 killed & 210 wounded. His own escape was almost miraculous. His horse was shot twice. A hole was shot through his saddle blanket, his bridle reins cut in two near his hand. An India rubber overcoat tied on behind his saddle has 15 holes through it made by a musket ball & piece of shell. His sword was shot off at the point, & shot half in two near the hilt, & his sword knob was also shot off. Besides all this he was struck on the shoulder with a grape shot (which bruised it severely) and was also struck on the breast & leg with fragments of spent shell.

I met him just as he was coming out of the fight and he was weeping

These miniatures show three casualties of the Battle of Glendale from the Palmetto Sharpshooters of Jenkins' brigade: Captain William W. Humphries (left) and Lieutenant William Poe (right) were wounded but survived. Lieutenant Joel H. Gleason was killed. The Palmetto Sharpshooters were nearly annihilated on June 30, losing 69 percent of their men.

like a child at the destruction of his brave, noble men. He told me that at one time when he saw how fast they were falling around him, he stopped and prayed to God to send a bullet through his heart. He says, too, that at times as he would ride up and down the line, his men would turn and give him a look as much as to say, "We can go no further," when he would wave his hand to them and they would again dash forward.

LIEUTENANT LEVI G. MCCAULTY

7th Pennsylvania Reserves, Meade's Brigade

At Glendale Meade's troops were in the thick of the fighting, as bloody charges and countercharges swept over Randol's battery until the battered Pennsylvanians conceded the field to Brigadier General Cadmus M. Wilcox's hard-bitten Alabamians. From June 25 to July 2, Meade's command lost 1,400 troops, with McCaulty's 7th Pennsylvania Reserves contributing 294 men to this unenviable total.

The ball soon opened. General Meade, our brigade commander, rode up and told our Col., E. B. Harvey, "Look out for this battery on your left, as that is about where they will aim for!" and rode away. But in three or four minutes Meade galloped up again, and said "Col. there they come, I want you to defend these guns." Just about then the first discharge of cannon in our division thundered forth by Captain Randall, whose guns opened before the infantry could discern the foe. After a few discharges the Eleventh Alabama emerged from the bushes into the open, charging directly across Randall's muzzles, almost within speaking distance of the guns. Col. Harvey ordered u[s] to charge, and moving by the left oblique, we rushed down in front of our cannon almost against the Alabamians, who "about faced" and took cover in the brush. Those of us in front delivered a volly into their ranks. We were recalled. My company, because of its position in the charge, (the left front of the mass,) was last to fall back to original position.

Randall's gunners in their eagerness to cut down the Alabama boys, slewed their guns too much to the right before we were all out of line of their range, cutting Sergeant S. W. Lascomb almost in two. . . . Randall's shot naturally created some confusion in the company, but soon forming in line followed back to the original position.

The Confederates reformed their lines and advanced on our guns a second time, in heavier column. But having gained wisdom at the cost of life in the first charge, we did not advance in front of our cannon to meet them. They were repulsed with grape and canister from Randall, Cooper and Kern, and buck and ball from the infantry. Four charges were made on the position held by the Second brigade that day, all of which were repulsed with terrible slaughter, which occupied the greater part of the day. The powerful divisions of Hill and Longstreet were on our front, who outnumbered our division three to one. At one time they drove us in the rear of the battery, and almost captured it when the

Colonel Seneca Simmons (above) was killed while leading his Pennsylvania brigade at Glendale in an effort to save a Pennsylvania light artillery battery from Micah Jenkins' onslaught. Michael Miller of Simmons' 1st Pennsylvania Reserves wrote, "If there was one Ball Whistled past my devoted head that day there was thousands."

boys suddenly "about faced" as they realized the situation, and drove the enemy back.

. . . Lt. Col. Tapper, of the Fourth Regiment, rescued his own colors from the hand of a Confederate Sergeant. A group of three or four of his regiment, and as many of the enemy, were fighting for this standard. Tapper watching them and fearing the loss of his colors, rushed to the front with drawn sword, and cut the confederate down, carrying the flag back to his own line in safety. Corporal Long of company "F," was in rear of a second battery (not enough men left to operate it) when in one of the charges a Confederate laid his hand on the gun muzzle and said "This here gun is mine." Long slipped the muzzle of his musket up over the wheel by which he stood, shot the soldier dead, exclaiming, "Not just yet."

During one of the stormy scenes, when both sides were falling at every heart beat, a tall, able young man of the eleventh Alabama rushed upon me, with his bayonet at a charge, thinking to kill the d——d Yankee officer. But I parried his thrust with my sword, which in the encounter, was broken off about ten inches from the hilt, when Bennie Small, of my company, seeing the disadvantage I was at, promptly came up on my left, and bayoneted the Confederate, then clubbing his musket struck him across the forehead, killing him within three feet of where I stood. . . .

On receiving the shot in my elbow, with my pocket knife I ripped the clothing from my shoulder, and got one of the men to tie my handkerchief around my arm, just below the shoulder. Then, with a small stick, twisted the handkerchief, thus stopping the flow of blood, which by this time had run down my arm and over my hand. Turning, I saw General Meade who rode up and asked, "What's the matter?" I replied, "I am shot in the elbow," when he told me to go to the rear, which order I obeyed cheerfully, i.e. I was as cheerful as could be expected under the circumstances.

When the Rebel attack against Randol's battery threatened to rout his regiment, Captain James Taggart (above) of the 5th Pennsylvania Reserves assisted in calming the panic and forming a new battle line. Taggart's bravery helped to check the Confederate advance, but he was killed during the renewed fighting.

Colorbearer Charley McNeil of the 11th Alabama leaped atop one of Randol's guns waving this banner but was mortally wounded; Yankee troops captured the flag.

BRIGADIER GENERAL CADMUS M. WILCOX

BRIGADE COMMANDER, R. H. ANDERSON'S DIVISION

Wilcox commended his Alabamians for behaving with "remarkable coolness and gallantry" during the clash, which claimed 471 casualties from his brigade. His most bloodied regiment, the 11th Alabama, ended up with only 176 unhurt but exhausted survivors of 357 who had entered the fray three hours earlier.

The Eleventh Alabama had experienced severe loss in crossing the open field while advancing against this battery. Here the enemy, at first repulsed and driven from the battery, retire to the woods both on our left and in rear of the battery, and from there, under the shelter of the woods and with superior numbers, deliver a terrible and destructive fire upon this regiment. With its ranks sadly thinned it heroically stands its ground and returns the enemy's fire with telling effect. The latter, under cover of trees on our left flank and directly in our front, confident and bold from their superior strength, and seeing this regiment isolated and unsupported, now advance from their cover against it. Our men do not flee from their prize so bravely and dearly won overwhelmed by superior numbers, but, with a determination and courage unsurpassed, they stubbornly hold their ground, men and officers alike engaging in the most desperate personal conflicts with the enemy. The sword and bayonet are freely used. Capt. W. C. Y. Parker had two successive encounters with Federal officers, both of whom he felled with his sword, and beset by others of the enemy he was severely wounded, having received two bayonet wounds in the breast and one in his side and a musket wound breaking his left thigh. Lieutenant Michie had a hand-to-hand collision with an officer and having just dealt a severe blow upon his adversary he fell, cut over the head with a saber-bayonet from behind, and had afterward three bayonet wounds in the face and two in the breast, all severe wounds, which he survived, however, for three days. Many of the men received and gave in return bayonet wounds.

COLONEL ALEXANDER HAYS

63D PENNSYLVANIA INFANTRY, ROBINSON'S BRIGADE

Hays' troops, part of Kearny's division, were posted along the Charles City road in support of Captain James Thompson's Battery G, 2d U.S. Artillery. Despite double canister blasts, a Confederate attack by soldiers from Longstreet's division nearly overran the battery. The assault was stymied, said Hays, when his soldiers rushed at the enemy "yelling like incarnate fiends."

Very soon afterward General Kearny, as also Captain Thompson, announced danger to the battery. Again the order was given to charge, and again the regiment moved forward, passing the battery, and were halted 50 feet in front, the enemy retiring to the woods and houses beyond. The order was given to lie down and open spaces for the artillery. Within good range of . . . the continued fire of the artillery we hurled into the enemy a perfect storm of shot. The enemy, however, replied vigorously and presented an obstinate resistance. The contest was thus carried on for an hour, when Captain Thompson announced to me that his ammunition was exhausted and the necessity of withdrawing his battery. To cover his withdrawal, as the enemy had been made emboldened by heavy re-enforcements, I ordered again a charge. At once the men sprang to their feet, and with leveled bayonets dashed upon the enemy. The conflict was short, but most desperate, especially around the buildings. It was muzzle to muzzle, and the powder actually burned the faces of the opposing men as they contended through the paling fences. The enemy fled, and I withdrew my force back to the position occupied by the battery—one piece of which still remained upon the field. I was here informed that another force was relieving us, and retired to our original position at the fence. Night was coming on. We had been under fire for five hours, in action half the time, and our loss very heavy.

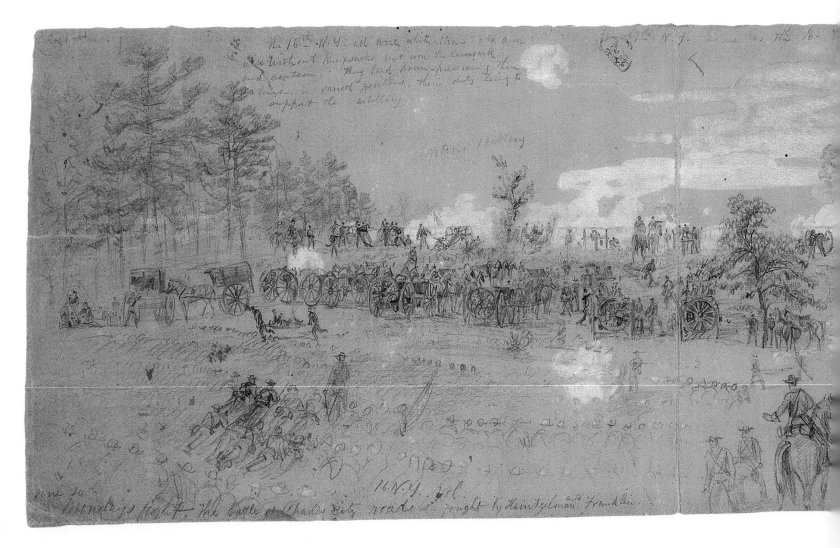

CAPTAIN BERNARD J. REID

63D PENNSYLVANIA INFANTRY, ROBINSON'S BRIGADE

After participating in his regiment's defense of Thompson's artillery, Reid resigned his commission for personal reasons on July 21 while at Harrison's Landing. He explained that he had wanted to leave the army after "Richmond should be taken; but that event being postponed, I am . . . constrained not to wait for it longer."

When the enemy first appeared and began its advance across the open space commanded by Captain Thompson's guns, the Sixty-third was faced about, marched a few paces to the rear, and ordered to lie low outside in the edge of the field. Here we then remained for half an hour, restive under shot and shell and whistling bullets, which we could not answer. We had nothing to do but watch with intense interest the effect of Captain Thompson's and Lieutenant Butler's splendid artillery practice in breaking the ranks of the advancing foe, and for a considerable time holding them in check. The enemy maddened, it seemed by the unexpected check, formed in new line with most likely new troops, and charged with a run and a yell as if determined to reach the battery and take it, cost what it might. Then "Up! up! boys! charge!" was the expected command of Colonel Hays, and away went the Sixty-third, with a counter yell and bristling bayonets, passing the field pieces, and bearing down with a rush on the enemy who, already staggered by the gaps made by the grape and canister at close range, fell back and sought safety in the woods. The Sixty-third then fell back and took a position close in front of the muzzles of

Alfred Waud drew this pencil sketch, published in the August 9, 1862, edition of Harper's Weekly, of Union field pieces shelling the attacking Confederates during what he termed the "Battle of Charles City Road" (Glendale). To the left, the straw-hatted 16th New York lies in reserve, "preserving their lines—in varied positions," as Waud put it. A lieutenant in the 2d Michigan of Kearny's division wrote that the Yankee artillery fire at Glendale seemed to make the attacking Rebel lines "sink into the ground." Said the awestruck Yankee, "I never saw such slaughter."

the field pieces, lying low so that the artillery could fire over us, and keeping up a relentless fire upon the rebels in the edge of the woods, and whenever they renewed the advance in the open fields, as they did repeatedly during the afternoon. During all this time they were subjected to a galling front and cover fire from the enemy's artillery and infantry posted in the woods on both fronts of the exposed position we were to hold. About 6 o'clock we were reinforced by a part of the Thirty-seventh New York sent by General Kearney to our assistance, but they deployed in the field behind us; the iron and lead hail they had to face was so fearful that their officers had difficulty in getting them up to our position in front of the guns.

Three times before darkness clouded the sun did the Sixty-third charge upon the advancing columns of the enemy and drive them back before the guns. All the time Captain Thompson and his gallant men were handling the pieces most beautifully, and the effect of grape, canister, shrapnel, and solid shot, as they alternated in the fight, was absolutely terrific, opening wide lanes in the advancing columns and piling the ground with heaps of dead and wounded. At sundown Captain Thompson informed Colonel Hays that his ammunition was about spent, and that if the enemy should make another charge he feared he might lose his guns. Just then a fresh line appeared from the opposite woods; it seemed as if they were ready with reserves, constantly brought forward to replace the shattered ranks of regiment after regiment that had attempted to take that battery and failed. "Give them another, Captain," said Colonel Hays, "and leave the rest to me." Captain Thompson withheld his fire until the enemy had advanced about half way and then, at very short range, opened on them with staggering effect, followed by the last charge of the Sixty-third. The two lines met at the negro house in the field. A portion of the rebel line gave way at first and fell back towards the woods, firing as they retreated, whilst the rest, under cover of the intervening house and garden, stood their ground for awhile until driven off in a hand-to-hand encounter. Meantime the exhausted battery was withdrawn and replaced by DeRussey's, and as it was growing dark, Meagher's Irish Brigade came up the road at the double quick, and the Sixty-third was relieved after one of the hardest fought five hours of the war.

LIEUTENANT E. BURD GRUBB

Staff, General George W. Taylor

Grubb, detailed as an aide de camp to brigade commander Taylor, recounted the moment when the brigade—consisting of the 1st, 2d, 3d, and 4th New Jersey regiments—plunged into the battle, eager to prove their mettle to General Kearny, a fellow Garden State resident. Grubb eventually became a colonel, and was brevetted a brigadier general at the close of the war. A wealthy iron manufacturer following the conflict, Grubb served as the U.S. minister to Spain from 1890 to 1892.

General Kearny was the idol and hero of our brigade from the time we first saw him. He and all his staff were well known to every man and officer of us; and when Captain Moore, of Kearny's staff, came riding down the road waving his hat and calling out that General Kearny had lost a battery, and wanted the Jersey Brigade to help him get it back, it seemed to me that the whole brigade heard him, because I am sure that no orders were given to do that which occurred, and I had barely time to scramble on my horse and join in the rushing throng. General Taylor called to me as I passed him: "Keep ahead of them and keep them from going too far. The enemy's line is in the woods right in front of our guns." Captain Moore, who was talking to him, had probably told him this. The guns that had been captured were not more than three hundred yards from us, a little advanced to the west of the road. I had noticed that they were not gone when I passed along on my ride to General Slocum's, but the melée was so confused that I have not and never had a very clear idea of it. When I got to where the guns were the road was somewhat sunken, and, as the bank was so steep that I could not ride my horse up, I jumped off and scrambled up. There were a good many men among the guns before I got there, and the guns were being re-captured. But I do know that when I passed near a gun, a sergeant of the First Regiment, whose name was either Hollins or Hollister, had a Rebel prisoner by the neck. The man, though captured, had not surrendered, and as I passed him in carrying out the order which I had, to stop the men from going beyond the guns, he thrust at our sergeant with his bayonet, missed him, and gave me a prod, the scar of which I carry to this day, though it did not disable me then or now, as it was on the inside of the thigh. I passed the order to halt to several of the officers of our brigade.

COLONEL FRANCIS C. BARLOW

61st New York Infantry, Caldwell's Brigade

After double-quicking from White Oak Swamp, Barlow's regiment helped stave off one last Rebel push at Kearny's frayed line. The aristocratic, Harvard-educated Barlow's tenacity earned him a promotion to brigadier general in September 1862. Wounded at Antietam and at Gettysburg, he returned to duty, rose to the rank of major general, and served through Appomattox.

My Regt. got separated from the rest of the Brigade in the confusion occasioned by some of our troops firing on each other and I put myself under the command of the First Brig. Gen. I came to—Genl. Robinson of Kearneys Division—our Troops had been firing upon the enemy from behind some fences and parapets but Genl Robinson stopped this fire and ordered us to charge over the parapet into the open field. We did this (my Regt. alone) at a charge bayonets and without firing. We went on a rush across the large open field. It was quite dark and very smokey so that we could not distinctly see the enemy on the open ground but they heard us coming and broke and ran leaving a flag on the ground with the inscriptions "Williamsburg" and "Seven Pines" thereon—which I captured and sent up to Genl Sumner. On arriving at the edge of the woods on the opposite side of the field the enemy shouted from the woods "What Regt. is that" to which my men answered "61st N.Y." The rebels then shouted "Throw down your arms or your are all dead men." I gave the order to fire and we poured in a volley . . . and a vigorous fire was kept up on both sides for a long time when I . . . succeeded in getting the 81st Penn. . . . to reinforce us. . . . After firing for a long time and losing many men we were withdrawn and subsequently ordered to Genl Kearney to occupy the parapets and hold them with the bayonet (our ammunition being expended). . . . About 12 midnight we were withdrawn and had a horrible march of several hours, the whole army retreating.

MAJOR ROY STONE

13TH PENNSYLVANIA RESERVES, REYNOLDS' BRIGADE

Darkness finally ended the bloodletting at Glendale, but the soldiers of both armies continued to blunder into one another. Stone managed to escape becoming a prisoner of the 47th Virginia in one such encounter in which his companion, Brigadier General George McCall, commander of the Pennsylvania Reserve Division, was captured. Stone later led the 149th Pennsylvania Bucktails.

At dusk I moved the whole battalion, which seemed to put itself under my command, forward in excellent line of battle toward the front, where the fight was raging in the dense woods. I should have been utterly at a loss as to where advantageously to place my command but for the superior judgment and accurate knowledge of the progress of the battle possessed by Mr. Lamborn, who had posted the other divisions of the fresh troops as they had come up, and knew from his own observation the position of every corps upon the field. Upon his advice I moved by flank up the Richmond road, and advancing steadily to the extreme front under sharp fire, halted to reconnoiter upon finding myself among the wreck of our own batteries where the action commenced. General McCall had come out of the woods wounded and alone, and taken his place at the head of the column.

After the halt the general took me forward a few paces with him, and suddenly in the darkness we found ourselves close upon the leveled muskets of a column of the enemy, which filled the road in front of us. We were ordered to "Halt; dismount"; but I turned and escaped only slightly hurt, though drawing two volleys from the enemy. General McCall was not so fortunate, and is in the enemy's hands. My men at the same time had captured the colonel of a rebel regiment with a small party who were scouting in our direction. I formed my first company across the road, and went to the rear in search of a cannon to sweep the road in front.

Sergeant James W. Staples (above) of Berdan's 1st U.S. Sharpshooters was among the 297 Union soldiers killed at Glendale while protecting the Federal route of retreat. The Rebels lost more than 630 dead in their failed bid to split and destroy the Army of the Potomac. Rebel artillery officer Major E. Porter Alexander later stated that "never, before or after, did the fates put such a prize within our reach."

Final Battle: Malvern Hill

On July 1 McClellan's infantry and artillery deployed on Malvern Hill, an open plateau about three miles south of Glendale. Reaching 100 feet at its crest, a mile and a quarter wide north and south, and three-quarters of a mile deep east and west, the plateau was flanked by creeks and ravines and separated from the James River by a strip of marshy ground. Malvern Hill was an ideal place to defend.

McClellan had arrayed his lines in a rough semicircle on the northern rim. The strongest concentration guarded the Federal left, which seemed the most likely avenue of attack. Here, at the base of the hill, Willis Church road emerged from belts of timber and swamp and climbed a gradual slope through cultivated fields.

At the top were three divisions of infantry and numerous batteries. Farther to the rear stood the bulk of the Artillery Reserve, nearly 100 guns lined up practically wheel to wheel, part of nearly 250 Yankee field pieces on Malvern Hill. The Federal gunboat flotilla, standing by on the James, added to the awesome array of firepower.

Some Confederates recognized the difficulty of assaulting Malvern Hill. "If General McClellan is there in force," said D. H. Hill, "we had better leave him alone." But Lee believed the Federals were exhausted and ripe for a licking.

By noon Lee had most of his men forming up in a mile-long crescent in the woods at the base of the plateau. W. H. C. Whiting, leading a division of Jackson's forces, was on the Confederate left with two brigades; D. H. Hill held the center astride the Willis Church road with five brigades; and two of Huger's brigades were on the right, where Magruder's six brigades were due to join them. In reserve were Ewell's division and Jackson's old division, now under Brigadier General Winder, on the left, and A. P. Hill and Longstreet on the right; Theophilus Holmes' small division was standing by, a few miles to the southwest.

On Longstreet's recommendation, Lee determined to establish 40 to 60 guns along a knoll west of the Willis Church road, and another 100 pieces east of the road in order to enfilade the Federal batteries and permit an infantry assault up Malvern Hill's front slope.

But Lee's orders for conducting the attack, drafted about 1:30 p.m. by his chief of staff, Colonel Robert H. Chilton, triggered a series of costly mistakes. The directive read: "Batteries have been established to rake the enemy's line. If it is broken, as is probable, Armistead, who can witness the effect of the fire, has been ordered to charge with a yell. Do the same."

Entrusting the start of a general assault to Brigadier General Lewis Armistead, a brigade commander in Huger's force, just because he happened to be in a good spot for observation was risky. Moreover, the batteries cited in Lee's order had not yet actually been deployed —nor had Lee figured out how they might be. His 80-gun artillery reserve was somewhere in the rear on the troop-clogged roads.

Division commanders tried to bring up their own batteries, but altogether they succeeded in deploying only about 20 pieces, and these were soon knocked out or forced to withdraw by Federal shellfire. By 3:00 p.m., Lee realized that he would not be able to get enough guns into place properly to support the assault. Then, around 4:00 p.m., an opportunity seemed to present itself and Lee pounced.

Whiting reported to Lee that the Federals in his sector were withdrawing, but the Yankees he had observed were merely shifting position. At the same time Magruder, who had just arrived on the Confederate right, notified Lee that Armistead had achieved a significant advance. But Magruder was also wrong. Armistead's brigade had only driven back some skirmishers and was now pinned down by Federal artillery.

The two reports were too much for Lee to resist. Determined not to let McClellan get away again, he ordered Magruder to advance immediately. But Magruder's own brigades had taken the wrong road to Malvern Hill and were not yet in position; so at 4:45 p.m. Magruder sent forward the troops at hand—two of Huger's brigades, under Mahone and Brigadier General Ambrose R. Wright, totaling about 2,500 men. Their line of attack would carry them for nearly half a mile through wheat field and meadow toward the bluff atop which Federal guns were clustered around the old Crew farmhouse.

When D. H. Hill, waiting near Willis Church road, heard the yells of the charging men he rushed his five brigades into the fray in accordance with Lee's original orders. From the edge of the woods where Hill launched his assault, it was about 800 yards to the Federal line. Marching over open ground against Federal cannon, Hill's men were cut to ribbons. The 3d Alabama lost more than half its strength, including six colorbearers.

By about 6:00 p.m. the survivors of Hill's brigades began falling back. On the right, the remnants of Huger's three brigades remained pinned down, still 75 yards from the Federal lines. To their right, Huger's last brigade, under Brigadier General Robert Ransom, fought to within 20 yards of the enemy before it, too, retreated. Meanwhile, Magruder had finally brought his own men into action, but they came up piecemeal and in confusion. Daylight was fading fast, hastened by clouds of sulfurous smoke.

Jackson began moving up his own troops and Ewell's to reinforce D. H. Hill, but it was too late. Whiting remained idle, and Lee did not call up Longstreet or A. P. Hill or Holmes. Toward 9:00 p.m. darkness fell and the sound of musketry died away, although Federal cannon boomed for another hour or so.

Confederate casualties in the failed attack had totaled 5,355—more than half of them victims of the accurate Federal artillery. The Army of the Potomac's casualties were 818 missing, 314 killed, and 1,875 wounded.

McClellan had again won a clear-cut defensive victory against Lee. But, as at Savage's Station, his reaction was to order a withdrawal, this time to Harrison's Landing. He was still closer to Richmond than to the tip of the Peninsula, whence he had begun his campaign, but the direction of his army's recent movement was not promising.

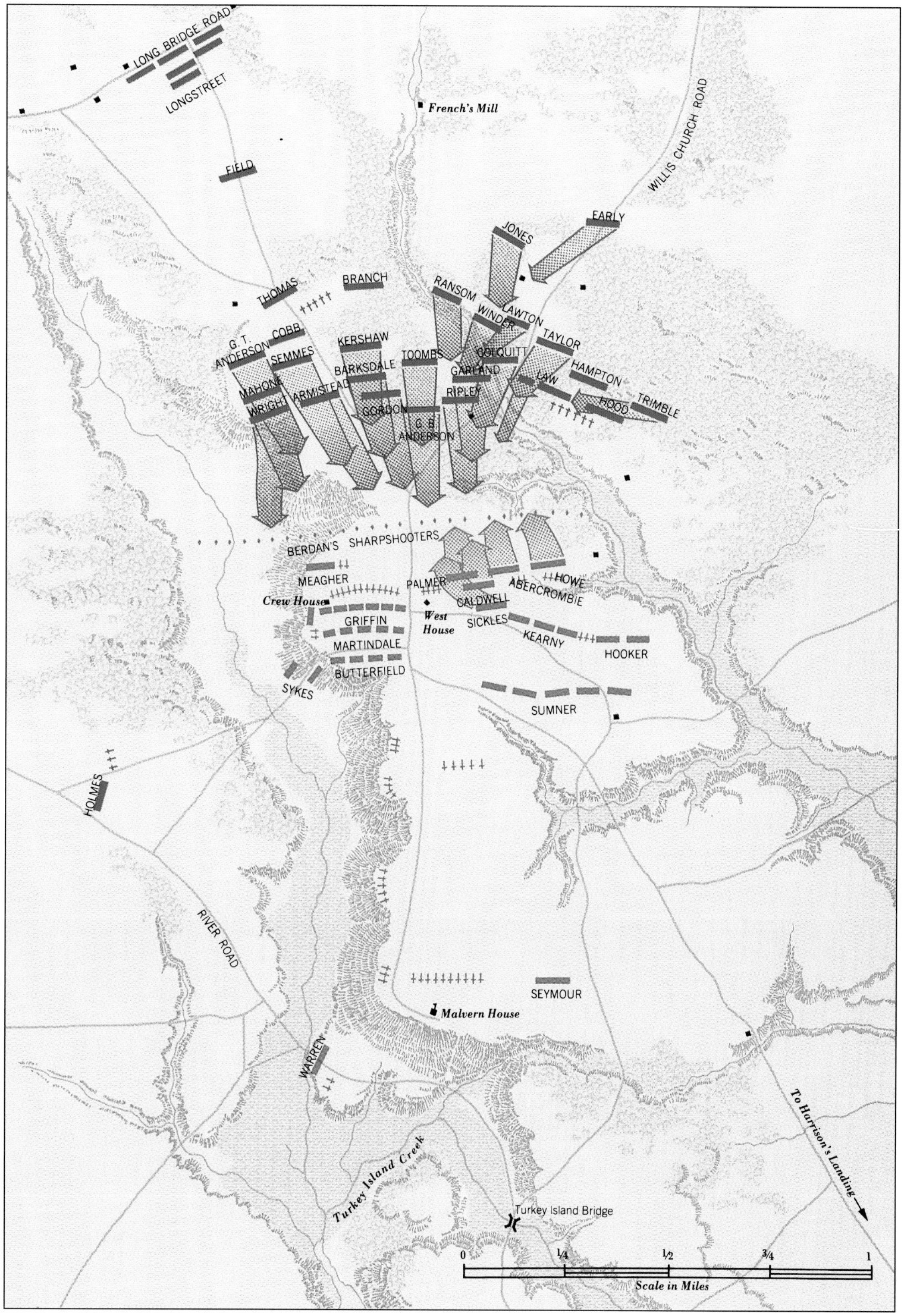

On July 1 McClellan's army turned to face Lee's pursuing Confederates, deploying infantry and 250 guns along the northern rim of Malvern Hill, a 100-foot rise near the James River. The overwhelming might of the Federal batteries easily suppressed the Confederate artillery. Late in the day, Lee sent five of his divisions against the Federal lines, where they were mowed down by massed Federal artillery and infantry fire. Despite dealing the Confederates a bloody repulse, McClellan ordered his army to evacuate Malvern Hill and retreat to Harrison's Landing.

SERGEANT JOHN G. ADAMS

19TH MASSACHUSETTS INFANTRY, DANA'S BRIGADE

Several hours after nightfall the fighting at Glendale finally ceased. Rebels stared nervously eastward across darkened, gore-stained fields, watching for any renewal of fighting from the Union side. Meanwhile, tired Yankee troops were pulling out of their defensive lines and stumbling southward on the next leg of their retreat. Upon reaching safety, Adams said, the men of the 19th Massachusetts fell asleep in "a sea of mud . . . without shelter, overcoats or blankets."

We held our position until midnight. It was the saddest night I ever spent. The dead and wounded of both armies lay between the lines. The wounded were constantly calling on their comrades for water, and we could hear calls for Mississippi, Georgia and Virginia, mingled with those for Michigan, New York and Massachusetts. Brave men from our regiment crawled over the field, giving water to friend and foe alike. About midnight the order was whispered down the line to move. I had been from right to left of the company keeping the men awake, as we expected the order. As still as possible we crawled over the field. We had gone but a short distance when, looking back, I saw one member of the company had not started. Thinking he had fallen asleep I returned, and shaking him said, "Come, come!" As I drew close to him my eyes rested on the face of Jonathan Hudson, cold in death. He had been killed in the early evening as we lay in line and his death was not known to his comrades near him. It was the saddest sensation I ever experienced. When we arrived at the road we found many of our wounded. Colonel Hincks was on a stretcher, and as the ambulances were full he was carried a long distance before one could be found. Captain Devereaux was also badly wounded and had to be carried. We started with the body of Major How in a blanket as we had no stretchers, but being so very heavy we were forced to leave him.

Without any regimental formation we began our weary march to Malvern Hill.

PRIVATE WILLIAM J. WRAY

23D PENNSYLVANIA INFANTRY, ABERCROMBIE'S BRIGADE

According to Wray, the cheers McClellan received at Malvern Hill showed that the army's morale and spirits remained high despite the events of the previous week. In further defense of Little Mac, Wray wrote, "The Seven Days' fight, as a retreat, was a masterly one, ending gloriously at Malvern Hill." At Fredericksburg a gunshot wound cost Wray the sight of his right eye. After more than seven months of painful convalescence, he joined the Veteran Reserve Corps in July 1863.

On the night of June 29, 1862, the regiment which I had the honor to carry a musket in . . . was on picket in White Oak Swamp. That night the countersign was "Austerlitz," and I think it was the toughest one we had to wrestle with during the war, as the three of us on the picket-post where we were stationed could only come as near to it as "Oystershitz." Notwithstanding it was a very important picket, it took all the will power we had to keep awake, as we were pretty well played out for want of rest.

Sometime after midnight we pulled out, and after a weary march through the tangled swamp and woods, came out about daylight of June 30 on a broad highway below Malvern Hill, bivouacking in the woods. It was my luck to be detailed on guard, which consisted of a sentry on the colors and each flank of the musket-stacks, to keep the stragglers and wounded who sought the shade along the edge of the woods from the thick dust of the road, along which was pouring prisoners, broken-down artillery, and other debris of the fight of the day before, from disturbing our boys while they took a short nap.

When all our division got in, we pushed up the long slopes of Malvern, and Gen. McClellan and staff passed along the road leading to the James, and such was the enthusiasm of the boys at that time for "Little Mac" that everybody's cap was in the air, mingled with their loudest cheers. It was a very hot, sultry day, and we all recall that climb up the Hill.

"As I stood here just a little after sunrise and looked for the first time upon our whole or very nearly our whole army I could hardly conceive *any* power that could overwhelm us."

CAPTAIN EDWARD A. ACTON

5TH NEW JERSEY INFANTRY, CARR'S BRIGADE

Despite being a pacifist Quaker, Acton had not hesitated to join the army shortly after Fort Sumter. Wounded in early May, he had just returned to duty when the Seven Days' campaign began. Arriving at Malvern Hill on July 1, he marveled at the breathtaking sight of the mighty Union army. Two months later he was killed at Second Manassas.

Soon after sunrise we marched into a large field, or rather a series of fields—the fences had all been destroyed giveing the appearance of a vast field to our camping ground. I think there must have been at least 500 or 600 acres of rolling ground entirely clear of fenceing and with very little timber. This tract was bounded in a circular manner in front by woods and in the rear by the river. In the center of it was a hill that commanded the whole and as I stood here just a little after sunrise and looked for the first time upon our whole or very nearly our whole army I could hardly conceive *any* power that could overwhelm us. It was a great and grand sight, the like of which in all probability I shall never see again. Lines of Battle were formed almost as far as the eye could reach. Troops were in almost every conceivable position—in Square—in Column at full distance—in Column at half distance—in Column closed in mass—in Echelon. Some moveing rapidly to their designated places, others with arms stacked resting on the ground. Some kindling fires and makeing coffee, others hastily slinging knapsacks and falling into line. Yonder is a squadron of Cavalry in line, *there* is another column, and here-away galloping like mad for that belt of woods is still another; now they are out of sight: they are sent out no doubt a[s] scouts. In looking over the field I see many of these squadrons. But yonder come Rushes Lancers, the tips of their long lances flashing in the sunlight and the red streamers flaunting sauceily from lance staffs as they move in stately regularity toward "Headquarters" near the River.

COMMANDER JOHN RODGERS

U.S.S. GALENA

The heavy guns of Rodgers' James River flotilla helped McClellan's concentrated forces decimate the attacking Rebels at Malvern Hill, but in this anxious dispatch Rodgers exceeds in pessimism even McClellan's own appraisals of the army's situation. In 1829 Rodgers began a career in the U.S. Navy that spanned 53 years. He achieved the rank of rear admiral in 1870 and died while on active duty in 1882.

The army is in a bad way; the gunboats may save them, but the points to be guarded are too many for the force at my disposal. I presume you will have to send some one to outrank me. To save the army, as far as we can, demands immediately all our disposable force. Fort Powhatan is a most important point; it should be strongly guarded. City Point commands the channel past it; that demands a strong force of gunboats to insure the passage of supplies. Each end of the encampment on the river banks demands a force of gunboats. We shelled the enemy with good effect, I hear, yesterday. . . .

The general (General McClellan) has come down here in this vessel to make a reconnoissance for the position of a new camp.

The use for more gunboats is pressing and immediate.

The army, continually pressed by largely superior numbers and fresh troops, falls back continually, in good order. The fighting has been continual; the losses very great. . . .

If, as I hope, we can get the army on a plain upon the river bank, and then protect each flank by gunboats, it can have time for rest.

The U.S.S. Galena (left), Commander John Rodgers' flagship, was built to one of the first three armored ship designs recommended by the navy's Ironclad Board. Initially passed over in favor of the Monitor, the Galena was built in February 1862. Carrying four 9-inch Dahlgren guns and two 200-pounder rifles, the Galena was battered—despite four inches of protective armor plate—on May 15, 1862, while engaging Rebel shore batteries at Drewry's Bluff on the James River. Her hull was pierced 13 times, but Rodgers withdrew her before she suffered irreversible damage. Besides service in the Peninsula campaign and the Seven Days' Battles, the Galena also saw action at Mobile Bay, Alabama. Outdated by the 1870s, she was broken up for scrap at the Norfolk Naval Yard.

SERGEANT FREDERICK E. GARNETT

74TH NEW YORK INFANTRY, SICKLES' BRIGADE

Weary after the Seven Days' Battles, the soldiers of the 74th—a unit of Brigadier General Daniel Sickles' Excelsior Brigade—still found the energy to chase a group of elusive pigs. Garnett was wounded at Malvern Hill, Second Manassas, and Gettysburg. In December 1863 he became a lieutenant of the 74th's Company H.

On reaching Malvern Hill our whole division halted in a compact mass and stacked arms, and there we remained until the enemy discovered us and opened on us with artillery, when we sought more comfortable quarters. Our brigade went at double-quick to the right and coming to a hollow descended into it and were hid from view. After we had been there some time a herd of swine was discovered roaming in the fields around us and as we were hungry, and at that period of the war we were generally hungry when not in camp, the sight of the pigs made quite an excitement. At last General Sickles was appealed to to give his consent to let us kill them. He acquiesced, stipulating, however, that not a shot was to be fired—the bayonet alone was to be used. Off we scampered pell-mell after the pigs, perhaps I ought to say the shoats, for that is the name they are known by in that locality.

It was a lively race, for like all the pigs in that section of the country they belonged to the long-legged breed. The men were yelling and the pigs squealing. Which made the most noise it would not be easy to determine. To the north of the field was a forest and some of the pigs were making tracks in that direction. On nearing the pigs those who were in pursuit of the pigs saw to their surprise that they were occupied by the enemy in force. They made no sign of their discovery, but wheeling gradually around went at once to General Sickles and reported what they had seen. The general at once handed his field glasses to one of the men and told him to climb a tree near by and report what he saw. Presently the pig chase was brought to a close, for the Confederates brought two pieces of artillery to the edge of the woods and began shelling us.

PRIVATE WILLIAM H. OSBORNE

29th Massachusetts Infantry, Meagher's Brigade

Situated on the right of the Union reserve line at Malvern Hill, Osborne's regiment—the newest contingent of the famous Irish Brigade—also enjoyed a repast of fresh meat on July 1. This time cattle, not pigs, were slaughtered. During the battle the 29th remained in the rear, enduring Rebel shellfire until it moved forward around 6:00 p.m. to help turn back one of the last Confederate assaults.

A large herd of cattle was feeding upon the meadows; the soldiers being without rations, a detail was made from each brigade, soon after noon, to slaughter a sufficient number of these animals to supply the troops; and when this was done, the meat—scarcely cold—was served out by regiments. When the turn of the Twenty-ninth came to have a "bite," it was late in the afternoon. The slaughtered animals lay upon the grass, and the men by scores swarmed around them, each soldier helping himself to a piece of such size and quality as his fancy dictated.

The meat having been cut, was placed upon the end of a sharp-pointed stick and thrust into the fire to broil. In the process of cooking, being very fresh, it swelled greatly, so that more than one soldier was astonished to find his small ration of meat suddenly grown to a ball of the size of his head. As the men stood about the fire gnawing their beef like so many half-famished dogs, the bugle sounded "fall in!" With his meat in one hand and his gun in the other, each soldier took his place in the ranks. It was amusing to look down the line and observe the disappointment marked upon the countenances of the men at being torn away from their rude but much-relished repast. Fault-finding and severe scolding—soldiers' privileges—were freely indulged in; while some of the witty ones and wags gave the incident a laughable turn by sticking their half-cooked pieces of meat upon the points of their bayonets, declaring their intention of carrying their rations with them.

PRIVATE EDWARD A. MOORE

Rockbridge (Virginia) Artillery, Winder's Brigade

Arrayed east of the Willis Church road, Moore's battery endured a storm of Yankee iron as it tried to support the Confederate infantry advance up Malvern Hill. The battery suffered 12 casualties, and Moore wrote bitterly that he hoped his enemies would take ill from "the poisonous vapors of the bogs" surrounding Harrison's Landing.

Taking the road to the left, we soon emerged from the woods into a wheat-field, the grain standing in shocks. While seated on a caisson, driving down this road at a trot, I was suddenly seized with a presentiment that I was to be killed in this battle, the only time such a feeling came over me during the war. Finding myself becoming rapidly demoralized, I felt that, in order to avoid disgrace, I must get down from that seat and shake the wretched thing off. So down I jumped and took it afoot, alongside of the gun, as we passed down a little ravine which was being raked from end to end by the enemy's shells. The diversion worked like a charm, for in two minutes the apprehension toned down to the normal proportions of "stage fright." We were soon in position with our six guns ablaze. The enemy's batteries were posted on considerably higher ground, with three times as many guns and of heavier caliber than ours, which served us the same galling fire that had wrecked the batteries preceding us. After having been engaged for an hour, a battery posted some two hundred yards to our left was stampeded and came by us under whip and spur, announcing, as they passed, that they were flanked by Federal cavalry. In the commotion, some one in our battery called out that we had orders to withdraw, and, before it could be corrected, eight or ten of the company, joining in the rout, beat a retreat to the woods, for which they were afterward punished; some being assigned as drivers, and one or two gallant fellows having it ever afterward to dim their glory. We soon, how-

"The concern as to one's own person affords sufficient entertainment, without being kept in suspense as to who went down when a shell explodes in proximity to another member of the family."

ever, recovered from the confusion, but with diminished numbers. I know that for a part of the time I filled the positions of 7, 5, and 2 at my gun, until a gallant little lieutenant named Day, of some general's staff, relieved me of part of the work. My brother John, working at the gun next to mine, received a painful shell-wound in the side and had to leave the field. His place was supplied by Doran, an Irishman, and in a few minutes Doran's arm was shattered by a shell, causing him to cry out most lustily. My brother David, shortly after this, was disabled by a blow on his arm, and, at my solicitation, left the field.

I would suggest to any young man when enlisting to select a company in which he has no near kindred. The concern as to one's own person affords sufficient entertainment, without being kept in suspense as to who went down when a shell explodes in proximity to another member of the family.

John Fuller, driver at the piece next on my right, was crouched down on his knees, with his head leaning forward, holding his horses. Seeing a large shell descending directly toward him, I called to him to look out! When he raised his head, this shell was within five feet of him and

In this sketch of the July 1 battle, the Union gunboats Galena (left) and Mahaska stand at anchor near the mouth of Turkey Run, adding their weight to the Federal artillery tempest by lobbing the huge shells the Rebel troops called "lampposts" into the gray ranks on Malvern Hill. In the center of the sketch, the guns of Colonel Henry Hunt's artillery reserve sit aligned in a field, awaiting orders to enter the battle. The smoke rising over the crest of the hill at left center is issuing from the dozens of Yankee cannon parked out of sight on the north slope, which were bombarding the massed Rebel ranks struggling to break through the Union line.

grazed his back before entering the ground close behind him. He was severely shocked, and for some days unfit for duty. At the first battle of Fredericksburg, more than a year after this, while holding his horses and kneeling in the same posture, a shell descending in like manner struck him square on his head and passed down through the length of his body. A month after the battle I saw all that was left of his cap—the morocco vizor—lying on the ground where he was killed.

Behind us, scattered over the wheat-field, were a number of loose artillery horses from the batteries that had been knocked out. Taking advantage of the opportunity to get a meal, one of these stood eating quietly at a shock of wheat, when another horse came galloping toward him from the woods. When within about thirty yards of the animal feeding, a shell burst between the two. The approaching horse instantly wheeled, and was flying for the woods when another shell burst a few feet in front of him, turning him again to the field as before; the old warrior ate away at his shock, perfectly unconcerned.

Private Andrew Jackson Ruth (above), a gunner in the Rowan (North Carolina) Artillery, fell wounded at Malvern Hill when a Union shell fragment hit him just above the left eye. The incident occurred in the action described at right. Ruth recovered in time to fight at Second Manassas and serve through the end of the war.

LIEUTENANT JOHN A. RAMSAY

ROWAN (NORTH CAROLINA) ARTILLERY, WHITING'S DIVISION

Ramsay, writing in the third person, describes the events that led to his battery's being ordered forward by Stonewall Jackson unsupported. In 15 minutes of action the North Carolinians discharged 121 rounds before retiring with a loss of 12 wounded—three of whom later died.

In front of Malvern Hill General Whiting ordered Captain Reilly and Lieutenant Ramsay to make a thorough reconnoissance of Malvern Hill and report to him. They had an excellent field glass, and rode over the field at a distance of about one thousand yards from the enemy's batteries. They reported that the enemy had thirty guns, in good position, on ground higher than the opposite side of the valley, and that six of the guns were, in their opinion, twenty-pound Parrotts, and all of the others were either rifles or Napoleons. General Whiting said: "From the examination made, what plan of attack would you suggest?" Captain Reilly replied: "Our guns, excepting those we captured from the enemy, are inferior to theirs; many of our batteries have only four guns, while all of theirs have six, and I suggest that we place eight in position at the same time. The distance is about one thousand yards, and smoothbore guns are effective at that distance; the only trouble is that the range is not accurate." General Whiting designated the eight batteries that were to be sent forward, and sent his couriers to bring them up at once. The batteries were nearly ready to advance, when General Jackson rode up and asked why this delay. General Whiting explained the plan of attack. General Jackson replied that one battery was sufficient, and ordered Captain Reilly to advance at once, take a good position and commence the action. The battery took the best position it could get, and opened fire on the enemy. The fire of the enemy's five batteries was concentrated on our one, and was terrific. The battery had been in action for fifteen or twenty minutes, when General Whiting rode into the battery, and seeing the situation, said: "Reilly, take your men out of this."

"From what I saw of Gen. Jackson, he is a very ordinary looking man of medium size, his uniform badly soiled as though it had seen hard service."

PRIVATE WILLIAM H. ANDREWS

1st Regiment Georgia Regulars, G. T. Anderson's Brigade

Although Stonewall Jackson had been on the Peninsula since the beginning of the Seven Days' campaign, he was still a stranger to many soldiers. At Malvern Hill Andrews and other soldiers could not keep up when their brigade was ordered on what Colonel George T. Anderson called an exasperating series of "marches and countermarches . . . over swamps, dense undergrowth, ravines, and hills."

While we were halted an officer was seen riding some 200 yards in front of us and going to our left. Such cheering I had never heard. The soldiers went wild as they tossed their caps in the air. The officer doffed his cap, spurred his horse, and was quickly out of sight. On asking who it was, I was told that it was Gen. T. J. Jackson, the hero of the valley. . . .

From what I saw of Gen. Jackson, he is a very ordinary looking man of medium size, his uniform badly soiled as though it had seen hard service. He wore a cap pulled down nearly to his nose and was riding a poor rawboned horse that did not look much like a charger, unless it would be on hay or clover. He certainly made a poor figure on a horseback, with his stirrup leather six inches too short putting his knees nearly level with his horse's back, and his heels turned out with his toes sticking behind his horse's foreshoulder. A sorry description of our most famous general, but a correct one.

Our line was then ordered by the right flank. Being subject to spells of rheumatism in my left knee and being almost past traveling that morning, I got permission to fall out of ranks and follow after the command doing the best I could. The command marched in the direction of the James River, and after going about two miles, halted, about-faced, and marched back over the same ground. I then asked Dr. Mayo for a pass, but he declined to give it to me but told me to hobble along and do the best I could. When the command turned back, I was no longer able to keep up, and was left behind. I will now tell what befell myself and follow the brigade later.

I struggled along, I suppose, for about one and a half miles to where the roads forked, one going to Malvern Hill. There was a farm house at the fork of the road that was afterwards used as a field hospital.

On reaching that point I decided to stop, as I had just about given out. I dropped down by the roadside where I remained some little time, it being then in the afternoon. Pretty soon the enemy's guns from Malvern Hill commenced shelling the woods. The first shells not reaching the road, but every one seemed to come nearer and nearer.

About the time I had decided to change my position, Sgt. L. B. Wheeler of Company B come staggering along the road with his head bound up, having been badly shocked by a shell. He proposed that we go down a steep bottom just back of the house, where we would be less exposed to the enemy's batteries. So we made for the bottom, he assisting me all he could, but the farther we went the farther the shells flew. When we got into the bottom, the shells got thicker if anything, so we decided to climb the hill. On getting to the top of that, the shells come faster than ever. In a field just beyond was several batteries of artillery feeding their horses. Pretty soon the shells reached them, and such a stampede as they had of it dashing to the rear.

About that time, Wheeler and myself was getting pretty badly scared as we could not outrun the shelling. We decided to move to our left and get out of range. I saw numbers of men running to the rear completely demoralized, and apparently scared half to death. Several regiments were marching in, and made efforts to stop the fleeing stragglers and carry them back, but nothing short of a bullet could stop them.

CAPTAIN G. CAMPBELL BROWN

STAFF, MAJOR GENERAL RICHARD S. EWELL

Confederate troops in the rear remained vulnerable to Union artillery fire. Brown watched as Private Willy Field of the 44th Virginia, an Orange County resident, was killed by the shock of a shell that struck the ground directly under his reclining form, although it neither touched him nor exploded.

As the troops moved forward into position, along the same narrow road, the shells came crashing thro' the pines, their noise & terror greatly exaggerated by the falling limbs—the sound of large guns on the boats was rendered additionally deep & solemn by the closeness & heat of the day—all the litter-bearers with wounded, the frightened stragglers & the broken caissons or ambulances met them in their advance—that by the time they were in position in reserve, they had been exposed to all the discouraging influences usually encountered by troops brought forward in the crisis of an action. As they lay for hours in reserve they were exposed to a cannonade the violence of which rendered rest impossible—and every now & then one of their number was stricken down. About 1 p.m. Gen'l Early, Col. J. A. Walker & his volunteer A.D.C., Willy Field, son of Judge Field and as fine & brave as possible, were lying together on the grass eating dinner, when a shell after passing through the body of a soldier struck just under Field's side (he was leaning on his left elbow with his back towards the enemy) and without actually touching him raised him a few inches from the ground. It stopped, fortunately without bursting, under Walker's very backbone. At first he thought Field was unhurt, but on examination found him dead—tho' his skin was unbroken & not even his clothing torn. The concussion had killed him.

PRIVATE ROBERT A. STILES

RICHMOND (VIRGINIA) HOWITZERS, GRIFFITH'S BRIGADE

The Confederate defeat at Malvern Hill, wrote Stiles in his postwar memoir "Four Years Under Marse Robert," had a "stunning and temporarily depressing effect" on Lee's men. Stiles expressed his "wonder . . . that any survived who were working . . . [his battery's] three pieces" on July 1. During the battle Stiles passed out from a combination of exhaustion and fear. Snapping out of this "semi-stupor," he staggered to the rear, joining the crowds of Rebel soldiers fleeing the slaughter.

Three of the guns of the old battery were put in action against McClellan's majestic aggregation of batteries, by way of at least making a diversion in favor of our assaulting infantry, a diversion which I presume we to some extent accomplished; for I never conceived anything approximating the shower and storm of projectiles and the overwhelming cataclysm of destruction which were at once turned upon our pitiful little popguns. In the short time they existed as effective pieces they were several times fired by fragments of Federal shell striking them after the lanyard was stretched and before it was pulled; and in almost less time than it takes to tell it the carriages were completely crushed, smashed, and splintered and the guns themselves so injured and defaced that we were compelled to send them to Richmond, after the battle, to be remoulded.

We were put in action, too, after a long, hot run. I was as sound and strong as human flesh could well be, and yet my lungs seemed to be pumped out, my brain reeled and my tongue clave to the roof of my mouth, which was burnt so dry that I experienced great difficulty in swallowing. Nevertheless, I managed to do my part in serving my gun, until, in a few moments, it was completely disabled, when I fell to the earth, a horror of great darkness came upon me, and the only distinct impression I can recall is that I felt I would be glad to compromise on annihilation.

PRIVATE JOHN S. SLATER

13th New York Infantry, Martindale's Brigade

Though outgunned, the Rebel army's artillery gamely shelled the Union lines throughout the engagement, in one instance precipitating a funny and inspiring incident involving one of Slater's comrades, a wisecracking fellow named Connolly. Slater, too, was known in his regiment for his flip attitude. His service record states that he was reduced from corporal to private in November 1861 for "the use of highly indecent and impertinent language to his superior officer."

A Confederate battery succeeded in getting into a position which enabled it to take the whole length of the Thirteenth New York Volunteers as the men lay in line. In the regiment was one man—Connolly, of "B" Company—an odd sort of genius, with a dash of the "Green Isle" in his nature, who, though a capital soldier, was inclined to be just a trifle too indulgent to himself in one respect: he never would bear a burden, not even a weapon, when he could find any way to get rid of it. A short time previous, while on the march, he had succeeded in getting his Remington rifle rendered unserviceable by carelessly fastening it to a wagon, from which it fell under the wheels, and the value of it was charged to him upon the payrolls. Just prior to the battle he received his new weapon. When the artillery opened he was lying flat upon the ground, his gun underneath him, the muzzle projecting a foot or so beyond his head, which was slightly elevated, "taking observations." The shells came in thick and fast for a few moments and most of the "boys" hugged their mother earth pretty closely; but not so Connolly. He still kept on the lookout, cracking jokes as missile after missile flew by without doing any harm. Presently a shell struck a slight elevation in front of the writer, ricochetted, struck again with a dull, heavy thud, and then glancing over the heads of the men on the left, exploded. When the shell struck for the second time, Connolly got up. In fact, he was obliged to do so, for the 12-pounder struck the muzzle of his rifle, ploughed a furrow underneath him the whole length of his body and gave him a most decided lift in life. As he afterward said, "he felt as if he had swallowed a barrel of powder and a friction primer." Of course, the concussion knocked the breath out of him, tore his clothing, bruised and lacerated his person, at the same time reducing his Remington to a complete wreck. Every one expected to see him fall dead, but for several moments he danced about, first upon one foot then upon the other, meantime rubbing his stomach and gasping like a drowning person. "Lie down! Lie down, you d—d fool, you!" (the situation demanded strong language) was shouted from every side, but Connolly paid no heed. Presently he stooped over, keeping his stomach well in hand, picked up his dismantled weapon, which looked like Rip Van Winkle's after the twenty years slumber, and, continuing to caress his astonished front, hobbled up to his commanding officer and drawled out: "I say, Cap, will I have to pay for this d—d old gun?" The effect was irresistible, and high above the boom of cannon and hissing and screaming of shot and shell, went up "three cheers for Connolly" from half a thousand throats. In response to the inquiry he was ordered to the rear to repair damages, and reluctantly obeyed: but it was many a weary day before he fully recovered from what he called his "attempt to ride a 12-pound shell bare-back."

COLONEL EDWARD C. EDMONDS

38th Virginia Infantry, Armistead's Brigade

An 1858 graduate of VMI, Edmonds was serving as the principal of the Danville Military Academy when the war began. At Malvern Hill his Virginians hugged the ground below the Crew house for three hours, incurring 96 casualties, including Lieutenant Colonel Powhatan B. Whittle, who lost an arm during the fight. Edmonds was killed at Gettysburg during Pickett's charge; his body was never recovered.

The skirmishers soon engaged the enemy, each holding his position, no orders as yet having been given to advance. During the skirmish, General Armistead and myself reconnoitered the position of the enemy from a good stand-point, and with the assistance of a strong glass readily detected his presence in force and the advantages of his position.

Major-Generals Magruder and Longstreet came up in turn and observed the enemy from the several points to which I conducted them, and left perfectly satisfied, as I supposed, of the impossibility of charging them from the position which our advance (Armistead's brigade) held, unless supported by a large amount of artillery, as Major-General Magruder remarked it would require thirty pieces of the heaviest caliber. This I supposed had been determined upon, as the colonels commanding the regiments were immediately ordered to pull down the fencing in their front, preparatory to advancing our skirmishers, supported by the regimental reserves, so as to force back the enemy's skirmishers, with a view of bringing up our artillery. So soon as the fencing was removed the order was given to drive in the enemy, which was being done in the most successful manner, when I received an order, or rather General Armistead, with hat off and arm uplifted, ordered us to charge; where and upon what I was at a loss to imagine. It could not have been to support our skirmishers; they needed none, for they were driving the enemy's pickets before them. It could only then have been the main position of the enemy upon which we were to charge. The charge was made most gallantly by my regiment and a portion of the Fourteenth and Fifty-third Virginia Regiments, under the lead of their respective colonels, up the hill, across the extensive plateau, and through the valley, until we arrived at the hill nearest the position of the enemy. We were here supported by a Georgia regiment, which, having charged under mistaken orders, soon returned to their original position with General Wright's brigade. Thus it was that my regiment, with a part of the Fourteenth Virginia, under the command of a captain, [and] a part of the Fifty-third, Colonel Tomlin, held this advanced position for three hours awaiting orders. Receiving none, I sent Major Cabell to General Armistead asking orders, who returned with instructions that we must hold our position, and that re-enforcements would soon be at hand. I am proud to say we did hold our position through all the storm of bullets, canister, grape, [and] shell, with occasional shells from the huge pieces playing upon us from the gunboats, until we saw the gallant Wright, with hat off and glittering blade, leading his brigade across the hill to our support.

His brigade subjected to a terrible fusillade at Malvern Hill, Confederate brigadier general Lewis Armistead (left) begged in vain for more artillery support for his beleaguered men. "What I wanted never arrived," he wrote, "that is, more guns and heavier ones"—a lament that reflected the overall experience of Lee's troops during this last of the Seven Days' Battles. Armistead was mortally wounded in Pickett's charge at Gettysburg.

BRIGADIER GENERAL JOHN H. MARTINDALE

Brigade Commander, Morell's Division

Martindale's Maine, Michigan, and New York regiments had been bivouacked atop the western edge of Malvern Hill since June 30. After a breakfast of coffee, sugar, and hardtack on the morning of July 1, the infantrymen relaxed and napped until noon, when their position was swept from the northeast by eight Rebel batteries of Stonewall Jackson's command parked along the Willis Church road. An officer in the 2d Maine recalled that the "roar of the artillery at this time was tremendous."

The battle was now an affair of artillery, and none of Porter's corps had yet engaged the infantry. Couch, however, was pressed severely on the right, but held his ground. I had encountered artillery before, but now it opened as I had never yet seen it. It was obvious that the whole Army of the Potomac was resting there for safety on the steadiness of the portion of it which was then confronting the enemy. I went along the line of my regiments and told them my dispositions for battle, and reminded them that a retreat would be annihilation. It would be better to face the enemy to the last than to retire—that there was no Washington to fall back upon, as at Bull Run; no Chickahominy to cross, as at Gaines' Mill. We must be victorious or perish. That statement of the case was true, and the men knew it and appreciated it.

During the progress of the cannonading my men were held inactive. I saw repeatedly the wounded rise from their places and retire to the shelter of a bank to our left and rear (which place was selected for a hospital), and those that could not go without aid borne by comrades, who deposited them with the surgeon, and promptly and quietly returned to their places. In this position a number of men were killed and were borne away in like manner, and the places thus made vacant were immediately closed again. Without contrasting the quiet, steady, resolute courage of my brigade with any other engaged that day, I am sure that no other furnished finer exhibitions of fortitude and heroism than my men displayed. At length the enemy ceased their cannonading. There was a calm, but the storm burst again speedily.

PRIVATE JOHN S. SLATER

13TH NEW YORK INFANTRY, MARTINDALE'S BRIGADE

Before the opening of the battle, Slater lay enraptured by the lush agricultural scene spread before him, which reminded him of his own farm in Portage, New York. Thundering field pieces and the seemingly endless ranks of gray-coated foes pouring from the woodlots to the north shattered his bucolic reverie. Another Union soldier said the advancing Rebels reminded him of "pictures of great battles in Europe."

I . . . shall never forget the panorama which lay spread out before me. Between my brigade and the timber from whence the foe were expected stretched a field of wheat ready for the harvest. Some of it had already been cut. I gazed out over the sea of waving grain rippling beneath the touch of each passing breeze up to the very breast of the high forest wall, whose dark green foliage formed a fitting background to the picture and was entranced. The sky, so high above me and so blue, was flecked with light, fleecy, silvery-white clouds, which cast soft shadows upon the scene below, and the hum of insect life impelled to drowsiness and called up cherished visions of home—of the old farm house, the meadow, the orchard—where I used to while away the hot, sultry "nooning" time—the fertile fields, the silent woods, filling my heart with tender thoughts and longing for the dear ones far away.

At 6 o'clock the profound stillness was rudely broken—the magic wand of memory was snapped in twain. The combined strength of the opposing artillery opened a furious fire upon the Fifth (Porter's) Corps and Couch's Division, under cover of which the Confederates, debouching from the timber, advanced to carry the heights. They came massed in solid column—"end on," as we used to term it—and it seemed as if the whole armed strength of the rebellion had lain behind that narrow belt of green only awaiting the signal to advance. I have seen some grand sights—some glorious and sublime spectacles in my day, and I have experienced some thrilling moments; but never have I beheld anything to compare in sublimity and grandeur with the scene upon which my eyes rested as column after column marched into view. Never have I felt the thrill that stirred my pulses as the serried ranks of gray entered the waving grain—marched into the golden sea.

472
HARPER'S WEEKLY.
473
BATTLE OF MALVERN HILL, VIRGINIA, JULY 1, 1862.—THE REBELS REPULSED BY THE UNION ARTILLERY.—[See Page 471.]

Although this drawing of Malvern Hill from the July 26, 1862, edition of Harper's Weekly mistakenly shows the Union gunboats (top right) to be in visual contact with the battlefield, it otherwise accurately depicts the gentle, open slope that made up the north side of the hill—a perfect killing ground for the rapidly firing Yankee artillery positioned near the summit. David Winn, a soldier in the 4th Georgia of Brigadier General Ambrose Wright's brigade, remembered that during his regiment's advance on the Federal lines "shell after shell, illuminating the whole atmosphere, burst over our heads, under our feet, and in our faces. . . . It is astonishing that every man did not fall."

MAJOR GENERAL JOHN B. MAGRUDER

DIVISION COMMANDER, ARMY OF NORTHERN VIRGINIA

On July 1 Magruder was suffering from indigestion, which his physicians were treating with mind-clouding morphine, and he had slept for only two of the previous 72 hours. Nonetheless, he was ordered to spearhead the attack at Malvern Hill, a harrowing assignment further complicated by Major General Benjamin Huger's lack of cooperation. Huger was relieved of field command shortly after the campaign.

I proceeded to address a few words to Mahone's brigade and ordered it forward. Returning rapidly to the center, I directed General Armistead to advance with the remainder of his brigade. Being informed by him that his best troops were already in front, those on hand being raw, I directed the three regiments of Cobb's brigade, then on the spot, instead of Armistead's force, to advance in line and attack the enemy in front, and they moved forward accordingly without delay.

At this moment I sent an order to General Ransom, on my left, to advance, and I proceeded in person to Colonel Barksdale's brigade, of my own division, superintended its formation, and directed him to advance to the support of the troops which had already preceded him on the right. Here the fire of the enemy's grape, shrapnel, and round-shot was terrific, stripping the limbs from trees and plowing up the ground under our feet.

This gallant brigade, not quailing for an instant, advanced, steadily into the fight. On my return to the position I had selected, and to which I directed my staff officers to report, I learned by note from General Ransom that neither he nor General Huger knew where the battery was, and that all orders coming to him must come through General Huger.

I sent several staff officers successively, urging him to advance to the front and attack on the left and in support of those who by this time were hotly engaged; but this gallant officer felt himself constrained to obey his instructions and withheld the desired support. He nevertheless afterward sent me one regiment, which was ordered into action on the left of those already engaged.

PRIVATE WILLIAM C. KENT

1ST U.S. SHARPSHOOTERS, MORELL'S DIVISION

Kent, seated next to his brother Evarts, was one of the marksmen posted in the wheat fields that fronted the Union position. Armed with accurate Sharp's breech-loading rifles, these crack shots opened with telling effect on the Rebel columns as they marched from the cover of a nearby woods in the early afternoon.

We sat down in the cornfield and a glaring sun which was insupportable. The time then passed till noon, or nearly noon when the gun boats which were hitherto silent opened up and did the thing up *brown.* A dozen shells used up the battery and all was silent. Our line was near enough for us to hear the word of command from the rebels, as they drew off and for an hour all was still. I took off my haversack and made a respectable dinner of sugar and garlic, all the while keeping a lookout for rebels. None came and I took a long quiet smoke. The men were too anxious to see the rebels to talk much. While smoking I could hear every now and then a rebel order from the woods in front and the rumble of artillery. A report being made to that effect, the batteries began to get the range of the woods by apparently careless shots here and there but which were of great use when we were finally attacked. I had just put up my haversack and pipe and girded up my loins when two or three shots from the left where they were on higher ground, brought every man to attention. I fired once before I well knew what I was about, when I saw a line of grey coats rush out of the woods towards us. I guess I didn't miss though, for it was only 400 yards, and clear as ever it could be. Apparently a large brigade of 3 or 4 thousand men had come out. I wish I could give some idea of the crash occasioned by the simultaneous discharge of 50 of our guns, beside those of the enemy's; but I can't. In a minute of time, the air was full of missiles of some sort of other. Our line did well, though only a few against a brigade. We stood up, and fired just as fast as we could and with good effect.

In this sketch by Allen C. Redwood, men of Colonel Hiram Berdan's 1st U.S Sharpshooters fire at enemy soldiers from behind stands of harvested wheat. As the Rebels reached canister range, the sharpshooters withdrew to the Union lines.

SERGEANT GEORGE S. BERNARD

12th Virginia Infantry, Mahone's Brigade

During a slight lull in the fighting on his front, Bernard watched as artillery devastated a Confederate unit, offering a foretaste of the fate of his own. "The poor fellows reeled and fell, it seemed, by the dozens. . . . The line, broken, was forced back to seek shelter under the brow of the hill." A teacher before the war, Bernard was wounded and captured at South Mountain in September 1862. Exchanged, he rejoined the army, serving until wounded again at Hatcher's Run in 1865.

In a few moments we are in motion, forming a line of battle with our faces in the direction of the Federal artillery, whose fire seems now to increase. Between us and the enemy intervenes the body of woods referred to, and we saw nothing of them as we move forward. A hundred or two yards of forward movement brought us into these woods, a body of large chestnuts and oaks. Through the tops of these tall trees, far above our heads, the shot and shell of the Federal artillery howl and crash, putting us in constant danger of injury from falling fragments of huge limbs of trees. But on we went until we reached a ravine or gully, along the bottom of which ran a small branch. Here we halted. In the ravine was a brigade of troops, all sitting with their backs to the wall of the gully next to the enemy, seemingly secure from danger, ensconced, as they were, in what appeared to be comparatively a bomb-proof, and looking far more comfortable than we felt under an order to charge a battery and on our way to execute this order. The occasion of our temporary halt just here was an examination of the route by which it would be best to go forward. In the dilemma one of the couriers attached to our regiment suggested to our colonel that we might go through a little gate in sight a short distance to our right. The courier's suggestion was taken

"My heart leaped with joy. The enemy are flying! Their artillery and infantry are routed! We are victors without firing a gun! But I was terribly mistaken."

and we moved to our right and filed through this gate.

We were now very close to the enemy. At the foot of the hill upon the table ground McClellan's army await our assault, so close that we feel the vibrations of the earth at each discharge of the Federal guns. Not three hundred yards intervened between us and these guns, the slope of the hill, however, perfectly protecting us, we being now opposite to the extreme left of the Federal line of battle. To our right in a beautiful field, the meadow mentioned by General Wright, with its yellow shocks of recently harvested wheat, are stationed the Federal sharpshooters against whom we have been warned. Posted behind the shocks of wheat, they see us, but we cannot see them while they pick off our men as they come up to take position in line of battle. . . .

As I marched along to this position I looked over towards the woods on Turkey creek skirting this meadow. The prospect was beautiful; everything in that direction was so tranquil that clear summer afternoon, in striking contrast with the harsh notes of war. The crisis was now at hand. General Mahone, seizing the colors of one of our regiments, commanded us to move forward. We rush up the slope of the hill towards the enemy, yelling at the top of our voices. Just near the brow of the hill I caught a glimpse of four artillery horses hitched to a gun, or to a caisson, dashing away at full speed. My heart leaped with joy. The enemy are flying! Their artillery and infantry are routed! We are victors without firing a gun! But I was terribly mistaken. I saw only those four horses in flight. No men, no other horses drawing pieces of artillery, no infantry, are flying. It was imagination, the wish being father to the thought, which, magnifying for the instant what was actually seen, had drawn the picture of the whole force of the enemy in full retreat.

Our line of battle was allowed to get well upon the hill when the enemy's infantry, stationed not more than one hundred and fifty or two hundred yards in front of us and their artillery in the rear of the infantry, suddenly opened upon us with terrific fury. Our men were driven back with terrible loss, but only to gain the protection of the brow of the hill, there to rally and to return to the charge.

Three Rebel "pards" (above) who would later be at Malvern Hill pose in Richmond in 1862. At left is Private Henry Simmons of the 1st Louisiana Infantry, wounded at Malvern Hill and at Chancellorsville. In the center stands Private John C. Kelly of the 1st Virginia Infantry. Both Simmons and Kelly ended the war as prisoners. At the right is another Louisianan, Charles Hurley, who also survived the conflict.

PRIVATE JOHN S. SLATER

13TH NEW YORK INFANTRY, MARTINDALE'S BRIGADE

Slater watched with apprehension, then amazement, as the closely aligned Rebel columns advanced in formation toward the Union positions, enjoying a few moments of calm before the Federal artillery barrage slashed into their ranks. Some 50 Union cannon—including a battery of 32-pounder siege guns—decimated the exposed Rebel lines. Slater adopted an almost biblical tone in describing the scene.

Out of the shadowy wood, into the golden sea on, on they came, until the long slanting bars of yellow sunlight glinted upon the weapons borne in brawny hands. On and yet onward beneath the fiery arches their covering guns were building with shot and shell above their heads. On and on, grim and silent as destiny itself, they pressed until they had traversed nearly half the distance between the forest and ourselves. Their artillery grew dumb, but the gray wall kept moving on. "Will it never stop?" We began to ask ourselves: "Must we be overwhelmed?" "Why are our cannon silent?" A little further, fifty yards, perhaps, and then over our heads hurtled and hissed and screamed the iron grape and deadly canister from nearly an hundred guns, through the frightened air rushed monster shells. Our ears were assailed by a roar as if the artillery of the whole earth, and heavens too, had been let off in unison. The ground shook as if with fear. Great wreathes of smoke, from out of which shot tongues of flame, curled upward, building lofty pyramids in ethereal space. The golden sea was ploughed into wide furrows, the bosom of the earth was gashed and scarred, the advancing wall of gray was rent and torn assunder. Men and banners, and forests of gleaming steel went down beneath the surface of the golden sea to rise no more. Those who continued to breast the fearful blast dashed bravely onward. The gaps were closed again and again, only to be reopened by each succeeding gust that swept above the heads of us who watched and waited. Behind us the cannoneers were handling

Union brigades stacked three deep stand in the foreground of this William Waud depiction, while to the right a hub-to-hub array of guns unleashes its deadly hail upon the distant ranks of the Army of Northern Virginia as they charge up Malvern Hill's northern face. Even against such formidable odds some Confederate troops threatened the Yankee line: The Rebel infantry sheltering in the closest stand of trees, for example, are engaging the first line of Union riflemen. The fruitless charge of Thomas Ware's 15th Georgia, however, was far more typical. Ware wrote in his journal, "We commenced ascending a hill in front of the enemy, where we suffered awful. . . . Men could be seen falling in every direction, the grape and bombs bursting just above our heads, taking off a great many heads & cutting some half into."

their pieces as if they were toys, not huge engines of suffering and death. The very guns themselves seemed endowed with life. We could feel the fiery breath as it came in short, sharp gasps from their blackened muzzles. We could hear them groan as they recoiled from each discharge. They shook and trembled, and yet came bravely to the front, time after time. Ammunition boxes were emptied and went rumbling to the rear for a fresh supply, but others took their places and the fearful work went on.

In a ceremony in 1861 Colonel Dwight Woodbury accepted this national flag for his 4th Michigan Infantry from the ladies of Adrian, Michigan, vowing he would never surrender it while alive. At Malvern Hill, as the 4th helped repel General Ambrose Wright's Rebels, Woodbury was killed and the flag shredded by gunfire.

SERGEANT DANIEL G. MACNAMARA

9th Massachusetts Infantry, Griffin's Brigade

Macnamara's regiment lost 24 men killed and wounded at Malvern Hill. Most of these casualties occurred when the regiment mounted a counterattack to save the imperiled guns of Captain John Edwards' two 3d U.S. Artillery batteries. Edwards gratefully acknowledged the 9th's help in his report, writing that the Massachusetts' men "rose up, gave a cheer, and advanced bravely," checking the oncoming Rebels.

The artillery fire was of short duration; as it ceased long lines of gray colored infantry came forth from the woods with a quick, long, swinging stride onto the open plain. Brigade followed brigade and regiment followed regiment into line of battle as they deployed along our front three-quarters of a mile away. As they manœuvred in their thousands they were watched with intense interest by thousands of eyes from our infantry, lying on the ground, and from our batteries of artillery, every gun of which was loaded with double-shotted canister, grape and shrapnel, and every battery man eager at his post. General Griffin rode up to his brigade, on his spirited bay horse, and, in his clear shrill tones, called on his regimental commanders to "get ready to charge." He likewise warned each brigade commander to be ready. Again, in a short time, he dashed on to the line of the Ninth and cried out "Colonel Cass! Get ready to charge! They are coming!"

Major Hanley, who was now acting lieutenant-colonel in command of the right wing of the regiment, saw General Griffin coming, and was on his feet in an instant ready to assume command, thinking, perhaps that Colonel Cass would be unable to go forward in the charge.

. . . Colonel Cass on hearing General Griffin's orders, which the latter supplemented by shouting, "Up Ninth and at them!" cried out at once, "Attention, battalion!" whereupon every man of the Ninth sprang from the ground like magic, eager for the fray.

In the meanwhile the enemy's long line of gray had steadily advanced up the slope. So far they had not fired a shot. Their guns were trailed and their long swinging march had increased to a rapid stride. No doubt they expected to be very soon among the guns of our artillery, which so far had waited for orders. The enemy's line was within a hundred and fifty yards of our guns. The heavy tramp of their feet could be heard. The order was then given to our batteries, "Fire!" The lanyards were pulled, and from the muzzles of fifty pieces of artillery death and dire destruction were spread amongst the lines of the gallant foe. Great gaps were instantly seen in the still advancing lines of gray. But they were as quickly closed without seeming to check their advance. Again and again our guns poured their death-dealing missiles into the foe as the brave fellows pressed forward with the hope of reaching and capturing our batteries, little heeding that their trail was marked by hundreds of their dead and wounded comrades. The artillery fire was then held back, and the orders rung out along our lines "Charge bayonets!" With a rush like the wind the Ninth went forward, joined by the 4th Michigan on the left and the 62d Pennsylvania on the right. With a defiant Irish cheer that broke into a prolonged yell, loud enough to almost raise the dead from the field, our blue line of glittering steel went over the ground with relentless impetuosity for sixty yards or more, to meet and drive back the now steadily advancing lines of the determined foe.

The solid line of blue, holding with a firm grip their rifles, with their glittering bayonets at a charge, go forward yelling like demons. The onset is terrible and resistless. The enemy's line hesitates, wavers, breaks, turns and flies. Along the Union line the cry rung out, "Back to your guns! Quick! Back to your guns!" The line of blue rushed back. The artillery was unmasked. Its deadly fire was then poured forth in flame and smoke into the backs of the wildly retreating foe. Our infantry joined in the slaughter with buck and ball and rifle shot "at will" until the enemy sought shelter in the ravines and woods and behind the natural protection of the elevated ground around them. In the meantime the brigades of D. H. Hill furiously assaulted the lines of Couch on our right and were driven back with great slaughter.

With a perfect recklessness that is wholly regardless of consequences the enemy's line is reformed and reinforced with fresh troops, and the charge is renewed. With a steady and rapid stride the long line of determined men push surely and swiftly up the slope. Soon they are falling thick and fast from our galling infantry fire and the heavy shells that burst along their front. Double-shotted canister cut great swaths in their ranks as they approach; still they do not hesitate or seem to waver in their forward movement, or notice the terrible slaughter in their midst; on the other hand, they draw together each moment and shoulder to shoulder increase the rapidity of their steps, hoping to reach and capture our guns, and force back our lines of infantry in confusion. But they are doomed to disappointment. Another wild rush and cheer, with furious yells, and our solid lines of blue are upon them driving them back in wild disorder and capturing many prisoners. "Back to your guns!" is the cry, and as soon as our batteries are unmasked the demoralized lines of the enemy are raked with canister, shell and rifle shot. Again and again Magruder and D. H. Hill charge their brave and resolute lines against the resistless fire of our splendid guns without avail. Our reserves are pushed forward to the front line and relieve our tired and war-worn men, who retire only to replenish their ammunition boxes and reform for another charge.

The enemy try desperately to pierce our lines. In vain they press forward in their thousands against Morell's front only to be repulsed with great slaughter. Fresh lines rush forward against Couch's and Kearney's front where they meet only death and disaster.

MAJOR GENERAL JOHN B. MAGRUDER

Division Commander, Army of Northern Virginia

Magruder wrote a dramatic report of Malvern Hill that emphasized grandeur and élan while ignoring the sacrifice of his overmatched troops. Disliked by many of his peers in Lee's army, Magruder was transferred to the District of Texas in November 1862, remaining in the Trans-Mississippi region for the rest of the war.

The fire of musketry and artillery now raged with terrific fury. The battle-field was enveloped in smoke, relieved only by flashes from the lines of the contending troops. Round shot and grape crashed through the woods, and shells of enormous size, which reached far beyond the headquarters of our gallant commander-in-chief, burst amid the artillery parked in the rear. Belgian missives and Minie balls lent their aid to this scene of surpassing grandeur and sublimity. Amid all our gallant troops in front pressed on to victory, now cheered by the rapid fire of friends on their left, as they had been encouraged in their advance by the gallant brigades on the right, commanded by Generals Wright and Mahone. Nevertheless the enemy, from his strong position and great numbers, resisted stoutly the onset of our heroic bands, and bringing into action his heavy reserves, some of our men were compelled to fall back. They were easily rallied, however, and led again with fury to the attack. The noble, accomplished, and gallant Harrison, commander of the Charles City Troop, uniting his exertions with my own, rallied regiment after regiment, and, leading one of them to the front, fell, pierced with seven wounds, near the enemy's batteries.

Captain Benjamin Harrison (left) led the Charles City Troop, a cavalry contingent from the Peninsula hamlet of the same name. Harrison's men, well acquainted with the region, performed a great deal of scouting and picket duty during the Peninsula and Seven Days' campaigns. Harrison voluntarily entered the fight at Malvern Hill, helping to lead several infantry assaults before he was killed.

"With faces wet with perspiration and begrimed with the smoke, in the light of the sudden flash from the guns they looked as much like devils as men."

SERGEANT J. J. MCDANIEL

7th South Carolina Infantry, Kershaw's Brigade

At 6:00 p.m. Brigadier General Joseph Kershaw was commanded to lead his brigade, including McDaniel's regiment, in an effort to turn the Union right flank. Given no information regarding the enemy's dispositions, Kershaw disgustedly complied with the order, marching his men into what he termed a "crushing shower of grape and canister." Believing, he said, a "further advance would lead to the destruction of my command," Kershaw ordered his men into a swale until night fell.

Our Brigade advanced through the thicket on the left of a large field, passing over two other Brigades as we advanced. One of the Brigades was retreating in disorder. Gen. Kershaw ordered ours to lie down, and let them pass out over us. But we jeered them so, that they lay down in front of us, when we rose up and passed over them. Some of their officers were making desperate efforts to rally them. We pressed forward to the edge of the woods, and there found one Brigade lying in a road which had formed a kind of a breastwork by wearing away the earth about 18 inches. With this alone to shield us, we lay down just in rear of that Brigade, ordered not to fire as we had other lines in front. This proved a mistake, as this was our advanced line in this part of the field. We lay here for some time exposed to the most fearful and destructive fire. The enemy's infantry were not over 100 yards, though rather obscured from view by weeds and briers. A perfect tempest of minie balls, grape shot and shells were rained upon us. Every tree round where we lay still testifies to the severity of the fire, from the great number of scars, from the ground to the height of 30 feet. At this crisis Gen. Kershaw was about to order a charge on the vast masses of the enemy, but having received orders when we were sent in to *support* other Brigades in advance, he declined advancing further. But to lay there would be too destructive, therefore we were ordered to fall back to a ravine. It was now growing late, and soon darkness closed in upon the dreadful scene.

SERGEANT FREDERICK E. GARNETT

74th New York Infantry, Sickles' Brigade

Moving from a reserve position onto the battlefield at 5:00 p.m., the 74th initially took shelter in a ravine. At that point Staten Island native Garnett was ordered to reconnoiter the front of his regiment, a mission in which he became one of the 54 casualties his regiment incurred during the Seven Days' campaign. After Garnett's wounding, the 74th moved to support Brigadier General Darius Couch's division of the IV Corps and remained deployed until the early-morning hours of July 2.

It was getting dark as we passed through the lines formed by our artillery. It was a magnificent sight to see that crescent of fire. How the brave fellows worked at their guns. With jackets off and shirt sleeves rolled up, with faces wet with perspiration and begrimed with the smoke, in the light of the sudden flash from the guns they looked as much like devils as men. The artillery kept up an almost constant booming, while from still further to the left came reports which seemed to make the earth rock, and following the reports came the sound of falling trees and crashing timbers. Our gunboats on the James were helping us with their enormous guns. Meanwhile we had continued to advance and were at last drawn up in line in front of our batteries.

Our Colonel, Charles K. Graham, not knowing where he was nor what was expected of him, dispatched a messenger to find General Sickles and get orders from him. The messenger not returning in a reasonable time, another one was sent. The Colonel, at this time, was in rear of our company, which was the right flank company of the regiment, and turning to me ordered me to go forward and ascertain if any of our own troops were in front of us. By this time it was just light enough for me to see that there were woods a few hundred yards in front of the open ground where we were standing; not that I could see the trees, but a heavy black mass rose up there which I knew must be woods. I could neither see nor hear indications that other troops of either army were in front of us. Forward I went with my rifle at a

SOUTHERN ILLUSTRATED NEWS

VOL. II. RICHMOND, SATURDAY, DECEMBER 12, 1863. No. 23.

"MALVERN HILL."

Above we present a picture of Malvern Hill *proper.* The battle-field of Malvern Hill extended over an area of ground about three-quarters of a mile. In the trees, on the hill presented above, was massed the batteries which were so destructive to our troops. The house, shown on the left of the picture, was used as the headquarters of McClellan. The battle of Malvern Hill was fought on the 1st day of July, 1862, and it was here that the Federal army under McClellan was defeated and utterly routed after seven days' hard fighting. Confederate loss 1,350 killed and 4,421 wounded. Federal loss 1,585 killed, [illegible],800 wounded and 6,000 taken prisoners

An engraving of Malvern Hill from an 1863 edition of Richmond's Southern Illustrated News shows no trace of the bloodbath of July 1, 1862. The Malvern house, Fitz-John Porter's headquarters, is at the upper left, incorrectly labeled as the "headquarters of McClellan." Little Mac spent much of the battle on board the Galena and at Harrison's Landing, not appearing on the battlefield until about 3:30 p.m.

"ready," with eye and ear on the alert, and when I had gone about fifty yards from the regiment there was the sudden flash of a rifle before me, and the next moment I was whirled around and fell to the ground. I had been hit in the side. I suppose the flash of our artillery behind me had revealed me to the enemy. The right general guide of our regiment, who was a particular friend of mine, heard the bullet strike me and at once came forward and assisted me to rise.

BRIGADIER GENERAL JOHN H. MARTINDALE

Brigade Commander, Morell's Division

Shortly after the battle finally ended, the roads behind the Union lines leading to Harrison's Landing—10 or so miles away—became clogged with a nearly impenetrable tangle of troops, artillery pieces, and supply wagons. The situation worsened on July 2, when a heavy, hours-long downpour set in early in the day, turning the roads into oozing bogs of mud. "We camped in mud & slept in mud. The enemy did not press," wrote a dispirited, fatigued Michigan officer.

At this time a considerable body of wounded men and stragglers were retiring from the lines. General Porter directed me to form a line to prevent straggling and collect the wounded. I proceeded to execute his orders, and took the Twenty-fifth New York and stretched it across the field for that purpose. The enemy had been driven back at all points. I was directed by General Porter to send out pickets to the front, and did so. My brigade, except the Twenty-fifth New York, bivouacked in line of battle on the advanced ground which had been won on the left, and which was part of the identical ground to which I had advanced the night before. The light of the fires, reflected on the clouds over the woods, and the report of the pickets disclosed that the enemy was using the night to retire out of reach of our cannon toward Richmond.

At about 10 o'clock, while preparing to bivouac, I learned that we must make a forced march that night 11 miles down the James River to Harrison's Bar. At a later hour the order was given me by General Morell in person to get in motion. My brigade, according to the order, was to lead, and I called in my pickets and moved my command back a mile to the summit of Malvern Hill. Descending, it was necessary to go through the long, dark passage which I have before described. General Morell met me there. The artillery was moving down the defile.

He told me to follow the artillery and left me, saying he would rejoin me there. I rested with the head of my column close to the moving artillery. Soon troops came on and attempted to pass the head of my column. I halted them. They pressed through to the other side of the artillery and moved on. I moved the head of my column down about 100 yards to a bend in the road to see if I could not stop the movement, and halted again.

But the tide on the other side rolled on. We were left in the rear, and the order of march was no longer maintained. I sent back an orderly for General Morell, but no tidings of him were brought to me. The head of my column still maintained its ground. In the darkness I discovered General Butterfield's assistant adjutant-general passing by me. I halted him. He informed me that Generals Butterfield and Porter had just passed. Thereupon I gave the order to the Second Maine, then in advance, to move forward. We advanced, groping through the darkness. At length we emerged from the long defile and came opposite to the ground where we had encamped the previous day. There I found General Morell. The troops were retiring in great disorder. It was fortunate for us that we had whipped the rebels so soundly a few hours before.

After the war Colonel Warren Moseley of the 8th Georgia was relating a story of the horrors of Malvern Hill to another Rebel veteran named R. W. Jemison. Moseley told of how a Union shell had crashed into a nearby Louisiana regiment, leaving a "Man standing headless, with bayonet drawn as in the charge, his blood spurting high in the air from the jugular vein." The shocked Jemison responded that the decapitated corpse had been his brother, Private Edwin Francis Jemison (left).

CAPTAIN G. CAMPBELL BROWN

Staff, Major General Richard S. Ewell

Brown tried, with considerable pessimism, to corral stragglers after the awful slaughter. Malvern Hill had cost the Confederates 5,650 casualties, as opposed to the enemy's 3,007—a bitter ending to the otherwise successful Seven Days' campaign. The bloodied Army of Northern Virginia needed rest, refitting, and revamping of its command structure before it would be ready for another major engagement.

About nightfall the crowd of stragglers from the front grew quite dense. Col. Jno. M. Jones, Maj. Nelson, Turner & I were now together without orders. Jones having just returned from Gen'l Ewell & reporting no need of anyone there—and with nothing special to do. So having communicated with Bradley Johnson, who approved of the idea & agreed to use his reg't. where it stood to stop all stragglers on that side of the road, we organized an impromptu provost-guard to stop stragglers & turn them back. Two only of our couriers out of eight detailed were with us—the rest having slipped off to the rear. These two were Sgt. Barrett & Sgt. or Corp'l Wright of Loudoun Co. Sometimes on foot, but mostly on horseback, we formed a little cordon across the road & started many men back for the front. How far they went, whether they sneaked round us in the dark or lay down behind trees or logs or (improbable) returned to their reg'ts., we had no means of telling. Most were from D. H. Hill's Divn & must have been lying some hours in the woods, as his troops had left our front early in the evening. One poor fellow, nearly scared to death, felt a great oppression on his chest when stopped & assured me he could hardly breathe, so badly had he been "stung with a bung"—shaken or contused by a shell. This excuse of "shocked by a bomb" became familiar to me that evening. One man had had a shell to burst "right in his face"—a cunning Irishman walked lame &c, &c. Amid all the noise I happened, being unoccupied at the instant, to hear Col. Jones about six feet from me in a sharp altercation with a straggler trying to pass him—all at once Col. J. fired on him at not more than six feet off & the man disappeared in a rapid trot towards Malvern Hill, as if bent on taking it single-handed. I called to Jones, "Great heavens Colonel, weren't you afraid of hitting him." "Oh no, I aimed a foot over his head—but it wouldn't have mattered much if I had killed him."

McClellan's Campaign Peters Out

Throughout the morning of July 2, the retreating Army of the Potomac slogged east along the River road toward Harrison's Landing, eight miles east of Malvern Hill on the north bank of the James. About 10:00 a.m. a hard rain began to fall.

The cohesion and discipline that had held McClellan's army together during the stress and strain of the past seven days seemed to dissolve in the downpour. Some men threw away their rifles; others dropped out of the line of march. Of the 818 Federal soldiers listed as missing at Malvern Hill practically all of them were lost not during the actual battle, but during the retreat. The number would have been even higher had not a provost guard, riding at the rear of the army, corralled 1,200 stragglers.

Many of McClellan's officers condemned his order to abandon Malvern Hill. "The idea of stealing away in the night from such a position, after such a victory, was simply galling," wrote Captain William Biddle of McClellan's own staff. A seething General Philip Kearny was even more blunt, charging that "such an order can only be prompted by cowardice or treason."

Longstreet and A. P. Hill mounted a half-hearted pursuit, but after struggling through the mud for about two miles they gave up. The next day the rain stopped, and the Confederates tried again. Finding River road an impassable quagmire, they took a roundabout route that approached Harrison's Landing from the north. But when Lee reconnoitered the Federal defenses he concluded that McClellan's encampment was unassailable.

The Seven Days' Battles were over. And, for now at least, Richmond was safe. President Davis issued an official proclamation of thanksgiving, and the Richmond press lionized Lee. But Lee was less than satisfied, for he believed, and stated in his official report, that he should have been able to destroy McClellan's army.

The sense of relief that pervaded the South was tempered by grief at the enormous cost of the campaign. Overall, Lee had lost 20,204 men, all but 952—those missing or captured—having been killed or wounded. The losses among Confederate officers were especially high: killed or wounded were 10 brigade com-

War-weary Lieutenants Abel Wright (left) and John Ford of the 3d Pennsylvania Cavalry were photographed by Alexander Gardner at Harrison's Landing. By the first week of July fewer than three-fifths of McClellan's troops remained fit for duty.

manders and 66 regimental commanders.

The Federal toll was 15,855, including the unusually large number of 6,055 missing and presumed captured. McClellan had saved most of his army—through a movement he brazenly termed "unparalleled in the annals of war." But no words of praise could disguise the failure of his campaign. "This army left well equipped with everything a soldier needs," one man lamented. "Now, what a change. And who is responsible? The men feel that something is loose and can't find what it is." Another soldier confessed he was unsure whether "we have made an inglorious skadaddle or a brilliant retreat."

Still, most Yankee soldiers felt they had fought the best Confederate troops on equal terms, and most of them retained faith in their beloved Little Mac—for whom, said one, they would "fight to the last."

Neither side had a clear idea of what to do next. In the North, the dream of a speedy restoration of the Union was gone, along with the grim resolve that had united the nation's contentious political factions after the humiliating rout at Bull Run a year before. Now, the Union was split along party lines, with Republicans blaming the Democrat McClellan for his army's failure to take Richmond, and Democrats accusing Republicans of a conspiracy to oust their champion.

In the South, critics called for an end to President Jefferson Davis' policy of defensive warfare. Under Davis' strategy, the Confederates would fight to protect their homeland, grinding down the Federal armies in the expectation that the Northern public would grow weary of heavy casualties and demand that the war be stopped. Davis also hoped that by refraining from taking the war northward he could convince the European powers that the South was a victim of Northern aggression. Combined with the pressure exerted on European economies by a self-imposed moratorium on cotton exports, this position might, he hoped, induce one or more of the European powers to intervene.

But now many Southerners demanded that the fighting be carried North—both to move the scourge of warfare from Virginia and to give the Yankees a taste of their own medicine.

Lee's first order of business, however, was to repair his battered army. On July 8 he began pulling his men back to Richmond, leaving behind a handful of cavalry to warn of any threatening Federal movement. He refurbished the army with captured Union supplies and began reorganizing it.

Eleven Confederate divisions had fought in the Seven Days' Battles—too many for Lee to control. He wanted to establish a few larger commands to ensure that the entire army would be more responsive to his orders. But to set up corps, Lee would have to circumvent a Confederate law that prohibited the formation of any unit larger than a division. While working behind the scenes to repeal the law—adopted to allow governors to maintain some authority over regiments recruited from their states—Lee split his army into two wings.

He chose Longstreet to lead one command and assigned him five divisions, to be headed by Major Generals Richard H. Anderson and David R. Jones and Brigadier Generals Cadmus M. Wilcox, James L. Kemper, and John Bell Hood. Lee put Jackson in charge of the second wing, assigning him two divisions: his, now led by Charles S. Winder, and that of Richard Ewell.

Lee temporarily retained the division of A. P. Hill under his personal direction and regularized the arrangements of his cavalry, assigning brigades to Brigadier Generals Wade Hampton, Fitzhugh Lee, and Beverly H. Robertson, under the overall command of Jeb Stuart. The commanders who Lee felt were ill-suited to a flexible, hard-hitting army—John Magruder and the aging, ineffective Theophilus Holmes and Benjamin Huger—were transferred to the West.

Reorganizing the Federal forces in Virginia was more complex. The central question for Lincoln and Secretary of War Stanton was what to do with McClellan and his army. If McClellan would renew his drive toward Richmond, and if at the same time a Federal attack could be mounted from the north, Lee's army might well be crushed in the huge pincers. But if McClellan would not make a timely assault, the only alternatives would be to replace him or transport his army off the Peninsula.

McClellan continued to bombard Washington with requests for reinforcements. "I need 50,000 more men," he had wired on July 1, "and with them I will retrieve our fortunes." Two days later he raised his requisition to 100,000, begging the president to be "fully impressed by the magnitude of the crisis in which we are placed."

Lincoln explained that reinforcements in the numbers McClellan demanded did not exist. The president had already persuaded the 16 Northern governors to petition the administration for approval to sign up 300,000 more volunteers. He also decided to call upon help of another sort, in the form of two highly regarded generals from the West.

Lincoln appointed Major General Henry W. Halleck general in chief and put Major General John Pope, instrumental in Union victories at New Madrid and Island No. 10 along the Mississippi, in charge of a newly formed Army of Virginia. Pope's command consisted of the two corps of Major Generals Nathaniel P. Banks and John Charles Frémont in the Shenandoah Valley and the corps of McDowell, split at the time between Fredericksburg and Manassas Junction.

On August 3, Lincoln's patience with McClellan expired. The president told Halleck to order McClellan to begin preparing his army for evacuation by sea to join Pope's force in northern Virginia. That same day, news reached Lee in Richmond that 14,000 Federal troops under Major General Ambrose E. Burnside, having been shipped to the Peninsula from the Carolinas, would not be reinforcing McClellan but would continue their journey up the Chesapeake.

Gambling that McClellan no longer posed any threat to Richmond, Lee gave Stonewall Jackson a mandate to begin a limited offensive against Pope. Not long afterward, on August 16, the last units of McClellan's army left Harrison's Landing and marched to Fort Monroe for embarkation to new battlefields farther north. The Peninsula campaign was over.

THE SEVEN DAYS' CASUALTIES

FEDERAL

Killed	1,734
Wounded	8,066
Missing	6,055
Total	15,855

CONFEDERATE

Killed	3,494
Wounded	15,758
Missing	952
Total	20,204

"We soon learned that Gen. McClellan was treating the enemy to a few rounds in admonition, to head off a possible night attack."

PRIVATE THEODORE V. BROWN

3D U.S. INFANTRY, BUCHANAN'S BRIGADE

Born Theodor Braun in Württemburg, Germany, the 22-year-old pharmacist joined the army in 1857 and was assigned to duty as a hospital steward with the 3d Infantry. At Malvern Hill, Brown spent a tense evening picking up wounded soldiers while near the Rebels. He remained in the army until 1879, although plagued by liver disease, a result of malaria contracted on the Peninsula. Brown died in 1914.

At dark, on July 1, the fighting at Malvern Hill ceased. "The Meadows," in front of our position, was covered with dead and wounded, the blue and the gray intermingled. We were about to sally with lanterns to do what we could for the wounded, when right alongside of us a most terrific cannonade, in which several hundred of our guns participated, began. We thought at first that the battle had been renewed in the darkness, but no answering shells greeted our expectant ears; for which we were duly thankful. We soon learned that Gen. McClellan was treating the enemy to a few rounds in admonition, to head off a possible night attack.

During the cannonade, which lasted, I should say, about 10 minutes, a young French priest, who followed the Irish Brigade, seeing by the light of the flashing guns that we were a hospital party, came rushing up to me: "You will have one fire built immediate," he said in a manner so peremptory and dictatorial that it made my blood boil. Dr. Sternberg was not at the time with us.

"You go to ——," I answered. The priest gave me a look of mingled rage and indignation, and rushed on.

My conscience smote me. "Here is a man who is trying to do his duty, and you treat him thus because he is full of holy zeal," I said to myself, and running after him I said, "Stop, Father, and we'll build the fire." The priest halted but did not deign to look at me. We soon had a good fire started, around which a circle of mortally-wounded men, chiefly of the Irish Brigade, was formed, as if by preconceived arrangement, and the priest hurriedly went from one to the other mumbling absolution and leaving with each dying man a small piece of lighted candle. Though the ceremony was conducted with a brisk business air, the zeal and sincerity of the ecclesiastic was too evident not to inspire respect, and I much regret my failure to learn the good man's name.

Upon the cessation of the cannonade Dr. Sternberg, who had rejoined us, led us down the slope of the hill, where, by the aid of lanterns, we found the ground strewn with dead and wounded. We could do absolutely nothing for the poor fellows, except to give some of them a drink of whisky; but our small supply of that often useful stimulant was very soon exhausted; even our supply of water did not last long.

We formed circles of wounded men under the larger trees to afford them protection against the night dews. Profound silence reigned. Though thousands of men with wounds of every description surrounded us, not a cry, not a groan was heard. We knew that the rebel pickets were near by and that we ran great risk of being fired on, and we were ourselves careful to make no noise.

COLONEL WILLIAM W. AVERELL

3D PENNSYLVANIA CAVALRY, III CORPS

The repulse of the Confederates at Malvern Hill left the Federals in command of the field. Nevertheless, McClellan ordered the heights abandoned, and Averell's regiment formed part of the rear guard. Later, Averell strikingly described the windrows of Confederate dead and wounded on the battlefield.

At daylight the cavalry advanced toward the front. There was a fog so dense that we could not see a man at fifty paces distance. Colonel Buchanan was met with his staff returning from the front on foot, their horses being led. He informed me that the enemy was threatening his pickets, and advancing on both flanks. I asked him to halt his command until further orders, and galloped to the front, where our line of battle had been the night before. I could see nothing, but could hear shrieks and groans and the murmur of a multitude, but no sounds of wheels nor trampling horses. I ordered the line re-established with skirmishers and a squadron of cavalry on either flank. Colonel Hall, with the Second Regiment Excelsior Brigade, also reported for duty, and took position in the line. The battery not having reported, some cavalry was organized into squads, resembling sections of artillery, at proper intervals behind the crest. By this time the level rays of the morning sun from our right were just penetrating the fog, and slowly lifting its clinging shreds and yellow masses. Our ears had been filled with agonizing cries from thousands before the fog was lifted, but now our eyes saw an appalling spectacle upon the slopes down to the woodlands half a mile away. Over five thousand dead and wounded men were on the ground, in every attitude of distress. A third of them were dead or dying, but enough were alive and moving to give to the field a singular crawling effect. The different stages of the ebbing tide are often marked by the lines of flotsam and jetsam left along the seashore. So here could be seen three distinct lines of dead and wounded marking the last front of three Confederate charges of the night before.

PRIVATE JOHN H. WORSHAM

21ST VIRGINIA INFANTRY, J. R. JONES' BRIGADE

Worsham, the 23-year-old son of a prosperous Richmond clothing merchant, was a veteran of the Valley and Gaines' Mill. At Malvern Hill, however, he sat out the battle in reserve. In his 1912 recollections, "One of Jackson's Foot Cavalry," he described encountering the wounded from the day's fight.

Just about dark the second brigade was ordered to march by the left flank, and entering the road, we marched towards Malvern Hill, crossed a creek, and soon were in a field at the edge of which we halted, staying there the remainder of the night. I sat down in a fence corner to get a little rest, and had not been there long before one of our men, wounded, came along, and was begging for water. Having some in my canteen, I stopped him and gave him a drink. He sat down and complained very much of being weak. I gave him something to eat from my scanty rations; he seemed very thankful, and revived a little, but soon complained of being cold. I unrolled my blanket, and made him lie down, and covered him with it; a little while after I got cold too, so crept under the blanket with the wounded man, fell asleep, and did not wake until morning. I then crawled from under the blanket as carefully as I could, to avoid disturbing him, went to the creek, took a wash, filled my canteen, and brought it to my friend, tried to arouse him, but he was dead.

The enemy fled during the night, and my division was ordered back, stopping at Willis' Church the remainder of the day. It had commenced to rain, and was very disagreeable. While we were here, I went to the spring for water, but found a dead Yankee lying with his face in the spring. I suppose the poor fellow had been wounded in the fight two days before with Longstreet's command, and going to the spring, had leaned down to drink, and death overtook him. The next morning we moved in pursuit of the enemy, and found them at Harrison's Landing on James river, busily fortifying.

"The men were subsisting on hard bread and drinking polluted surface water."

BRIGADIER GENERAL JOHN H. MARTINDALE

Brigade Commander, Morell's Division

Martindale graduated from West Point in 1835 but resigned the following year. In 1861 he left his New York law practice to accept a brigadier general's commission. After Malvern Hill he was exonerated by a court of inquiry for allegedly swearing that he would rather surrender than abandon his wounded.

The rain had commenced to fall early in the morning and continued during most of the day. During the forenoon my brigade was encamped in close proximity to the Eighteenth Massachusetts, over which regiment, from the time that I joined it, I resumed command as brigade commander. The continued rain and inpouring of troops, teams, and wagons were cutting up the soil, through which movement grew more and more difficult.

The following night was passed in great discomfort. The men were subsisting on hard bread and drinking polluted surface water.

The morning of the 3d of July came. All around us was a sea of deep mud, through which the mules were struggling and goaded to drag the loads behind them. At length there was the sound of cannon. The enemy were shelling us. I got my regiments into line of battle by battalions in mass, agreeably to orders. A few solid shots plowed the earth right in our midst, but without doing any damage, except in a single instance, where a shot went crushing through a transportation wagon. At length some troops (not of our division) were sent in the direction of the firing, and the enemy retired. Then I moved my brigade about three-quarters of a mile into the edge of woods which bounded the broad plain at Harrison's Bar and skirted the Westover marshes.

CAPTAIN WILLIAM H. OWEN

Assistant Quartermaster, Birney's Brigade

Commissioned into the 3d Maine Infantry in August 1861, Owen was made a quartermaster the following May. He conducted a brigade train of 42 wagons during the Federal withdrawal to Harrison's Landing. During the retreat the teamsters driving the wagons had to deal with wretched road conditions, traffic jams, and the constant threat of capture by the pursuing Rebels. In his report Owen stated just how near to disaster the trains came after the Battle of Malvern Hill.

Nearly the whole transportation of the army was parked on the great plateau of Malvern Hill during Monday night, and remained there Tuesday morning in plain view of the enemy and within easy reach of his shells. It was not until this began to be demonstrated that the trains commenced to move down the hill out of range. I could not learn, though I sought the information in many quarters, that any orders whatever were given about the trains. It would seem that each quartermaster acted on his own responsibility and according to the best of his judgment, unenlightened by any knowledge of the roads, the position of the enemy, or the intended future movements of our own troops. Our own train did not get in range until late in the afternoon. It was fortunately hidden from the enemy by a clump of trees, and though some shells fell in close proximity, no damage was done. The teamsters, partly citizens (white) and partly soldiers, showed no timidity or disposition to abandon their teams. We parked that night about two miles beyond Malvern Hill, near Haxall's Landing, having been informed that that line of defense would be held and this would be the depot of supplies. That night it was decided otherwise, and before morning nearly the whole army had passed us, going toward Harrison's Landing. We had received no notification of the fact.

At daylight Wednesday, the 2d, we fell in with the line of wagons, marching that day about four miles, the single road being blocked with troops, artillery, and army wagons, and now become almost impassable by reason of the heavy rain and the passage of the immense artillery trains. We passed that night in the road without unhitching the teams or unsaddling horses, expecting momentarily to move on, but unable to do so, the roads being blocked in front. Thursday, July 3, found us still in the road not ten feet from where we were at dark the night before. A gloomy and unpromising prospect was before us. We were six miles from Harrison's Landing. The whole army had passed. Not a corporal's guard was left for rear defense. At least 1,500 wagons in a dozen long lines, pointing toward a narrow road (possible but for a single line), struggled for precedence and neutralized each other's efforts in the struggle. The mud was almost unfathomable. As the day advanced with scarcely a diminution in the almost interminable string of wagons, matters began to grow more critical. The gun-boats were shelling the woods in our rear. The enemy might be expected momentarily. There was nothing to prevent them, if they had chosen to come. Five hundred mounted resolute men might, in my opinion, have captured 1,000 prisoners and half the transportation of the army. Almost a panic ensued. Many wagons stuck in the mud, which might have been extricated with a little effort, were abandoned, with their loads. Many one-horse ambulances were burned. An immense quantity of public stores and private baggage was thrown out of the wagons and plundered and destroyed by stragglers. Several companies of cavalry sent to hurry up the wagons, and to assist them, I suppose, employed their time, with the exception of a few men who worked of their own accord, in breaking open and rifling trunks and other private baggage, undeterred by their officers, who either would not or could not control them, and were deaf to all entreaties for assistance. I saw wagons stuck in the mud block the road for half an hour in front of a large squad of these men without their making the least effort to extricate them, the commanding officer of the regiment at the same time saying that he had orders to destroy every wagon that had not passed that point by a given time. I sent forward to the brigade for a detail of fifty men. They came promptly. By their aid I not only got my own train through without loss of any kind, but was able to render assistance to many others. As the enemy did not advance upon this road most of the wagons were saved, but it might have easily been otherwise.

Soldiers of Leroy Stafford's Louisiana Brigade gather up some of the more than 1,100 corpses on Malvern Hill. The dead of both armies were buried, said a Confederate officer, "as well as circumstances would permit." This engraving, from a sketch by an unknown artist, appeared in the Southern Illustrated News in December 1863.

PRIVATE LEVI J. FRITZ

53D PENNSYLVANIA INFANTRY, FRENCH'S BRIGADE

Late in July the first exchanged Federal prisoners of the Seven Days' fighting arrived at Harrison's Landing. In a letter to the Montgomery (Pennsylvania) Ledger Fritz reported the experiences of a comrade, Private Andrew Missimer, who had been captured at White Oak Swamp. While Missimer said that his treatment as a prisoner had been, for the most part, fair, he complained that he and his fellows were "most starved on the limited amount of rations dealt out" to them.

When they found that the rebels were coming on them, and they would have to surrender, some of them broke their muskets, and a number of guns and cartridge boxes were thrown down a well, thus preventing them from falling into the hands of the enemy. The whole squad was immediately marched towards Richmond. As they passed along they were greeted in various ways by the citizens and soldiers. Jackson's men appear to be the most gentlemanly. Remarks like the following would be made: "Well, your bound to have your Fourth of July dinner in Richmond after all." "You don't know when McClellan is gone to stop running—do you?"—Some of the boys answered that they should "go on, he would stop to-day somewheres for them—he had done so every day yet." Some of the women were very outspoken, and very fierce. One of this class of crinoline secesh, cryed out for the guard to "kill the Yankees, kill them on the spot, kill every one of them!" Others appeared to be really ladies, and either kept modestly silent, or spoke to them kindly. A lady pressed into the hands of one of the boys a confederate five dollar note, and a few gave bread to our hungry soldiers. A number of sutlers of our army, were captured, and our boys, greatly to the amusement of their rebel guards tantalized them, saying: "All you come in the army for was to make money of all us, now you are in for it and will have to spend some of it." They passed through the camp of the 1st Louisiana Regiment, and there saw the flag of the 31st New York, the staff stuck in the ground upside down. But one line of breastworks was noticed, and two small half moon shaped forts, one mounting two guns and the other three. When they arrived in the rebel capitol they were marched at once to one of the tobacco warehouses along the river, a building that accommodated three thousand prisoners, there known as "Prison, No. 3." The first day they had nothing to eat, the next they got a few crackers, and after that, their regular rations, which consisted of one fourth loaf of bread per day, the loafes about the size of our half dime ones, and a small piece of fresh beef without salt. This prison was under charge of Lieut. Shinn of Alexandria, who appears to have been a gentleman though an ardent secessionist. He endeavored to satisfy the wishes of our unfortunate soldiers as far as possible. Our boys are under

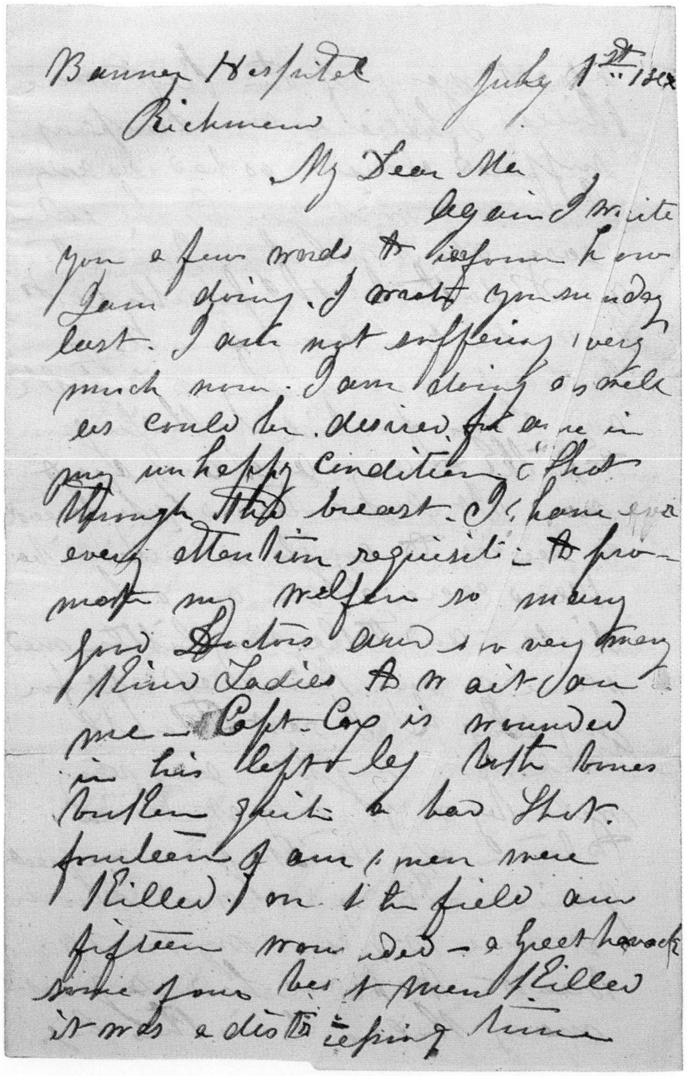
Banner Hospital July 1st 1862
Richmond
My Dear Ma
Again I write
you a few words to inform how
I am doing. I wrote you sunday
last. I am not suffering very
much now. I am doing as well
as could be desired for one in
my unhappy condition & shot
through the breast. I have every
every attention requisite to promote my welfare so many
good Doctors and so very many
kind Ladies to wait on
me — Capt. Cox is wounded
in his left leg both bones
broken quite a bad shot.
fourteen of our men were
killed on the field and
fifteen wounded — a great havock
some of our best men killed
it was a distressing time

Lieutenant William C. Norris of the 1st South Carolina Rifles wrote this letter to his mother from his bed in the Banner Hospital in Richmond. He had been shot through the chest while leading his company at Gaines' Mill. In his letter Norris complained that the pain "almost tears my breast to pieces." He died on July 10.

obligations to him for favors at his hands. While there, they on several occasions saw Gen Winder, the iron hearted superintendent of the Richmond prison houses. They were kept for eleven days in the over-crowded and poorly ventilated warehouse, then they were removed to Belle Island in the James, opposite Richmond. Here they were in tents —most of them being captured from us. There was thirty five hundred prisoners on this Island, including the whole of the 14th Reserves (Penna) and 4th N.J., and about three hundred of the Bucktails. The Tredegar iron works was opposite their camp, and every day the rebels would take cannons out to try them, and almost every day one or more of the iron dogs would burst, "then our boys would yell." I am satisfied that there is a number of union men and women in Richmond. When any of them was taken sick on the Island, they had to tend to them as best they could, as there was no doctors to call in. Everybody appeared to be anxious to get hold of our money. And dealers of almost every kind prefer our notes (treasury or bank) to Confederate script. Their officers bought up money from the prisoners, giving them six dollars of theirs for five of ours. Daily there were persons in their midst, many of them Confederate officers, bargaining and buying our "green backs." At one time they asked a rebel Captain who appeared to be very anxious to trade money with them. "Why they wanted our notes if their Confederacy was all O.K.?" The officer said he had friends north that he wished to send it to. (The usual answer they gave to such questions.) Our boys told him "they could'nt see it."

Major Henry A. Barnham (above) of the 12th New York was shot through the abdomen and captured at Malvern Hill. Exchanged a few days later, he recovered partially and returned to duty, rising to command a brigade. Recurring infections compelled Barnham to keep a linen thread passed through the wound to promote drainage.

PRIVATE JOHN W. F. HATTON

1st Maryland (C.S.) Battery, A. P. Hill's Division

Hatton was severely wounded in the left arm while manning an artillery piece at Mechanicsville. In a postwar memoir he recalled the circumstances of his removal from the battlefield to a Richmond hospital. Because both armies quickly moved on after the fighting, many of the wounded were left untended, awaiting makeshift arrangements and, in Hatton's case, the kindness and care of local citizens.

After the troops passed on from the Mechanicsville Battlefield, we, the wounded, were gathered up by the Hospital details, placed in Ambulances, and carried to the cars to be transported to Richmond. When the train arrived, the cars were too much crowded with the wounded to accommodate us, and we were left over for the next trip. When we were left alone and helpless, we suffered for water and attention, which we could not render each other. We knew that there was plenty of nice cool and clean water a few hundred yards away in a stream we could almost see in a small gully, but it may as well have been on the moon as far as it was contributing to our comfort. We had to remain on our backs where placed upon the ground, not having our burning thirst quenched, nor the dust and powder of the battle-field washed from our hands and faces, nor any attention whatever, except what each could render to himself in the way of twisting about to find an easy position and whisking the flies away from face and wound. As good fortune would have it, we did not have to suffer this disagreeable predicament very long, but long enough, nevertheless, to give us an insight into the great misery endured by soldiers left wounded and helpless upon the battlefield without succour, without a friend to soothe their dying agonies, which was often the case. To our great joy, we saw coming up the road, intuitively feeling it was for our relief, a two-horse spring wagon with a man and a boy in it. They approached, stopped the wagon in the road opposite to us, dismounted, and, coming to us with a smiling and benevolent face, said "Ah! You are wounded are you not? Thank God you have whipped the Yankees! I drove out this morning to see if I could not give assistance to our wounded braves! My wife put straw and blankets in the wagon. Hey Johny, drive the wagon around here my son!" He seemed to know so well what to do and so bent on rendering what help he could, he went on cheering us up and arranging his wagon without giving us time to thank him or make any exclamation. But as he helped us, one by one, into his wagon using a great deal of care and forethought for our comfort, he was given to understand that his kindness was duly recognized and appreciated. Major Barker, Sergeant Gale and myself, with two or three infantrymen, were made somewhat comfortable in the wagon, three or four less wounded sitting up. When we started the farmer produced a jug of water, a flask of whiskey and a cup, which he said his wife had provided for the "poor soldiers." These requisitions were refreshing and stimulating, but the water was sufficient for me; while Sergeant Gale and some others paid their respects quite often and lavishly to the contents of the flask. Notwithstanding careful driving, the wagon would jolt sometimes and cause the wounded considerable pain. Having travelled five or six miles, we arrived at the City in the after noon, and was carried to the St. James Hotel which had been converted into a hospital and were lodged on the second floor, in a large room to accommodate about twenty small beds, arranged ten on a side with heads to the wall and an aisle up the center. I was conveyed to the far end of the room, and placed in a bed on the left hand side. The first thing in order of treatment, I was administered a dram of strong raw whiskey; it burned my throat as it went down, and I made a wry face. The Matron, a kind, attentive, bright faced young lady, said, "Oh! You are not use to that—never mind, it will do you good." I replied under a frown, "So it may, but I don't fancy any more such fiery doses." She laughed and turned away to direct the next proceeding. Every piece of my clothes was stripped off; clean under garments furnished and put on me; face and hands washed; wound dressed; and food set before me, a cup of rye Coffee, two slices of baker's bread and a slice of tenderly stewed steak with gravy. This repast was far superior to our field rations, and was eagerly dispached. I then pulled the props from under my shoulders, stretched out under the white sheet and dropped off into a sound sleep.

MAJOR GENERAL GEORGE B. MCCLELLAN
Commander, Army of the Potomac

On July 4, 1862, McClellan ordered the distribution of this congratulatory address to the army at Harrison's Landing. The message praised the army for beating off attacks by "vastly superior forces" and promised to renew the offensive against Richmond. The order was publicly read in the midst of Independence Day celebrations, during which, as one soldier recorded, "Gen. McClellan came around to see us & we all cheered most heartily for country, cause & leader."

Soldiers of the Army of the Potomac

Your achievements of the last ten days have illustrated the valor and endurance of the American soldier. Attacked by vastly superior forces, and without hope of re-enforcements, you have succeeded in changing your base of operations by a flank movement, always regarded as the most hazardous of military expedients. You have saved all your material, all your trains, all your guns, except a few lost in battle, taking in return guns and colors from the enemy. Upon your march you have been assailed day after day with desperate fury by men of the same race and nation skillfully massed and led; and under every disadvantage of numbers, and necessarily of position also, you have in every conflict beaten back your foes with enormous slaughter.

Your conduct ranks you among the celebrated armies of history. No one will now question that each of you may always say with pride, "I belonged to the Army of the Potomac!"

You have reached this new base complete in organization and unimpaired in spirit. The enemy may at any moment attack you. We are prepared to receive them. I have personally established your lines. Let them come, and we will convert their repulse into a final defeat. Your Government is strengthening you with the resources of a great people.

On this our nation's birthday we declare to our foes, who are rebels against the best interests of mankind, that this army shall enter the capital of their so-called Confederacy; that our National Constitution shall prevail, and that the Union which can alone insure internal peace and external security to each State, must and shall be preserved, cost what it may in time, treasure, and blood.

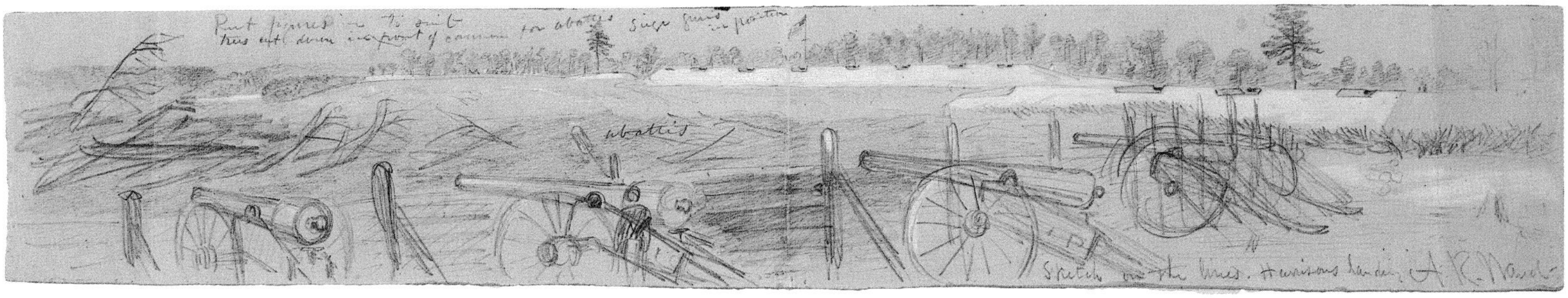

In this Alfred Waud drawing, siege rifles, posted behind earthworks and an abatis of felled trees, dominate part of McClellan's ring of fortifications at Harrison's Landing. Between two marshy creeks, the Federal artillery, backed by gunboats anchored in the James River, presented a formidable obstacle to any Confederate attack.

CAPTAIN ALFRED C. HILLS

71st Pennsylvania Infantry, Burns' Brigade

Confidence in McClellan, while still common among members of the Army of the Potomac after the retreat from Malvern Hill, was not universal. In late July Hills unburdened his feelings in a letter to a friend. A Philadelphian, Hills had joined the 71st in 1861 and was soon promoted to captain. In August 1862 he resigned his commission to accept a staff appointment with General Nathaniel Banks.

The newspapers lie about us like Satan. They say we are in excellent health and spirits, with plenty of food and full of enthusiasm for McClellan. It is all a lie—as bare-faced and absolute a lie as was ever told. We are in miserable health and worse spirits. We are suffering for wholesome food, and our enthusiasm has been left in the trenches and swamps of Yorktown & Richmond. We have lost confidence in McClellan; it is up-hill business to conceal it. This Campaign has proved a most absolute and miserable failure. He kept us doing nigger's work in trenches where we should have been fighting. All the advantage of Fair Oaks—in itself a blunder—was thus thrown away, and, finally we are compelled to make a disastrous retreat—fighting bravely and successfully, to be sure, but suffering all that human fortitude can bear, and losing the fruits of all the blood and toil which have been wasted on this God-forsaken Peninsula. As for myself, although I

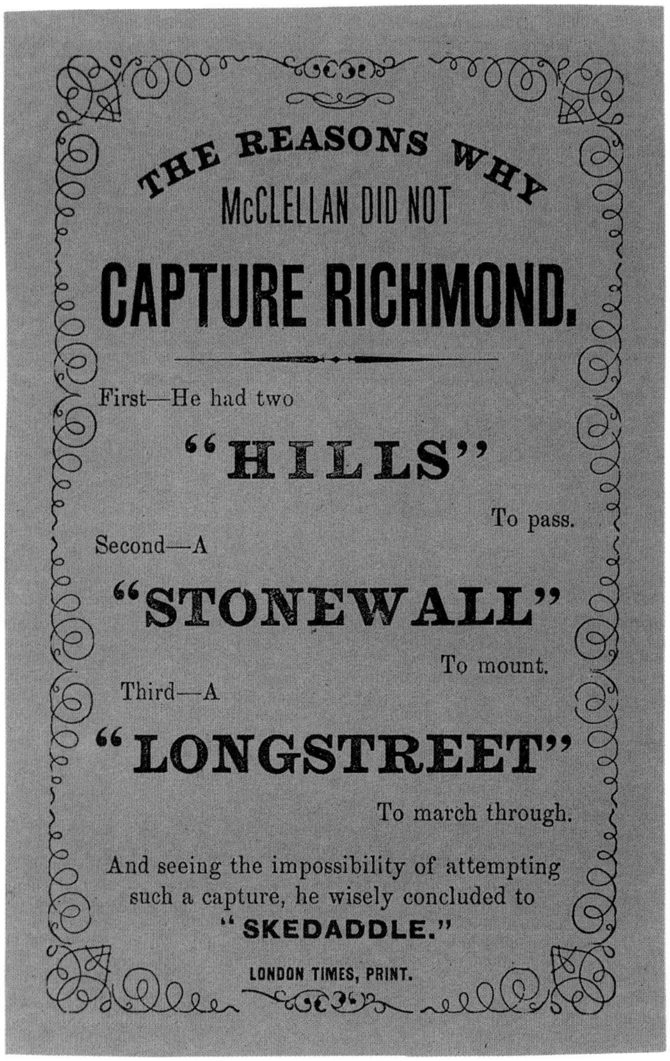

THE REASONS WHY
McCLELLAN DID NOT
CAPTURE RICHMOND.

First—He had two
"HILLS"
To pass.
Second—A
"STONEWALL"
To mount.
Third—A
"LONGSTREET"
To march through.

And seeing the impossibility of attempting such a capture, he wisely concluded to
"SKEDADDLE."

LONDON TIMES, PRINT.

Based on a jest current in Richmond following the Seven Days' Battles, a broadside issued by the London Times offers a series of punning "reasons" why McClellan's campaign to capture the Confederate capital ended in failure.

was in every fight, and, I believe, did my duty fully, I fainted and fell twice on the march from heat and with exhaustion; but, bless God, I was in every place of danger which the Regiment saw, and my heart swells with pride when I think how nobly the California boys did their duty.

It is all very well to talk about a change of the base of operations; but every one knows we have been out generaled and defeated, and nothing can convince us to the contrary. Nothing but the unsurpassed bravery of our troops saved the army from utter annihilation. The papers say it was the "consummate strategy" of McClellan. I say it was the consummate bravery of our soldiers.

"The government by wickedly witholding the reinforcements, which little Mac has required for two months, has almost caused the annihilation of this army."

LIEUTENANT CHARLES O. BALLOU

5th New Hampshire Infantry, Caldwell's Brigade

In a letter to his sister, written from Harrison's Landing on July 10, Ballou claimed that the army had been sabotaged by a sinister "abolition party" determined to withhold reinforcements from McClellan until the government adopted its agenda. This conviction was shared by many—including, most notably, McClellan himself, who warned President Lincoln that a pro-abolition stance would "rapidly disintegrate our present armies." Ballou was killed at Fredericksburg on December 13, 1862.

I shall if my health permits continue in the service until the war is over, provided my life is spared. After that perhaps I may return to California, but it is a long way ahead, till this war is over. And indeed when I see the attemps of the abolition party in Congress to prevent McClellan's sucess by withholding supplies and reinforcements, for his army at the time when he most needs them, I almost dont care whether we have a Union or not. Make this a war for the abolition of Slavery, and you will see how quick Congress will send troops to prosecute the war, but unless this object can be effected they had rather see McClellan defeated—our flag disgraced—and the union forever destroyed, And the entire army begins to perceive, what they are being used for. Insted of vigorously prosecuting the war, raising men and means, Congress passes its time in petty squabbling about a little "free nigger school" by one Vincent Colyer, in North Carolina. One thing is certain! Unless they pursue a different course, they will have not many officers to fight for them, for just as sure as Congress proposes emancipation of the slaves, one half if not more, of the officers will resign, I should most certainly do so.

ALFRED R. WAUD

Special Correspondent, Harper's Weekly

Waud, an Englishman, sketched scenes throughout the Peninsula campaign and the Seven Days' Battles and was among those who blamed the government for McClellan's failures. Trained at the School of Design of the Royal Academy in London, Waud moved to the United States in 1850. His brother, William, covered the campaign for Leslie's Illustrated.

Will talks of coming home soon, to save his health although he is better than he has been. To tell you the truth, no amount of money can pay a man for going through what we have had to suffer lately, and being to my great astonishment alive, I feel a good deal like leaving myself. The government by wickedly witholding the reinforcements, which little Mac has required for two months, has almost caused the annihilation of this army. The enemy almost surrounded us two or three to one on the Chickahominy and the only chance left us was to fight our way to the James river and the protection of our gun boats. For seven days against immense odds this gallant

Army has fought like heroes, covering the retreat of the baggage trains, and rolling back the devilish greycoats in every attack. Only think of it, seven days almost without food or sleep, night and day being attacked by overwhelming masses of infuriate rebels then driving at us from all sides, and finally securing our position, utterly worn out, in a drenching rain, with a loss of nearly 35000 men 80 pieces of artillery and 300 wagons destroyed, to keep them out of the enemies hands. So dogged have our men fought that the enemies loss foots up to a much higher figure than ours. At the last days fight, they made sure they had us, but with such fury did our soldiers stand at bay, that 10000 of the rebels fell, and our loss was but 1000. Where the rebels were, the ground looked like a burnt prairie so thickly the grey bodies covered the ground.

Alfred Waud sketched this view of a line of rifle pits overlooking Kimmidges Creek and the James River on the left flank of the strong Federal line of fortifications defending the camp at Harrison's Landing. Yankee axmen had chopped down trees in front of the works to create a clear field of fire, leaving the fallen trunks as obstacles.

PRIVATE WATSON D. WILLIAMS

5TH TEXAS INFANTRY, HOOD'S BRIGADE

In a letter to Miss Laura Bryan of Liberty, Texas, Williams announced the Rebels' "great victory" in saving Richmond. Of the Yankees' frustrated expectations he wrote, "But alas! how frail are human calculations," unaware of that sentiment's ironic relevance to his own prediction that "before six month more passes away the balmy breezes of peace will be blowing over all sunny South and our newly adopted flag will be classed with the standards of the superior nations of the earth."

The principal subject of conversation among the boys now is a speedy termination of the war. They all believe the war will end this year and they think by the 1st of January, next, if not earlier they will be at home. It is very pleasant to have such a belief but almost too good a hope to cherish. And they have pretty good reason for believing so. The great battle upon which so much depended has been fought and won by us. The Federal army so lately posted in fortified position before Richmond was perhaps the largest and most splendidly equipped this continent has ever produced. They had no lack of men, nor arms nor means. And led by the man they claimed as the greatest warrior of the age. Of course they thought Richmond would become an easy prey to their arms. But alas! how frail are human calculations. McClellan's Army a few days ago occupied a solidly entrenched front before Richmond extending ten miles and were holding a position from which they boasted they could not be driven. And indeed they were most formidably posted and only desperate men fighting for their homes and firesides and all else they held dear could have stormed their fortifications with anything like success. But before an army composed of the material that characterizes the Southern people his earthwork fortifications could not keep them back. Made more desperate by the threat of his Gun boats on the James river, afraid to meet in fair fields the Rebel forces they so vauntingly threatened to "bag" and subjugate. The great army is now nearly thirty miles away from Richmond, badly whipped, confused, and disorganized and it will take them six months at least if not a year to reorganize and get in the good condition they were two weeks ago. And upon the great victory we have so gloriously won over this army the boys base their hopes of the war ending soon.

JEFFERSON DAVIS

PRESIDENT OF THE CONFEDERATE STATES OF AMERICA

On July 5 Davis sent this address to the men of the Army of Northern Virginia, praising their valor and congratulating them for their "brilliant victories." During the Seven Days' Battles Davis had traveled to the front lines and personally witnessed the fighting at Mechanicsville, Gaines' Mill, and Glendale.

Soldiers: I congratulate you on the series of brilliant victories which, under a favor of Divine Providence, you have lately won, and, as the President of the Confederate States, do heartily tender to you the thanks of the country whose just cause you have so skillfully and heroically served. Ten days ago an invading army, vastly superior to you in numbers and in the material of war, closely beleaguered your capital, and vauntingly proclaimed its speedy conquest. You marched to attack the enemy in his intrenchments with well-directed movements and death-defying valor. You charged upon him in his strong positions, drove him from field to field over a distance of more than 35 miles, and, despite his re-enforcements, compelled him to seek safety under cover of his gunboats, where he now lies cowering before the army so lately derided and threatened with entire subjugation. The fortitude with which you have borne toil and privation, the gallantry with which you have entered into each successive battle, must have been witnessed to be fully appreciated, but a grateful people will not fail to recognize your deeds and to bear you in loved remembrance. Well may it be said of you that you have "done enough for glory," but duty to a suffering country and to the cause of constitutional liberty claims from you yet further effort. Let it be your pride to relax in nothing which can promote your future efficiency, your one great object being to drive the invader from your soil and carry your standards beyond the outer boundaries of the Confederacy, to wring from an unscrupulous foe the recognition of your birthright, community independence.

"Under ordinary circumstances the Federal Army should have been destroyed."

GENERAL ROBERT E. LEE

COMMANDER, ARMY OF NORTHERN VIRGINIA

In the conclusion of his official report of the Seven Days' Battles, Lee refers to his disappointment that McClellan's army had not been crushed. To his wife, Mary, he confided, "our success has not been so great or complete as we could have desired." Nevertheless, Lee expressed considerable pride in the valor of his officers and men.

Under ordinary circumstances the Federal Army should have been destroyed. Its escape was due to the causes already stated. Prominent among these is the want of correct and timely information. This fact, attributable chiefly to the character of the country, enabled General McClellan skillfully to conceal his retreat and to add much to the obstructions with which nature had beset the way of our pursuing columns; but regret that more was not accomplished gives way to gratitude to the Sovereign Ruler of the Universe for the results achieved. The siege of Richmond was raised, and the object of a campaign, which had been prosecuted after months of preparation at an enormous expenditure of men and money, completely frustrated. More than 10,000 prisoners, including officers of rank, 52 pieces of artillery, and upward of 35,000 stands of small-arms were captured. The stores and supplies of every description which fell into our hands were great in amount and value, but small in comparison to those destroyed by the enemy. His losses in battle exceeded our own, as attested by the thousands of dead and wounded left on every field, while his subsequent inaction shows in what condition the survivors reached the protection to which they fled. . . .

Among the dead will be found many whose names will ever be associated with the great events in which they all bore so honorable a part. For these, as well as for the names of their no less distinguished surviving comrades, who earned for themselves the high honor of special commendation, where all so well discharged their duty, reference must necessarily be made to the accompanying reports. But I cannot forbear expressing my admiration of the noble qualities displayed, with rare exceptions, by officers and men, under circumstances which demanded the exercise of every soldierly virtue.

GLOSSARY

abatis—A defensive barrier of fallen trees with branches pointed toward the enemy.
adjutant—A staff officer assisting the commanding officer, usually with correspondence.
battery—The basic unit of artillery, consisting of four to six guns. Or, an emplacement where artillery is mounted for attack or defense. A battery is generally open or lightly defended in the rear.
bee gum hat—A broad-brimmed slouch hat with a conical crown resembling a bee gum, or hive.
Belgian—A Belgian-made musket, usually a flintlock, refitted with rifling, or grooves cut in the barrel, and modified to take a percussion cap.
Berdan's Sharpshooters—The 1st U.S. Sharpshooters Regiment, named after its founder, Hiram Berdan, a well-known marksman.
breastwork—A temporary fortification, usually of earth and about chest high, over which a soldier could fire.
buck and ball—A round of ammunition consisting of a bullet and three buckshot.
Bucktails—Nickname for the 13th Pennsylvania Reserves. Recruits were required to bring in a deer's tail as proof of their prowess with a rifle. The men then wore the tails in their hats.
butternut—The color, variously described as yellowish brown, tan, or brownish gray, of the common homespun Confederate uniform for those who could not afford to acquire cloth of the official gray. It became a general Northern term for a Confederate soldier.
caisson—A cart with large chests for carrying artillery ammunition; connected to a horse-drawn limber when moved.
canister—A tin can containing lead or iron balls that scattered when fired from a cannon. Used primarily in defense of a position as an antipersonnel weapon.
clubbed musket—A musket swung like a club in hand-to-hand combat.
contraband—A slave who sought the protection of Union forces.
corduroy road—A road with a surface of logs laid together transversely.
double-quick—A trotting pace.
double-shotted artillery—Artillery charged with two projectiles rather than the normal one.
echelon—A staggered or stairsteplike formation of parallel units of troops.
embrasure—An opening in a fort wall through which a cannon was fired.
flank—The right or left end of a military formation. To flank is to attack or go around the enemy's position on one end or the other.
forage—To search for and acquire provisions from nonmilitary sources. To soldiers of the Civil War it often meant, simply, stealing.
grapeshot—Iron balls (usually nine) bound together and fired from a cannon. Resembling a cluster of grapes, the balls broke apart and scattered on impact. Although references to grape or grapeshot are numerous in the literature, some experts claim that it was not used on Civil War battlefields.
guidon—A small flag used to identify a mounted military unit.
haversack—A shoulder bag, usually strapped over the right shoulder to rest on the left hip, for carrying personal items and rations.
howitzer—A short-barreled artillery piece that fired its projectile in a relatively high trajectory.
limber—A two-wheeled horse-drawn vehicle to which a gun carriage or a caisson was attached.
mess—A group of soldiers who prepare and eat meals together, or to eat such a meal; the place where such a meal is prepared and eaten.
Minié ball—The standard bullet-shaped projectile fired from the rifled muskets of the time. Designed by French army officers Henri-Gustave Delvigne and Claude-Étienne Minié, the bullet had a hollow base that expanded, forcing its sides into the grooves, or rifling, of the musket's barrel. This caused the bullet to spiral in flight, giving it greater range and accuracy. Appears as minie, minnie, and minni.
musket—A smoothbore, muzzleloading shoulder arm.
muster—To assemble. To be "mustered in" is to be enlisted or enrolled in service. To be "mustered out" is to be discharged from service, usually on expiration of a set time.
Napoleon—A smoothbore, muzzleloading artillery piece developed under the direction of Napoleon III. It fired a 12-pound projectile (and therefore was sometimes called a 12-pounder). Napoleons were originally cast in bronze; when that material became scarce in the South, iron was used.
oblique—At an angle. Units would be ordered to fire or move in a direction other than straight ahead.
orderly—A soldier assigned to a superior officer for various duties, such as carrying messages.
parapet—A defensive elevation raised above a fort's main wall, or rampart.
Parrott gun—A muzzleloading, rifled artillery piece—of various calibers—made of cast iron, with a unique wrought-iron reinforcing band around the breech. Patented in 1861 by Union officer Robert Parker Parrott, this gun was more accurate at longer range than its smoothbore predecessors.
picket—One or more soldiers on guard to protect the larger unit from surprise attack.
pioneer—A construction engineer.
provost guard—A detail of soldiers acting as

police under the supervision of an officer called a provost marshal.
rammer—An artillerist's tool used to force the powder charge and projectile down the barrel of a gun and seat them firmly in the breech.
rifle—Any weapon with spiral grooves cut into the bore, which give spin to the projectile, adding range and accuracy. Usually applied to cannon or shoulder-fired weapons.
round shot—A solid, spherical artillery projectile.
secesh—A slang term for secessionist.
shrapnel—An artillery projectile in the form of a hollow sphere filled with metal balls packed around an explosive charge. Developed by British general Henry Shrapnel during the Napoleonic Wars, it was used as an antipersonnel weapon. A fuse ignited the charge at a set distance from the gun, raining the balls down on the enemy. Also called spherical case.
skirmisher—A soldier sent in advance of the main body of troops to scout out and probe the enemy's position. Also, one who participated in a skirmish, a small fight usually incidental to the main action.
solid shot—A solid artillery projectile, oblong for rifled pieces and spherical for smoothbores, used primarily against fortifications and matériel.
spherical case—See shrapnel.
sutler—A peddler with a permit to remain with troops in camp or in the field and sell food, drink, and other supplies.
vedette—A sentry on horseback (also *vidette*).
Zouaves—Regiments, both Union and Confederate, that modeled themselves after the original Zouaves of French Colonial Algeria. Known for spectacular uniforms featuring bright colors—usually reds and blues—baggy trousers, gaiters, short and open jackets, and a turban or fez, they specialized in precision drill and loading and firing muskets from the prone position.

ACKNOWLEDGMENTS

The editors wish to thank the following for their valuable assistance in the preparation of this volume:
Rickie Brunner, Alabama Dept. of Archives and History, Montgomery; Ann Christiansen, Minnesota Historical Society, St. Paul; George C. Esker III, Metairie, La.; Terri Hudgins, Museum of the Confederacy, Richmond; Mary Ison and staff, Library of Congress, Washington, D.C.; Bill Jackson, Gil Ford Photography, Jackson, Miss.; JoAnna M. McDonald, Capitol Preservation Committee, Harrisburg, Pa.; Steve Massengill, North Carolina Dept. of Archives and History, Raleigh; Nelson Morgan, Hargrett Rare Book and Manuscript Library, University of Georgia, Athens; Roseanne O'Canas, High Impact, Baltimore; Joan Redding, National Museum of Health and Medicine, Washington, D.C.; Michael Rhode, National Museum of Health and Medicine, Washington, D.C.; Teresa Roane, Valentine Museum, Richmond; Bobby Roberts, Little Rock, Ark.; Paul Romaine, Gilder Lehrman Collection, New York; Mary L. Sluskonis, Museum of Fine Arts, Boston; Sandra M. Trenholm, Gilder Lehrman Collection, New York.

PICTURE CREDITS

The sources for the illustrations are listed below. Credits from left to right are separated by semicolons; credits from from top to bottom are separated by dashes.

Dust Jacket: front, courtesy Mark Katz; rear, Library of Congress, neg. no. B8171-7576.
All calligraphy by Mary O'Brian/Inkwell, Inc.
6, 7: Map by Paul Salmon. 8: Massachusetts Commandery of the Military Order of the Loyal Legion and the U.S. Army Military History Institute (MASS-MOLLUS/USAMHI), copied by A. Pierce Bounds. 15: From the Frank and Marie-Thérèse Wood Print Collections, Alexandria, Va. 16: Courtesy William B. Styple, photographed by Henry Groskinsky. 17: Print Collection, Miriam and Ira D. Wallach Division of Art, Prints and Photographs, The New York Public Library, Astor, Lenox and Tilden Foundations. 18: Minnesota Historical Society. 19: Bellamy Mansion Museum, Wilmington, N.C.; MASS-MOLLUS/USAMHI, copied by A. Pierce Bounds. 20: Public Health Service Photo Number 90 cm-385 in The National Archives—courtesy of the North Carolina Division of Archives and History, Raleigh. 21: The Gilder Lehrman Collection at the Pierpont Morgan Library, New York. 22: Courtesy Harris Andrews. 23: From the Frank and Marie-Thérèse Wood Print Collections, Alexandria, Va. 24: The Valentine Museum, Richmond. 25: From *War Diary and Letters of Stephen Minot Weld,* privately printed by The Riverside Press, 1912. 26: MASS-MOLLUS/USAMHI, copied by A. Pierce Bounds. 27: Courtesy Museum of Fine Arts, Boston, M. & M. Karolik Collection. 28, 29: From the Frank and Marie-Thérèse Wood Print Collections, Alexandria, Va.; MASS-MOLLUS/USAMHI, copied by A. Pierce Bounds. 30: Cook Collection, The Valentine Museum, Richmond—MASS-MOLLUS/USAMHI, copied by A. Pierce Bounds. 33: From the Frank and Marie-Thérèse Wood Print Collections, Alexandria, Va. 35: Courtesy Doug Bast/Boonsboro Museum of History, photographed by Larry Sherer. 36: MASS-MOLLUS/USAMHI, copied

by A. Pierce Bounds. 39: From the Frank and Marie-Thérèse Wood Print Collections, Alexandria, Va. 40: Print Collection, Miriam and Ira D. Wallach Division of Art, Prints and Photographs, The New York Public Library, Astor, Lenox and Tilden Foundations. 41: Courtesy Dr. Glen Cangliosi, New Orleans, La., photographed by Larry Sherer—MASS-MOLLUS/USAMHI, copied by A. Pierce Bounds. 42: Museum of the Confederacy, Richmond. 43: Courtesy Paul Loane, photographed by Robert J. Laramie. 44: Library of Congress, Waud #407. 46: Duke University, Special Collections Library, Durham, N.C. 47: MASS-MOLLUS/USAMHI, copied by A. Pierce Bounds; courtesy Paul Loane, photographed by Robert J. Laramie. 48, 49: Library of Congress, Waud #694(B). 50: Courtesy of South Caroliniana Library, University of South Carolina, Columbia—Library of Congress, Waud #652(A). 51: Courtesy of the North Carolina Division of Archives and History, Raleigh—courtesy Mary Gordon Elliott, photographed by Henry Mintz. 52: Courtesy Harris Andrews; photograph courtesy of the North Carolina Division of Archives and History, Raleigh. 53: National Archives, neg. no. 90-CM-497. 55: Library of Congress, Waud #177. 57: Map by Walter W. Roberts. 58: Michigan Historical Collections, Bentley Historical Library, University of Michigan. 59: From *War Years with Jeb Stuart,* by W. W. Blackford, Charles Scribner's Sons, New York 1945, copied by Philip Brandt George. 60: MASS-MOLLUS/USAMHI, copied by A. Pierce Bounds. 61: Collection of Michael J. McAfee. 62: Pennsylvania Capitol Preservation Committee, Harrisburg; courtesy of the South Caroliniana Library, University of South Carolina, Columbia. 63: Confederate Relic Room, Columbia, S.C., photographed by Larry Sherer. 64: Collection of Michael J. McAfee. 66: From *Gentle Tiger: The Gallant Life of Roberdeau Wheat,* by Charles L. Dufour, Louisiana State University Press, Baton Rouge, 1957; from *Four Years on the Firing Line,* by James Cooper Nisbet, McCowat-Mercer Press, Jackson, Tenn., 1963, copied by Philip Brandt George. 67: Mississippi Department of Archives and History, photographed by Gil Ford. 68: Photograph by Douglas Christian, courtesy Bureau of State Office Buildings, Commonwealth of Massachusetts. 70: The Cabin Museum, copied by Henry Mintz—courtesy of the North Carolina Division of Archives and History, Raleigh, copied by A. Pierce Bounds. 71: Civil War Library & Museum, Philadelphia, copied by A. Piece Bounds; courtesy of Mr. and Mrs. James A. Bass, photographed by Henry Mintz. 72: Roger D. Hunt Collection at USAMHI, copied by A. Pierce Bounds. 73: Courtesy Larry B. Williford, photographed by Henry Mintz. 75: Library of Congress, Waud #272. 76: Cook Collection, The Valentine Museum, Richmond. 77: From *The Long Arm of Lee, or the History of the Artillery of the Army of Northern Virginia,* Vol. 2, by Jennings Cropper Wise, J. P. Bell Company, Inc., Lynchburg, Va., 1915. 79: MASS-MOLLUS/USAMHI, copied by A. Pierce Bounds. 80: From the Frank and Marie-Thérèse Wood Print Collections, Alexandria, Va. 81: MASS-MOLLUS/USAMHI, copied by A. Pierce Bounds—photograph by Douglas Christian, courtesy Bureau of State Office Buildings, Commonwealth of Massachusetts. 82: Courtesy Paul Loane, photographed by Robert J. Laramie; collection of Michael J. McAfee. 84: Courtesy Paul Loane Collection, photographed by Robert J. Laramie; photograph by Douglas Christian, courtesy Bureau of State Office Buildings, Commonwealth of Massachusetts. 85: William A. Turner Collection. 87: Map by Walter W. Roberts. 90: Library of Congress, neg. no. LC-15508-BH82-4453. 92, 93: Lightfoot Collection, photographed originally by E. & H. T. Anthony; Massachusetts Historical Society, Boston—Library of Congress, Waud #580(A). 94: Courtesy George Esker. 95: Courtesy Gregory A. Coco Collection. 97: MASS-MOLLUS/USAMHI, copied by A. Pierce Bounds. 99: Library of Congress, Waud. 101: Library of Congress, Waud #548. 102: Minnesota Historical Society. 104: Library of Congress, Waud #1102(A). 105: David Wynn Vaughan. 106: MASS-MOLLUS/USAMHI, copied by A. Pierce Bounds. 107: Collection of Michael J. McAfee. 108: Painting by Julian Scott, courtesy Union League Club, New York, photographed by Henry Groskinsky. 109: Courtesy of The Atwater Kent Museum; from *Der Turner Soldat; A Turner Soldier in the Civil War: Germany to Antietam,* by C. Eugene Miller and Forrest F. Steinlage, Calmar Publications, Louisville, Ky., 1988. 110: Library of Congress, Waud #737(B). 112: *From Under the Red Patch: The Story of the Sixty-Third Regiment Pennsylvania Volunteers,* compiled by Gilbert Adams Hays, Pittsburgh, published by Sixty-Third Pennsylvania Volunteers Regimental Association, 1908; from *The Story of a Confederate Boy in the Civil War,* by David E. Johnson, Glass & Prudhomme Co., Portland, Oreg., 1914. 113: Museum of the Confederacy, Richmond, photographed by Larry Sherer. 114: Courtesy Mrs. L. B. Hopkins, photographed by Henry Mintz. 115: Courtesy Paul Loane, photographed by Robert J. Laramie. 116: Courtesy Paul Loane, photographed by Robert J. Laramie; Museum of the Confederacy, Richmond, photographed by Larry Sherer. 117: Private collection, copied by Evan H. Sheppard; courtesy Brian Pohanka. 118, 119: Library of Congress, Waud #746(B). 120: National Archives, neg. no. 111-B-2670. 121: Roger D. Hunt Collection at USAMHI, copied by A. Pierce Bounds; courtesy Paul Loane, photographed by Robert J. Laramie. 123: Map by Walter W. Roberts. 125: Bureau of Archives and History, New Jersey State Library, copied by A. Pierce Bounds. 126: MASS-MOLLUS/USAMHI, copied by A. Pierce Bounds—U.S. Army Military History Institute, copied by A. Pierce Bounds. 127: From *The Story of a Cannoneer Under Stonewall Jackson,* by Edward A. Moore, published by J. P. Bell, Lynchburg, Va., 1910, copied by Larry Sherer. 128: M. & M. Karolik Collection, courtesy of Museum of Fine Arts, Boston. 129: Courtesy Francis J. Ruth, photographed by Henry Mintz; courtesy John E. Ramsay Jr., copied by Henry Mintz. 131: Courtesy Tennessee State Library and Archives, Nashville. 133: Library of Congress, neg. no. LC-10421-B812-256. 134: From the Frank and Marie-Thérèse Wood Print Collections, Alexandria, Va. 135: Department of Archives and Manuscripts, Louisiana State University, Baton Rouge; from *Civil War Times Illustrated,* Vol. XV, no. 2, May 1976. 136: From *Battles and Leaders of the Civil War: North to Antietam,* edited by Robert Underwood Johnson and Clarence Clough Buel, Castle Books, New York, 1887. 137: Museum of the Confederacy, Richmond. 138: From the Frank and Marie-Thérèse Wood Print Collections, Alexandria, Va. 139: Michigan Capitol Committee, photographed by Peter Glendinning. 140: Cook Collection, The Valentine Museum, Richmond. 142: From the original in the Hargrett Rare Book and Manuscript Library, University of Georgia Libraries. 143: From *Divided We Fought: A Pictorial History of the War of 1861–1865,* David Donald, The Macmillan Company, New York, 1956. 144: Library of Congress, neg. no. 26543 BS171 622. 149: Library of Congress, neg. no. B8171-7576; from *One of Jackson's Foot Cavalry,* by John H. Worsham, The Neal Publishing Company, 1912. 150: From *The Photographic History of the Civil War,* Vol. 10, edited by Francis Trevelyan Miller, The Review of Reviews Co., New York, 1912. 151: University of Georgia, Main Library. 152: Courtesy of South Caroliniana Library, University of South Carolina, Columbia. 153: Otis Historical Archives, National Museum of Health & Medicine, Armed Forces Institute of Pathology, SP93. 155: Library of Congress, Waud #692(B); Providence Public Library. 156: Civil War Library & Museum, Philadelphia, copied by A. Pierce Bounds. 157: Library of Congress, Waud #116. 158: Library of Congress neg. no. B4146. 159: The Gilder Lehrman Collection at the Pierpont Morgan Library, New York.

BIBLIOGRAPHY

BOOKS

Adams, John G. B. *Reminiscences of the Nineteenth Massachusetts Regiment.* Boston: Wright & Potter, 1899.

Andrews, W. H. *Footprints of a Regiment.* Atlanta: Longstreet Press, 1992.

Averell, William Woods. *Ten Years in the Saddle.* Ed. by Edward K. Eckert and Nicholas J. Amato. San Rafael, Calif.: Presidio Press, 1978.

Baquet, Camille (comp.). *History of the First Brigade, New Jersey Volunteers.* Trenton: State of New Jersey, 1910.

Beale, G. W. *A Lieutenant of Cavalry in Lee's Army.* Boston: Gorham Press, 1918.

Bellard, Alfred. *Gone for a Soldier.* Ed. by David Herbert Donald. Boston: Little, Brown, 1975.

Blackford, William W. *War Years with Jeb Stuart.* New York: Charles Scribner's Sons, 1945.

Bowen, Roland E. *From Ball's Bluff to Gettysburg . . . and Beyond.* Ed. by Gregory A. Coco. Gettysburg, Pa.: Thomas Publications, 1994.

Brewster, Charles Harvey. *When This Cruel War Is Over.* Ed. by David W. Blight. Amherst: University of Massachusetts Press, 1992.

Caldwell, J. F. J. *The History of a Brigade of South Carolinians.* Dayton: Morningside Press, 1984 (reprint of 1866 edition).

Clark, Walter (ed.). *Histories of the Several Regiments and Battalions from North Carolina in the Great War, 1861–'65* (Vol. 2). Wendell, N.C.: Broadfoot's Bookmark, 1982 (reprint of 1901 edition).

Cooke, John Esten. *Wearing of the Gray.* Bloomington: Indiana University Press, 1959.

Cullen, Joseph P. *The Peninsula Campaign 1862.* New York: Bonanza Books, 1973.

Davis, Nicholas A. *Chaplain Davis and Hood's Texas Brigade.* Ed. by Donald E. Everett. San Antonio: Principia Press of Trinity University, 1962.

Davis, William C. (ed.). *The Confederate General* (Vol. 5). Harrisburg, Pa.: National Historical Society, 1991.

Dawson, Francis W. *Reminiscences of Confederate Service: 1861–1865.* Ed. by Bell Irvin Wiley. Baton Rouge: Louisiana State University Press, 1980.

Dickert, D. Augustus. *History of Kershaw's Brigade.* Dayton: Press of Morningside Bookshop, 1973.

Douglas, Henry Kyd. *I Rode with Stonewall.* Chapel Hill: University of North Carolina Press, 1968.

Dowdey, Clifford. *The Seven Days.* New York: Fairfax Press (Barre Publishing), 1978.

Eckenrode, H. J., and Bryan Conrad. *George B. McClellan.* Chapel Hill: University of North Carolina Press, 1941.

Fletcher, William A. *Rebel Private.* New York: Dutton, 1995.

Fuller, Richard F. *Chaplain Fuller.* Boston: Walker, Wise, 1863.

Fulton, William Frierson, II. *The War Reminiscences of William Frierson Fulton II.* Gaithersburg, Md.: Butternut Press, n.d.

Goree, Thomas J. *The Civil War Letters of Major Thomas J. Goree.* Ed. by Thomas W. Cutrer. Charlottesville: University Press of Virginia, 1995.

Handerson, Henry E. *Yankee in Gray.* Cleveland: Press of Western Reserve University, 1962.

Haskell, John Cheves. *The Haskell Memoirs.* Ed. by Gilbert E. Govan and James W. Livingood. New York: G. P. Putnam's Sons, 1960.

Hayes, Gilbert Adams (comp.). *Under the Red Patch.* Pittsburgh: Sixty-Third Pennsylvania Volunteers Regimental Association, 1908.

Heitman, Francis B. *Historical Register and Dictionary of the United Stated Army* (Vol. 1). Urbana: University of Illinois Press, 1965 (reprint of 1903 edition).

Hill, A. F. *Our Boys.* Philadelphia: John E. Potter, 1864.

Holt, David. *A Mississippi Rebel in the Army of Northern Virginia.* Ed. by Thomas D. Cockrell and Michael B. Ballard. Baton Rouge: Louisiana State University Press, 1995.

Johnston, David E. "Charge of Kemper's Brigade at Frazier's Farm." In Vol. 18 of *Southern Historical Society Papers,* ed. by R. A. Brock. Wilmington, N.C.: Broadfoot Publishing, 1990.

Kearny, Philip. *Letters from the Peninsula.* Ed. by William B. Styple. Kearny, N. J.: Belle Grove Publishing, 1988.

Krick, Robert K. *Lee's Colonels.* Dayton: Press of Morningside Bookshop, 1979.

Le Duc, William G. *Recollections of a Civil War Quartermaster.* St. Paul: North Central Publishing, 1963.

McDaniel, J. J. *Diary of Battles, Marches, and Incidents of the Seventh S.C. Regiment.* N.p.: 1862.

MacNamara, Daniel George. *The History of the Ninth Regiment.* Boston: E. B. Stillings, 1899.

Maxfield, Albert, and Robert Brady Jr. *Roster and Statistical Record of Company D, of the Eleventh Regiment Maine Infantry Volunteers.* New York: Press of Thos. Humphrey, 1890.

Meyers, Augustus. *Ten Years in the Ranks, U.S. Army.* New York: Stirling Press, 1914.

Miller, C. Eugene. *Der Turner Soldat.* Louisville, Ky.: Calmar Publications, 1988.

Miller, William J. *The Peninsula Campaign of 1862* (Vol. 2). Campbell, Calif.: Savas Woodbury, n.d.

Moore, Edward A. *The Story of a Cannoneer under Stonewall Jackson.* New York: Neale Publishing, 1907.

Mosby, John S. "The Ride around General McClellan." In *Southern Historical Society Papers* (Vol. 26). Wilmington, N.C.: Broadfoot Publishing, 1991.

Nichols, G. W. *A Soldier's Story of His Regiment.* Kennesaw, Ga.: Continental Book, 1961.

Nisbet, James Cooper. *Four Years on the Firing Line.* Ed. by Bell Irvin Wiley. Jackson, Tenn.: McCowat-Mercer Press, 1963.

North Carolina Troops, 1861–1865: A Roster (Vol. 6—Infantry). Comp. by Weymouth T. Jordan Jr. Raleigh, N.C.: State Division of Archives and History, 1990.

Norton, Oliver Willcox. *Army Letters: 1861–1865.* Dayton: Morningside, 1990.

Oates, William C. *The War between the Union and the Confederacy and Its Lost Opportunities.* Dayton: Morningside, 1974.

Osborne, William H. *The History of the Twenty-Ninth Regiment of Massachusetts Volunteer Infantry, in the Late War of the Rebellion.* Boston: Albert J. Wright, 1877.

Owen, William Miller. *In Camp and Battle with the Washington Artillery of New Orleans.* Boston: Ticknor, 1885.

Park, Robert Emory. *Sketch of the Twelfth Alabama Infantry of Battle's Brigade.* Richmond: W. E. Jones, 1906.

Post, Lydia Minturn, ed. *Soldiers' Letters: From Camp, Battle-Field, and Prison.* New York: Bunce & Huntington, 1865.

Robins, W. T. "Stuart's Ride around McClellan." In *Battles and Leaders of the Civil War* (Vol. 1). Ed. by Robert Underwood Johnson and Clarence Clough Buel. New York: Thomas Yoseloff, 1956.

Rodgers, John. Report, July 1, 1862. In *Official Records of the Union and Confederate Navies in the War of the Rebellion* (Series I, Vol. 7). Washington, D.C.: GPO, 1898.

Sears, Stephen W. *To the Gates of Richmond: The Peninsula Campaign.* New York: Ticknor & Fields, 1992.

Southwick, Thomas P. *A Duryee Zouave.* Brookneal, Va.: Patrick A. Schroeder Publications, 1995.

Stevens, John W. *Reminiscences of the Civil War.* Hillsboro, Tex.: Hillsboro Mirror Print, 1902.

Stiles, Robert. *Four Years under Marse Robert.* New York: Neale, 1903.

Toon, William H. "Report of Major William H. Toon." In *The Supplement to the Official Record* (Vol. 2). Wilming-

ton, N.C.: Broadfoot Publishing, n.d.
U.S. Army. *Official Army Register of the Volunteer Force of the United States Army* (Vol. 2, part 2). Gaithersburg, Md.: Olde Soldier Books, 1987 (reprint of 1865 edition).
U.S. War Department. *The War of the Rebellion: A Compilation of the Official Records of the Union and Confederate Armies* (Series 1, Vol. 11, part 2). Harrisburg, Pa.: National Historical Society, 1971 (reprint of 1884 edition).
Warner, Ezra J. *Generals in Blue.* Baton Rouge: Louisiana State University Press, 1964.
Weld, Stephen Minot. *War Diary and Letters of Stephen Minot Weld, 1861-1865* (2d ed.). Boston: Massachusetts Historical Society, 1979.
Wood, William Nathaniel. *Reminiscences of Big I.* Ed. by Bell Irvin Wiley. Jackson, Tenn.: McCowat-Mercer Press, 1956.
Wormeley, Katharine Prescott. *The Other Side of War with the Army of the Potomac.* Boston: Ticknor, 1889.
Worsham, John H. *One of Jackson's Foot Cavalry.* New York: Neale Publishing, 1912.

PERIODICALS
Acton, Edward A. " 'Dear Mollie.' " Ed. by Mary Acton Hammond. *Pennsylvania Magazine of History and Biography,* 1965, Vol. 89.
Alcorn, Alexander. Letter. *The Lawrence Journal* (New Castle, Pa.), July 26, 1862.
Alexander, Bates. "Pennsylvania Reserves." *Hummelstown Sun* (Pa.), July 13, 1894.
Anderson, Carter S. "Train Running for the Confederacy." *Locomotive Engineering,* Aug. 1892.
Bernard, George S. "A Virginian Victory." *Weekly Times* (Philadelphia), Jan. 14, 1888.
Brown, Theo. V. "Gaines's Mill." *National Tribune,* July 2, 1900.
Burton, Isaac M. "Vermont Veterans." *National Tribune,* June 28, 1883.
Chambers, C. C. "Mississippians at Gaines Mill." *Confederate Veteran,* Vol. 19, n.d.
Davenport, Alfred. "One of the Seven Days." *National Tribune,* 1894, Vol. 13.
Eskildson, Robert. "Gaines's Mill: With the 2d U.S. Horse Artillery." *National Tribune,* Feb. 28, 1905.
Evans, Thomas H. "At Malvern Hill." *Civil War Times Illustrated,* Dec. 1967.
Fritz, Levi J. "Letter from the Army." *Montgomery Ledger,* July 22, 1862.
Garnett, F. E. "The Retreat to Malvern." *Weekly Times* (Philadelphia), June 23, 1883.
Kent, William C. "Sharpshooting with Berdan." *Civil War Times Illustrated,* May 1976.
McCormick, John. "On the Peninsula." *National Tribune,* Feb. 21, 1901.
Miller, James Cooper. "With McClellan on the Peninsula." *Civil War Times Illustrated,* June 1969.
Slater, John S. "Scenes at Malvern Hill." *Weekly Times* (Philadelphia), Dec. 11, 1880.
Soderman, John G. "Charles City Crossroads." *National Tribune,* Aug. 28, 1902.
Sullivan, Eugene. "Bringing Up the Rear." *National Tribune,* Jan. 7, 1904.
Thurber, Charles H. Letter, July 6, 1862. *Bloomville Mirror* (N.Y.), July 22, 1862.
Tinsley, Fannie Gaines. "Mrs. Tinsley's War Recollections, 1862-1865." *Virginia Historical Magazine of History and Biography,* 1968, Vol. 35.
Wray, William J. "Malvern Hill." *National Tribune,* April 17, 1890.

OTHER SOURCES
Ashenfelter, Benjamin F. Letter, July 7, 1862. Carlisle Barracks, Pa.: U.S. Army Military History Institute, *Civil War Times Illustrated* Collection.
Alexander, E. Porter. Letter, July, 24 1862, from the Doubleday/Catton Papers. Washington, D.C.: Library of Congress, Manuscript Division.
Babcock, John C. Letter, June 6, 1862. Washington, D.C.: Library of Congress, Manuscript Division.
Ballou, Charles. Letter, July 4, 1862. Ballou Family Papers. Worcester, Mass.: American Antiquarian Society.
Bellamy, William James Harriss. Diary, 1862. Chapel Hill: University of North Carolina, Southern Historical Collection.
Blackford, Eugene. Unpublished memoir, n.d. Carlisle Barracks, Pa.: U.S. Army Military History Institute.
Fite, John A. Memoirs, n.d., Civil War Collection: Confederate and Federal, 1861-1865, Confederate Collection, Box 13, Folder 7. Nashville: Tennessee State Archives.
Hatton, John William Ford. Memoirs, n.d. Washington, D.C.: Library of Congress, Manuscript Division.
Hills, Alfred C. Letter, July 21, 1862. Washington, D.C.: Library of Congress, Manuscript Division.
Hollis, J. Rufus. Memoirs, n.d., Box 13, Folder 7, Confederate Collection, Civil War Collection: Confederate and Federal, 1861-1865. Nashville: Tennessee State Archives.
Malloy, Stephen. Letter, June 30, 1862, from the Doubleday/Catton Papers. Washington, D.C.: Library of Congress, Manuscript Division.
Waud, Alfred R. Letter, July 5, 1862. Washington, D.C.: Library of Congress, Manuscript Division.
Williams, Watson Dugat. Letter, Sept. 13, 1861. Hillsboro, Tex.: Hill Junior College.

INDEX

Numerals in italics indicate an illustration of the subject mentioned.

TIME® LIFE BOOKS Time-Life Books is a division of Time Life Inc.

TIME LIFE INC.
PRESIDENT and CEO: George Artandi

TIME-LIFE BOOKS
PRESIDENT: Stephen R. Frary
PUBLISHER/MANAGING EDITOR: Neil Kagan

VOICES OF THE CIVIL WAR

DIRECTOR OF MARKETING: Pamela R. Farrell

THE SEVEN DAYS

EDITOR: Paul Mathless
Deputy Editors: Harris J. Andrews (principal), Kirk Denkler, Philip Brandt George
Design Director: Barbara M. Sheppard
Associate Editor/Research and Writing: Gemma Slack
Senior Copyeditors: Judith Klein, Mary Beth Oelkers-Keegan
Picture Coordinators: Daryl Beard (principal), Lisa Groseclose
Editorial Assistant: Christine Higgins

Initial Series Design: Studio A

Special Contributors: John Newton, Brian C. Pohanka, Dana B. Shoaf (text); Charles F. Cooney, Steve Hill, Robert Lee Hodge, Susan V. Kelly, Beth Levin, Michael McAfee, Henry Mintz, Dr. Richard A. Sauers, Dana B. Shoaf (research); Janet Dell Russell Johnson (design and production); Jayne Rohrich Wood (copyediting); Roy Nanovic (index).

Correspondent: Christina Lieberman (New York).

Director of Finance: Christopher Hearing
Directors of Book Production: Marjann Caldwell, Patricia Pascale
Director of Publishing Technology: Betsi McGrath
Director of Photography and Research: John Conrad Weiser
Director of Editorial Administration: Barbara Levitt
Production Manager: Marlene Zack
Quality Assurance Manager: James King
Chief Librarian: Louise D. Forstall

Consultant
Brian C. Pohanka, a Civil War historian and author, spent six years as a researcher and writer for the Time-Life Books series The Civil War and the three-volume work Echoes of Glory. He is the author of *Distant Thunder: A Photographic Essay on the American Civil War* and has written and edited numerous works on American military history. He has acted as historical consultant for projects including the feature film *Glory* and television's *Civil War Journal.* Pohanka participates in Civil War reenactments and living-history demonstrations with the 5th New York Volunteers, and he is active in Civil War battlefield preservation.

First printing. Printed in U.S.A.
School and library distribution by Time-Life Education, P.O. Box 85026, Richmond, Virginia 23285-5026.

TIME-LIFE is a trademark of Time Warner Inc. U.S.A.

Library of Congress Cataloging-in-Publication Data
The seven days / by the editors of Time-Life Books.
p. cm.—(Voices of the Civil War)
Includes bibliographical references and index.
ISBN 0-7835-4720-X
1. Seven Days' Battles, 1862 I. Time-Life Books.
II. Series.
E473.68.S48 1998
973.7'32—dc21 98-4774
CIP